Europe's Relations with the United States and China in the 21st Century

INTERNATIONAL RELATIONS IN ASIA, AFRICA AND THE AMERICAS

Politics, Economy, Society - Transdisciplinary Perspectives

The series International Relations in Asia, Africa and the Americas is edited by the Centre for International Studies and Development of the Jagiellonian University in Kraków.

Andrzej Mania & Marcin Grabowski (eds)

VOL. 22

Łukasz Stach, Przemysław Łukasik and Przemysław Furgacz

Europe's Relations with the United States and China in the 21st Century

PETER LANG
Berlin · Bruxelles · Chennai · Lausanne · New York · Oxford

Bibliographic Information published by the Deutsche Nationalbibliothek
The Deutsche Nationalbibliothek lists this publication in the Deutsche Nationalbibliografie; detailed bibliographic data is available online at http://dnb.d-nb.de.

A CIP catalog record for this book has been applied for at the Library of Congress.
Library of Congress Control Number: 2025030913

The linguistic proofreading of the publication was carried out from the funds of the Vice-Rector for Science of the University of National Education in Kraków.

Proofreading of this publication has been supported by a grant from the Faculty of International and Political Studies under the Strategic Programme Excellence Initiative at Jagiellonian University.

ISSN 2511-588X
ISBN 978-3-631-92889-9 (Print)
ISBN 978-3-631-92890-5 (ePDF)
ISBN 978-3-631-94010-5 (ePUB)
DOI 10.3726/b23024

Published by Peter Lang GmbH, Berlin (Germany)

info@peterlang.com

This publication has been peer reviewed.

www.peterlang.com

Acknowledgement

The linguistic proofreading of the publication was carried out from the funds of the Vice-Rector for Science of the University of National Education in Kraków.

The proofreading of this publication has been supported by a grant from the Faculty of International and Political Studies under the Strategic Programme Excellence Initiative at Jagiellonian University.

Table of Contents

Introduction

Przemysław Furgacz

The northern hemisphere is undoubtedly the dominant region of the world, in which the prevailing majority of population, landmass and economic activity is concentrated. There are areas in the northern hemisphere that traditionally have crucial importance – North America, Europe and the Far East. The United States of America has been the leading state in North America for over 150 years, since they gained superpower status at the end of World War II. Traditionally, over the ages – except for a relatively short period of Japanese hegemony and imperialism in the first half of the twentieth century – the prominent power of Eastern Asia has been China in all its incarnations. Europe dominated the rest of the globe between the sixteenth and nineteenth centuries, with the culmination of its power and advantage over the rest of the globe in the late nineteenth century. That situation forces any scholar or analyst who wants to predict the future development of global political, economic and military relations to turn their attention to these three geopolitical and geoeconomic centres of the world, which in the twenty-first century still are: the US, China and Europe.

The objective of this book is to succinctly and briefly present some select aspects of Europe's evolving relations with two foreign powers struggling for primacy in world affairs – the US and China. International relations specialists agree that the United States are the current hegemon of the world and the most serious contender to take this preeminent place in the global hierarchy of states is the People's Republic of China – the unquestionable emerging great power with enormous ambitions for creating a new world order in which its position would be much stronger than nowadays. In the third decade of the twenty-first century, Europe has become the object of competition between these two major economic, military, and political powers. Moreover, the rivalry between these great powers is intensifying. Even worse, with Russia's invasion of Ukraine, interstate war has come to Europe once again, after a peace lasting many decades. Naturally, the attitudes of all three centres of geopolitical and geoeconomic power towards the conflict have become important.

The EU's general attitude toward Chinese investments has been described in the first chapter of the book. Attention has been paid in particular to the semiconductor and electrical vehicle industry, which have become an object of intensifying contention of major centres of technological and economic power. The specific pressures Europe is subject to were presented based on the example of Germany, the United Kingdom, Lithuania, Italy, and France. The German case is particularly important in the context of the China-US rivalry. As the largest country in the European Union, with the greatest sway on decisions taken by the European Commission in Brussels, and as Europe's biggest economy, Germany has become the object of intensifying competition between Washington and Beijing. Both competing superpowers want to redirect Berlin's foreign and economic policies in directions favourable to them. They do not hesitate to use typical geoeconomic instruments to achieve this objective. The US wants to convince European partners to de-risk – or perhaps even more ambitiously – entirely decouple their economies from China, thus making them less reliant on this communist Asian power and less vulnerable to China's economic and political pressure as well as espionage activities. Certain EU countries are reluctant and sceptical about de-risking and decoupling from China, perceiving them as the pursuit of essentially American – not European – interests and a far-reaching interference in the EU independence. For instance, the case of broad anti-Huawei worldwide campaign launched by the US is depicted at the end of the chapter. To some degree Washington attained its aim and indeed managed to stop the expansion of Huawei in European markets.

Łukasz Stach expanded this subject in the next section of the book, portraying the thriving economic relations between Europe, China and the US. In this context there is a risk that Europe may find itself between a rock and a hard place if bilateral U.S-China relations evolve into trade or actual war in the future. Considerable implications of the Sino-American competition for the European Union were scrupulously described. Łukasz Stach accentuated that the EU, due to the fact that it is a supranational political unit and because of its complicated decision-making procedures quite often has serious problems taking quick and effective political action, as well as formulating coherent policies vis-à-vis its main economic partners – the People's Republic of China and the United States of America. The author did not hesitate to point out the failures of European integration, like the European sovereign debt crisis, prolonged malaise of the Eurozone, and the failure to fully and effectively implement the Lisbon Strategy. All these problems weakened the EU's position towards China and the US. According to Łukasz Stach, Europe has an issue with adequate adaptation to the new international environment, the most distinctive feature of which is the aggravating Sino-American rivalry. Undoubtedly, any further worsening of bilateral US-China relations would risk the EU being caught between these two struggling powers. Obviously, such a development would not be beneficial to the long-term prosperity of the European economy. Furthermore, the intra-EU differences make it difficult to reach a consensus within the EU itself and to agree with Washington on a coordinated policy towards communist China. It is the approach to cooperation with the Middle Kingdom that seems to be the principle obstacle to the development of a more politically united Western world.

In the third chapter of the book, the same author describes the divergence between expectations and reality as regards the EU's policies towards China and the US. According to the author, forming a common EU security policy in particular would be a serious challenge in a divided Europe. Łukasz Stach does not hide his scepticism as to the probability of overcoming different existing divisions in Europe and the formation of a viable European army. Though often raised in public political discussions, so far these concepts still mostly remain unrealised. The author notes that the European Union has been ineffective in creating a common security and defence policy, even as the Russian invasion of Ukraine exposed the urgent need to bolster European defence capabilities, both in terms of armed forces as well as the defence industry.

Przemysław Łukasik in turn outlined the similarities and differences between China's and the United States' soft power on the European continent. This must be accurately highlighted, because softness in soft power is not tantamount to weakness. Soft power policy is unquestionably a considerable element of great power politics. The author observes that during Donald Trump's first presidential term, many European politicians openly phrased their mistrust of the US. At the time, the strength of American soft power in the eyes of some Europeans had somewhat weakened. Przemysław Łukasik argues that Chinese soft power fundamentally derives from the thought of Confucius, who advocated for the pursuit of harmonious relations not only within the state, but also in international relations. Thus, Confucianism became a source of Chinese soft power. The Chinese government goes to great lengths to consolidate the positive image of the Middle Kingdom on the European continent, seeing this also as creating a friendly environment for itself in the broader geopolitical confrontation with the USA. The author pays particular attention to the New Silk Road, Xi Jinping's flagship project. The chapter lists the distinctive characteristics of China's soft power policy. Moreover, throughout the chapter, the evolution of the US public diplomacy in the twentieth and twenty-first centuries was skilfully presented.

In the fifth chapter of the book, the same scholar outlined the difficult position of the countries of Central and Eastern Europe. These smaller, weaker and poorer states of the European family, situated in close proximity to Russia, which in the past has often displayed expansionist and hostile intentions towards them, traditionally seek a protector in a strong external power. These states have found such a defender and ally in the United States. On the other hand, they cannot be indifferent to the flourishing influence and importance of the Middle Kingdom, which they would like to trade and do business with. These quandaries were painstakingly characterised. In the next part of the book, the author discussed the ongoing debate on what the EU's global policy and the possible power status of the EU should look like. At the same time, Przemysław Łukasik places his argument in the context of various theories of international relations. Hence, the theoretical concept of power and other important categories of international relations were presented in the context of the ongoing process of European integration. This part of the book stresses the evolution of the EU's power status. The author is staunchly convinced that the EU decisively prefers soft policy methods in its political practices, concentrating much more on advancing mutually beneficial cooperation than competition with other states and global centres of power. Such a delicate approach distinguishes the EU in a positive manner, against the background of belligerent and hard power-loving Russia or Erdoğan's adventurous and haggling Turkey. This also creates an image of the EU as a stable partner that does not make sudden and abrupt 180-degree political turns to the surprise of its partners. Which of these approaches is more effective and beneficial in the long term is still a contentious issue amongst scholars and analysts today.

The last but not least chapter of the book discusses the joint and coordinated response of the United States and Europe to the Russian invasion of Ukraine. One can get an impression that Moscow's unfortunate move unwittingly reinvigorated the transatlantic alliance. First, the chapter outlines the growing diplomatic consultations and the formation of the foundations of a common coordinated policy towards the conflict on the eve of its second and most acute phase, which was the open invasion of Ukraine in February 2023. Washington's main aims are briefly outlined, followed by an outline of the key moves in economic warfare – unprecedented in world history. Never before has such a large country and such an important economy – at least in terms of raw materials – been subjected to such harsh and wide-ranging economic sanctions. Undoubtedly, this is an unprecedented situation, unmatched by anything in history. The ramifications of this state of affairs for the global economy and the evolution of the geopolitical and geoeconomic system around the globe will only fully materialise in the future. Already today, however, we can see a sort of progressive disintegration of the global economy into two blocs – a Western bloc led by the USA and an anti-Western bloc, BRICS+, under China's leadership. This section of the book also presents the considerable and comprehensive assistance that the US and Europe together provided to struggling Ukraine in a quite coordinated and harmonised manner. The volume and comprehensiveness of the aid is indeed immense, in fact, arguably the largest since the Lend-Lease Act. In addition, the war also provided the impetus for a serious empowering of the transatlantic energy partnership between the European nations and the US. In order to compensate for the loss of Russian hydrocarbon supplies on the European market, which is highly dependent on the import of the predominant majority of mineral resources, Washington and Brussels had to step up and deepen their cooperation.

Why did the authors decide to design the book in this way? The book we are handing over to readers is not a full and in-depth discussion of the entirety of European states' relations with the great non-European powers. Because of the necessarily limited scope of the book, the authors have been compelled to review and depict only painstakingly selected – albeit, in their opinion, quintessential – matters and dimensions of these relations. Economic issues are crucial in the relations between the US, the EU and China. Previous decades enhanced the interdependencies between the main global economies, but in the age of great power rivalry, it became a problem in mutual relations, especially that Western powers underline the fact, that the PRC is the main beneficiary of globalisation and growing interconnections. However, the West unwillingly admits that the prospects of huge profits from access to the Chinese market and cheap labour there have tempted many Western companies to relocate production to China. Nowadays, issues like electric vehicles, the Huawei case, attitudes to Chinese investments, the chips/semiconductors dispute have a significant influence on the EU, the US, and the PRC relations. Moreover, Germany (whose economy is the largest in the EU) is strongly bound both with the US and the PRC economies, which makes the whole thing an even more complicated jigsaw puzzle.

Economic growth and increasing innovation in the economy are allowing Beijing to develop its military capabilities, which is causing concern in Washington. When it comes to the military, the European army is still hypothetical, and it remains in the realm of rhetoric and plans. However, the EU can and should do more to strengthen European defence, especially that full-scale Russian invasion of Ukraine highlighted the importance of military power in politics, so this factor was also analysed. In international relations, it is not only hard power that counts but also soft power. Therefore, this topic has also been included, especially in terms of how great powers use soft power tools to achieve their foreign policy goals.

This study mostly employs desk research and descriptive data analysis methodology. The authors have used data and information from existing literature and readily accessible sources to critically assess the situation and make a substantive conclusion with a well-grounded foundation. The necessary data has been provided by institutions such as the World Bank (Gross Domestic Product (GDP) growth, GDP and purchasing power parity (PPP) values, GDP per capita, import/export of goods and services, research and development expenditures, etc.), Observatory of Economic Complexity (trade values, trade partners) and Stockholm International Peace Research Institute (military expenditures, arms trade).

This book is intended for readers who want a quick overview of the basic dimensions of this very complex and wide-ranging issue. The book tries to summarise the EU's position and response to the US-China rivalry, as well as the state of research and European Union's subjectivity in international relations. For this reason, the book does not analyse all aspects of the EU-US-PRC relations. However, areas of rivalry, such as the economy, military power, technology, or soft power, have almost always been points of reference in superpower clashes and are therefore the main focus of the work. The book was written before Donald Trump won the presidential election in 2024. Since then, US policy toward the PRC and the EU has undergone some changes that are not reflected in this book.

—Przemysław Furgacz

The Silk Road Versus the Atlantic Community – Europe's Relations with the US and China

Przemysław Furgacz

In the twenty-first century, the two leading powers in the world are the United States and China. Geopoliticians generally see the Middle Kingdom as the main candidate to replace the US as the global hegemon. European countries, which have numerous economic ties with both superpowers, try to pursue policies that do not alienate either of them. This chapter of the book focuses on selected aspects of European states' positions and attitudes in the face of the US-China rivalry, which has intensified in recent years, forcing European capitals to make difficult choices between Washington and Beijing.

EU attitudes to Chinese investment

Economic relations seem to have dominated EU-China relations in recent years. In 2020, China will overtake the US as the European Union's largest trading partner for goods. China is by far the EU's biggest import market. On average, EU-China trade reaches €1 billion a day.[1] Various economic disputes have characterised EU-China economic relations over the last two decades, if not longer.

One issue that the European Union is increasingly looking at is investment from China. Enthusiasts of Chinese FDI have insisted that Chinese investment will go mainly into struggling European companies. They argued that such an influx of Chinese capital would help them get back on their feet. This approach began to change after a Chinese company bought Kuka – a famous German manufacturer of industrial robots and production machinery. It turned out that Chinese firms were mainly interested in European high-tech companies, presumably to acquire the most advanced Western technologies and know-how to make Chinese industry even more competitive in the future.[2] This made Chinese FDI less attractive from the point of view of Western European businessmen and politicians. Put simply, the EU does not want to see a repeat of the success of Haier – a Chinese company that over the years has consistently made acquisitions of its Western competitors in order to acquire their well-known brands and, most importantly, access to their technologies. This strategy has brought the company great success, as it has become a global leader in the home appliances market, undermining the position of European companies.[3]

Since 2013, the EU and China have been trying to reach an agreement on an EU-China investment agreement for 2020, called the Comprehensive Agreement on Investment. So far it has not materialised. The formal reason for this impasse was the EU's decision to sanction Chinese officials for human rights abuses, and Beijing's retaliatory counter-sanctions. There are growing concerns in Europe about which side stands to gain more from the implementation of this agreement, although some circles in Brussels, Berlin and Paris still hope to revive the pact. The EU generally wants to trade and invest with China to support and develop the European economy, but at the same time European politicians and businessmen are finally beginning to realise that China's rapidly growing economic power could at some point pose a threat to the European economy, if only because products made by Chinese companies in China will displace European products not only from third country markets but also from the European market itself.

Electric cars and semiconductors

The best example is electric vehicles, widely seen as the future of the global car industry. Chinese cars with internal combustion engines have not been particularly successful either at home or abroad. For decades, Chinese carmakers were not serious competitors to the likes of Volkswagen, BMW or Stellantis. This changed when the Chinese car industry changed its strategy and focused on the next generation of cars with plug-in hybrid electric vehicles and electric engines. The authorities in Beijing have consistently supported the development of this industry in China, mostly through subsidies and tax exemptions. Beijing has been pushing hard to develop the battery industry for years, and after many years these efforts have borne fruit. Around 75% of the world's batteries are now produced in China.

Interestingly, Chinese companies are also at the technological forefront in the production of lithium-ion and sodium batteries used in electric car motors. Suddenly, European carmakers have realised that they are not only behind the US, but also behind the Middle Kingdom when it comes to electric vehicles. And this is an industry that is widely regarded as very promising and forward-looking. Beijing's goal is to dominate the entire value chain, from the extraction of raw materials to the delivery of electric vehicles to consumers.[4]

Central European countries are concerned that as Europe moves away from the internal combustion engine car, in the production of which suppliers from the Visegrad countries and Romania play a significant role, their position will be replaced by suppliers from China.[5] Western Europeans, on the other hand, are concerned that the share of their car companies in the global and even European market will gradually decline in favour of Chinese and US car companies. It is important to emphasise that the automotive sector is of vital importance to the EU economy. Suffice it to say that in 2021, the automotive industry had a positive trade balance of €112.2 billion for the EU, making it the second-largest generator of trade profit after the chemical industry.[6] Occasionally, European states bow to US pressure and acquiesce to measures that harm China, even if the same measures also harm their own industries. That's the case with the Netherlands and ASML – Advanced Semiconductor Manufacturing Lithography. ASML is the world's leading manufacturer of the very technologically advanced equipment used to make semiconductors. In October 2022, the Joe Biden administration introduced a very comprehensive export control law, which amounts to a ban on the export of the most advanced chips, software for designing and manufacturing chips, devices for manufacturing semiconductors and related technologies. The White House put pressure on the Netherlands and Japan, trying to persuade them to ban or at least reduce exports of the most advanced chip etching equipment. Japan's Nikon and the Netherlands' ASML are essentially a global duopoly in the production of high-end lithography machines, which are essential for the production of advanced semiconductors.[7] There are certain indications that Amsterdam and Tokyo have informally decided to restrict ASML's high-end machines to China, despite the fact that the Chinese market is very profitable for ASML.

On the one hand, Europe is increasingly being pressured by Washington to toughen its policy towards China, and on the other hand, China is putting pressure on Europe not to bend to the will of the U.S. Both of these rival powers are sometimes subtly, sometimes overtly implying that if Europe does not toe their preferred line, it could be punished economically with various measures harmful to European business.

US diplomats sometimes bluntly warn European governments that they must choose between the US and China. For example, the US ambassador to Portugal said so openly in 2021, trying to persuade the government not to sell the port terminal to the Chinese company.[8] Beijing sometimes uses its economic leverage over European states to push through EU-level policies that benefit China. Smaller and economically weaker states are more likely to play into Beijing's hands. Greece is a case in point. During the infamous Greek debt crisis, the Chinese state-owned shipping company COSCO bought the port of Piraeus on the cheap, thus gaining economic leverage over Athens. The Greek government vetoed EU policy statements attacking China both for its numerous territorial disputes with neighbours and for human rights abuses.[9] Beijing therefore used its economic influence in Greece to slightly redirect EU policy in the direction it saw fit.

Germany as an object of Sino-American rivalry

Similar to what has happened over the past two decades in US-Russian relations, where both powers have courted Berlin in various ways in their efforts to steer German foreign and economic policy in their favour, Beijing and Washington are currently trying to persuade the German government to distance itself and its economy from the other power. In particular, the Greens and the FDP have adopted positions that are generally closest to US wishes. The SPD, on the other hand, is more nuanced. Both Angela Merkel and her successor, Chancellor Olaf Scholz, were wary of pursuing a policy that could lead to retaliatory measures by China that would hurt German companies. Annalena Baerbock, as foreign minister, was trying to create a new German China policy, which in her vision would be more in line with the US position, but Olaf Scholz seems to be much more sceptical about the robust China policy pushed by the Greens.[10]

Policy towards the People's Republic of China (PRC) has become a hotly debated issue among German politicians. For example, the Greens and the FDP were adamantly opposed to allowing the Chinese state-owned shipping company COSCO to acquire a stake in a port terminal in Hamburg in 2022, while the SPD opted to go ahead with the deal. Eventually, coalition members compromised on the divisive issue and allowed COSCO to acquire a limited stake. Interestingly, according to a study, between 2017 and 2021, China accounted for 7% of Germany's foreign direct investment and 12–16% of its annual business revenue. Interestingly, analogous indicators for the US were very similar.[11] This means that the economies of both rival powers are equally important to Germany.

German big business puts pressure on the German government to maintain positive relations with the PRC. Otherwise, its lucrative profits from numerous business contracts in and with China could collapse. By the end of 2020, German direct investment in China reached €89.5 billion, making Chinese direct investment in Germany of €9 billion insignificant.[12] Germany, like other European economies, has notoriously high trade deficits in bilateral trade with China. In 2022, Germany imported €192 bn worth of goods from China while exporting only €107 bn.[13] German industrial giants such as Volkswagen, BASF, Bosch and Siemens make much of their profits in the Middle Kingdom, as do the German so-called Mittelstand – the medium-sized companies for which the German economy is world famous. All these corporate giants, along with the Mittelstand, have invested large quotas in China and do not want to lose this money. Volkswagen alone has 30 factories in China. It is precisely these big German companies that have enough influence in German politics to have a say in the Bundestag, the Bundesrat, the Foreign Office and the Chancellery. German carmakers and the chemical industry in particular are heavily dependent on unrestricted access to the Chinese market. This dependency has given Beijing serious leverage over Berlin that could one day be exploited.

Moreover, German businesspeople, politicians and pundits are increasingly frightened by the apparent growing strength of Chinese companies in the global market. In other words, Chinese companies in many industries are becoming more serious – and more threatening – competition for German and European counterparts year after year, not only in the Chinese and European markets, but in other markets as well. German business and political elites are aware that this expansion of Chinese companies is to some extent the result of unfair trade practices and massive intellectual property theft, of which Western companies are the victims. For many years, Western – including European – companies have complained that the People's Republic of China applies numerous, sometimes more disguised, sometimes less hidden, formalised or informal barriers and impediments to their expansion. These practices are causing European capitals to exercise a degree of caution and suspicion in their relations with China. The alarm raised in German business and political circles after the Chinese takeover of Kuka in 2016 prompted Berlin to intensify its screening of non-EU, mainly Chinese, investments in strategic sectors. Since then, the scrutiny of Chinese investments in the EU has increased significantly. Germany has since become more assertive in its economic relations with China. One example of this more assertive policy is the German government's refusal to allow the takeover of the German manufacturing company Leifeld by Chinese capital. Moreover, when the prospect of a Chinese takeover of the German electricity distribution company 50Hertz became real, Berlin increased its stake in the company in order to torpedo this possible transaction in advance.[14]

US power to influence Europe's China policy – the cases of the UK, Lithuania, Italy and France

When China set up the Asian Infrastructure Investment Bank, it was obviously sabotaged by Washington and Tokyo. The U.S. did not want to see another international financial institution that could reduce the influence of the World Bank Group, the International Monetary Fund and the Asian Development Bank, in which the U.S. has by far the largest voting power. From the US perspective, China's initiative could, in the long run, undermine the strength and importance of these institutions and, consequently, of the US. For a long time, therefore, US and Japanese diplomacy tried to persuade European allies not to join the AIIB, although both Washington and Tokyo publicly denied that they were in any way opposed to the concept. And for a while it seemed that this behind-the-scenes pressure was working, but in early 2015 the United Kingdom became the first major European state to declare that it would join Beijing's initiative. Leaders of other European countries concluded that since the closest European ally of the US had decided to join the AIIB, their countries should do so as well.

Reportedly, the White House was furious with David Cameron for taking such a decision openly against US interests. There are two main – and to some extent complementary – explanations for the UK's move. According to one explanation, the main reason for such a decision was the intention to support London's position as the leading European financial centre vis-à-vis the competing Frankfurt am Main.[15] If this is indeed true, it is evidence that Beijing is adept at exploiting the differences between Europe and the United States. Proponents of the second explanation claim that the British authorities signed up to the Asian Infrastructure Investment Bank because they believed it would attract more lucrative Chinese investment to the UK.[16] Perhaps the British government hoped for some lucrative future contracts in China for British companies. Some subsequent events support this thesis. For example, in October 2015, during Xi Jinping's official visit to the UK, many important economic deals worth about £40 billion were sealed. The British Prime Minister at the time was so pleased with the deals that he declared the beginning of a 'golden age' in UK-China relations.[17] In any case, the case clearly shows that the US has not always been able to steer the policies of its European allies in the direction it wants, especially when large European companies have been lured by Beijing with lucrative deals.

Some unilateral decisions by European states on China policy have caused controversy not only in Washington but also in Brussels. A good example is the Italian government's decision to sign an agreement with the PRC on cooperation in infrastructure development under Xi Jinping's well-known Belt and Road Initiative. Italy concluded an agreement with China on this matter in March 2019, probably without prior consultation with the EU and the U.S. In any case, U.S. and EU diplomats condemned this action by the Italian authorities. Other European states were concerned that Italy had taken such a step at a time when the EU was trying to form a more coherent collective policy towards the Middle Kingdom.[18] Italy did not change its mind under pressure, but weaker European states proved to be much more vulnerable to EU and US pressure on their China policies. An excellent example of this is the case of Croatia, which in the face of concerted pressure from the US and the EU in 2021 backed down and – in line with the US and the EU – cancelled the approval of the management of the port of Rijeka by a Chinese investor.[19]

In contrast to the major European powers, Washington's power of persuasion over small European states is much greater, especially if they border possessive and unpredictable Russia. A case in point is Lithuania, which suddenly toughened its China policy in 2021, infuriating Beijing. In 2022, Lithuania not only withdrew from the 17+1 initiative, which brings together China and Central and Eastern European states but also tightened relations with Taiwan. Beijing reacted strongly to these actions. The Chinese government recalled its ambassador from Lithuania, accused Vilnius of caving in to US pressure, and restricted Lithuanian companies' access to its huge market.[20] Within the EU, Vilnius is strongly in favour of closer transatlantic cooperation and partnership, which it sees as a priority. China, through diplomatic contacts with individual states, has attempted to torpedo Lithuania's proposals in the EU forum, which generally move towards closer relations with the US.[21] It seems that Washington has been pushing Vilnius behind the scenes to redirect EU policy to be more confrontational towards China, which would obviously be beneficial to the US.

In contrast to Croatia and Lithuania, France more often decides to resist Washington's pressure and trust. For example, French President Emmanuel Macron's visit to Beijing in April 2023 has caused a great stir on both sides of the Atlantic. The French president has explicitly distanced himself from US-China policy, stressing that Europe needs to move towards greater 'strategic autonomy', which can be interpreted as greater independence from the US and a lot of room to promote European (or perhaps more French) interests regardless of Washington's preferences. Macron argued that Europe should escape the 'bloc-versus-bloc logic'. Moreover, according to Macron, Europe should not automatically and blindly follow the US stance on the Taiwan issue – the most explosive flashpoint in US-China relations.[22] The French president admonished the EU not to become 'America's follower'.[23] Macron incessantly promotes the concept of European strategic autonomy, and in such an approach he essentially continues the policy of his predecessors in the Élysée Palace.

Naturally, Beijing will take every opportunity to drive a wedge between the US and its most influential European partners such as France. Xi Jinping welcomed Macron's words distancing France and Europe from the U.S. with unconcealed satisfaction.[24] Perhaps these controversial statements by Macron, which certainly did not please the politicians in Washington, London and Canberra, are a kind of retaliation for AUKUS and deprive France of a very lucrative asset of 56 billion contract to sell submarines to Australia.

However, Macron's words have led to an even greater rupture in European unity on China policy.[25] Polish experts and politicians have criticised Macron's behaviour. For example, Sławomir Dębski, the then director of the Polish Institute of Foreign Affairs, commented on Macron's behaviour as follows: 'This is a very dangerous signal, which shows that no matter how much peace in Europe is threatened, the most important thing for the French president is to be independent, not from China, not from Russia, but from the US, on which peace in Europe depends'.[26]

The cases described previously show that the major European states do not hesitate to make their own unilateral decisions on China policy, even if their moves provoke certain controversies on one or both sides of the Atlantic. They also show that Washington has not only been closely monitoring European policy towards China for many years but has also been trying to redirect it in a direction favourable to the United States.

The Huawei case

A very interesting case of Washington's pressure on Europe to change its policies is the case of the US global campaign against Huawei. In 2019, Washington initiated a series of various coordinated measures against Huawei Technologies Company – the Chinese national champion that developed quite rapidly and gained a huge share in the global smartphone market, especially in poorer markets. US diplomacy is trying to persuade other states to blacklist Huawei as well and prevent companies from entering their markets, especially in the 5G network. Basically, the US claims that Huawei in fact works intensively with Chinese intelligence services and that allowing it to develop 5G networks would be a huge threat to the national security of the states that would unwisely do so.

Soon after the US imposed its first sanctions on Huawei, it began to lobby European states to follow suit. The position of European politicians on whether or not to join the anti-Huawei campaign was differentiated. For example, Czech President Miloš Zeman strongly opposed any anti-Huawei measures. The Polish government's stance was more balanced. Prime Minister Mateusz Morawiecki gave a soft assurance in 2019 that Warsaw would stop Huawei's expansion in Poland, but the Polish government apparently preferred to pursue a coordinated policy on this issue at the EU level, fearing that Beijing might retaliate economically if Poland had unilaterally restricted Huawei's access to the Polish market.[27]

Ultimately, US diplomats were able to convince European governments to significantly curb Huawei's expansion on the continent. Most European authorities restricted the access of Chinese telecom companies (mainly Huawei and ZTE), but without naming them. However, the Swedish government did not hesitate to explicitly ban Huawei and ZTE from supplying their equipment and devices to the emerging Swedish 5G networks. Interestingly, the Scandinavian states – Sweden and Finland – have a vested economic interest in preventing Huawei and ZTE from expanding in the global telecom market, as Sweden's Ericsson and Finland's Nokia are the Chinese companies' main competitors in the global market for the supply of telecom equipment, including equipment used in 5G networks.[28] Thus, as Huawei's de facto only serious competitors in the promising 5G market, Stockholm and Helsinki willingly followed Washington's lead. In retrospect, US pressure to curb Huawei's presence and progress in Europe proved to be quite effective. Significantly, the UK under Boris Johnson was the ally that most resisted Washington's pressure to limit Huawei's presence in Europe. Once again, it was the prospect of money flowing from the PRC to British companies that made London less inclined to block Huawei.[29] It is worth noting that prominent US politicians, such as Secretary of State Mike Pompeo in Trump's administration, warned that if Europe allowed Huawei to participate in the construction of its 5G networks, the US might limit intelligence sharing with countries that did so, for fear that it would leak to Chinese intelligence.[30]

In general, European states have simply wavered on the Huawei issue, choosing between what is more relevant and beneficial to them – security and good relations with the US, or profitable business deals with China and access to the highly absorptive Chinese domestic market.

Conclusion

The EU's whole approach to China can be summed up by the opinion of the President of the European Commission, Ursula von der Leyen, that the EU must maintain its engagement with the People's Republic of China, but at the same time devise and implement a strategy aimed at 'de-risking' its relations and dependencies on China.[31] The global COVID-19 pandemic mercilessly exposed the consequences of over-reliance on imports from China. We should be aware that some turbulence and disruption in imports from the Middle Kingdom could be caused not only by a pandemic, but also by naval blockades or other military hostilities in the event of, exempli gratia, China's invasion of Taiwan.

In effect, then, Europe is caught between Scylla and Charybdis, between the US – a faltering global superpower desperately struggling to maintain its hegemonic position – and China – a rising demographic and economic colossus seeking to replace the US as the world's leading superpower. As bilateral relations between the US and the PRC deteriorate, Europe will find it increasingly difficult to manoeuvre between these two giants. Worse still, the EU is divided over the right policy to adopt in these circumstances. Traditionally pro-American states on NATO's Eastern flank, such as Lithuania, Poland or Romania, which see Russia as the most dangerous security threat for them, are adamantly in favour of maintaining close ties with the United States, even at the expense of relations with China. Western European countries, traditionally more sceptical of the US, are more mixed in their approaches and policy choices. Ideally, however, no European state would like to be drawn directly into a bitter dispute between the American eagle and the Chinese dragon. Having to take sides would be particularly painful for Germany, whose export-driven economy is as dependent on exports to the huge US market as it is on exports to China.

The EU's China and US policies are also quite vulnerable to sometimes overlapping pressures from different lobby groups. The EU's China policy is to a large extent a derivative of the various business interests of different industries. In conclusion, it seems that in the future, even more than in the past, Europe will have to try to juggle, weave and manoeuvre skilfully between the US and China.

Notes

1 Norman, Laurence / Mackrael, Kim: 'China Wants to Be at Center of New World Order, Top EU Official Says'. *Wall Street Journal*, March 30, 2023, retrieved 20.04.2023, from <https://www.wsj.com/articles/china-wants-to-be-at-center-of-new-world-order-top-eu-official-says-22987030>.

2 Popławski, Konrad: 'Capital does have nationality: Germany's fears of Chinese investments'. *Komentarze OSW*, 230, January 25, 2017, pp. 4–5, retrieved 04.06.2023

from <https://www.osw.waw.pl/en/publikacje/osw-commentary/2017-01-25/capital-does-have-nationality-germanys-fears-chinese>.

3 Hage, Simon et al.: 'Chinese Expansion Has Germany on the Defensive'. *Der Spiegel,* May 24, 2018, retrieved 01.06.2018, from <https://www.spiegel.de/international/business/chinese-economic-expansion-has-germany-worried-a-1209325.html>.

4 Popławski, Konrad: 'Globalne starcie o elektromobilność zagrożeniem dla Europy Środkowej?', p. 3.

5 Ibidem. p. 6.

6 Ibidem. p. 1.

7 'The U.S., Japan and the Netherlands Mull New Restrictions on China's Tech Sector'. *Stratfor.com,* June, 02, 2023, retrieved 11.02.2023, from <https://cc.bingj.com/cache.aspx?q=%22The+U.S.%2c+Japan+and+the+Netherlands+Mull+New+Restrictions+on+China%27s+Tech+Sector%22&d=4351532448908&mkt=pl-PL&setlang=pl-PL&w=oLTWziHDbtZ70fdhCFB6Uhf2_csCzzoQ>.

8 Fairless, Tom: 'In Battle With U.S. for Global Sway, China Showers Money on Europe's Neglected Areas'. *Wall Street Journal,* April 13, 2021, retrieved 13.04.2021, from <https://www.wsj.com/articles/in-battle-with-u-s-for-global-sway-china-showers-money-on-europes-neglected-areas-11618310350?mod=hp_lead_pos7>.

9 Wong, Audrye: 'China's Economic Statecraft: Lessons Learned from Ukraine'. *The Washington Quarterly,* 46(1), 2023, pp. 121–136.

10 'The conundrum of Germany's business ties with China'. *The Economist,* April 27, 2023, retrieved 04.05.2023 2023, from <https://www.economist.com/business/2023/04/27/the-conundrum-of-germanys-business-ties-with-china>.

11 'The conundrum of Germany's business ties with China'. *The Economist,* April 27, 2023, retrieved 04.05.2023 2023, from <https://www.economist.com/business/2023/04/27/the-conundrum-of-germanys-business-ties-with-china>.

12 Hage, Simon et al.: 'German Companies Ignore Major Risks in China'. *Der Spiegel,* January 01, 2022, retrieved 04.11.2022, from <https://www.spiegel.de/international/business/business-as-usual-german-companies-ignore-major-risks-in-china-a-27b66d20-f228-47d0-b2bf-95f3cc976e6c>.

13 'The conundrum of Germany's business ties with China'. *The Economist,* April 27, 2023.

14 'The Future of Chinese Investment in Europe'. *Stratfor,* February 25, 2021, retrieved 02.04.2023, from <https://webcache.googleusercontent.com/search?q=cache:-bX8ATMT8NMJ:<https://worldview.stratfor.com/article/future-chinese-investment-europe+&cd=1&hl=pl&ct=clnk&gl=pl>.

15 Hong, Yelin: 'The AIIB Is Seen Very Differently in the US, Europe, and China'. *The Diplomat,* May 08, 2015, retrieved 03.04.2023, from <https://thediplomat.com/2015/05/the-aiib-is-seen-very-differently-in-the-us-europe-and-china/>.

16 'America's Special Relationship Changes'. *Stratfor,* April 21, 2016, retrieved 05.05.2023, from <https://webcache.googleusercontent.com/search?q=cache:mv2AK-hNae8J:<https://www.stratfor.com/geopolitical-diary/americas-special-relationship-changes+&cd=1&hl=pl&ct=clnk&gl=pl>.

17 Kaczmarski, Marcin: 'The UK shows its openness to China'. *Centre for Eastern Studies,* October 28, 2015, retrieved 29.05.2023, from <https://www.osw.waw.pl/en/publikacje/analyses/2015-10-28/uk-shows-its-openness-to-china>.

18 Legorano, Giovanni: 'Italy Signs Up to China's Global Infrastructure Plan Despite U.S. Ire'. *Wall Street Journal*, March 23, 2019, retrieved 23.05.2023, from <https://www.wsj.com/articles/italy-signs-up-to-chinas-global-infrastructure-plan-despite-u-s-ire-11553341408>.

19 Kolarz, Stefania: 'EU Targets Insufficient Monitoring of Foreign Investment'. *PISM Bulletin*, 2664(43), April 13, 2023, p. 1, retrieved 04.05.2023, from <https://www.pism.pl/publications/eu-targets-insufficient-monitoring-of-foreign-investment>.

20 Przychodniak, Marcin: 'Regression and Pro-Russia Rhetoric. China's Reaction to Lithuania's Change of Policy'. *PISM Bulletin*, 2389(19), November 16, 2021, p. 1, retrieved 04.05.2023, from <https://www.pism.pl/publications/regression-and-pro-russia-rhetoric-chinas-reaction-to-lithuanias-change-of-policy>.

21 Ibidem. p. 2.

22 Ramzy, Austin: 'China's Xi Jinping Seeks to Shake Trans-Atlantic Solidarity With Flurry of Diplomacy'. *Wall Street Journal*, April 17, 2023, retrieved 19.04.2023, from <https://www.wsj.com/articles/chinas-xi-jinping-seeks-to-shake-trans-atlantic-solidarity-with-flurry-of-diplomacy-b671c6af?mod=world_major_1_pos1>.

23 Barigazzi, Jacopo: 'France and Poland spar as EU plan to buy Ukraine ammo idles in legal limbo'. *Politico.eu*, April 19, 2023, retrieved 20.05.2023, from <https://www.politico.eu/article/france-poland-eu-plan-buy-ukraine-ammunition-war/>.

24 It is quite frequent for French and German political leaders to present their national interests as purportedly European interest in general, whereas not always this is true.

25 Janke, Igor / Bielecki, Jędrzej: 'Prezydent Francji podważa rolę USA. Znaczenie wizyty Macrona w Chinach dla Europy - Jędrzej Bielecki'. *Układ Otwarty*, April 04, 2023, minutes: 8:00-9:00, retrieved 20.04.2023, from <https://www.youtube.com/watch?v=45TvjpOLf-4>.

26 Rawicz, Marta / Mazurek, Robert: 'Sławomir Dębski: To od USA zależy pokój w Europie'. *Poranna rozmowa w RMF FM*, April 12, 2023, retrieved 21.04.2023, from <https://www.rmf24.pl/tylko-w-rmf24/poranna-rozmowa/news-slawomir-debski-to-od-usa-zalezy-pokoj-w-europie,nId,6711044?utm_source=www.rmf24.pl&utm_medium=link&utm_campaign=rozmowa_kolumna#crp_state=1>.

27 Hinshaw, Drew / Woo, Stu: 'U.S. Campaign Against Huawei Faces Challenge in Eastern Europe'. *Wall Street Journal*, February 10, 2019, retrieved 11.02.2023, from <https://www.wsj.com/articles/u-s-campaign-against-huawei-faces-challenge-in-eastern-europe-11549833381>.

28 Woo, Stu: 'Beijing Shuns Ericsson, Nokia as the West Curbs Huawei'. *Wall Street Journal*, August 03, 2021, retrieved 03.08.2023, from <https://www.wsj.com/articles/beijing-shuns-ericsson-nokia-as-the-west-curbs-huawei-11627982882?mod=hp_lista_pos1>.

29 'Kłótnia w rodzinie z Huawei w tle'. *Gazeta Finansowa*, May 28, 2020, retrieved 10.06.2023, from <https://www.gf24.pl/wydarzenia/swiat/item/2734-klotnia-w-rodzinie-z-huawei-w-tle>.

30 Hinshaw, Drew: 'Allies Wary of U.S. Stance on Huawei and 5G'. *Wall Street Journal*, April 09, 2020, retrieved 13.06.2023, from <https://www.wsj.com/articles/allies-wary-of-u-s-stance-on-huawei-and-5g-11586460582?mod=ig_fivegtechnologyreport>.

[31] Norman, Laurence / Mackrael, Kim: 'China Wants to Be at Center of New World Order, Top EU Official Says'. *Wall Street Journal,* March 30, 2023, retrieved 20.04.2023, from <https://www.wsj.com/articles/china-wants-to-be-at-center-of-new-world-order-top-eu-official-says-22987030>.

Bibliography

'America's Special Relationship Changes'. *Stratfor,* April 21, 2016, retrieved 05.05.2023, from <https://webcache.googleusercontent.com/search?q=cache:mv2AK-hNae8J:<https://www.stratfor.com/geopolitical-diary/americas-special-relationship-changes+&cd=1&hl=pl&ct=clnk&gl=pl>.

Barigazzi, Jacopo: 'France and Poland spar as EU plan to buy Ukraine ammo idles in legal limbo'. *Politico.eu,* April 19, 2023, retrieved 20.05.2023, from <https://www.politico.eu/article/france-poland-eu-plan-buy-ukraine-ammunition-war/>.

Becker, Markus et al.: 'Germany Prepares for Possible Re-Election of Donald Trump'. *Der Spiegel,* April 28, 2023, retrieved 29.04.2023, from <https://www.spiegel.de/international/germany/horror-scenario-germans-prepare-for-possible-re-election-of-donald-trump-a-8668044c-f299-45a8-b6ea-ba3691cddb5f>.

Fairless, Tom: 'In Battle With U.S. for Global Sway, China Showers Money on Europe's Neglected Areas'. *Wall Street Journal,* April 13, 2021, retrieved 13.04.2021, from <https://www.wsj.com/articles/in-battle-with-u-s-for-global-sway-china-showers-money-on-europes-neglected-areas-11618310350?mod=hp_lead_pos7>.

Hage, Simon et al.: 'Chinese Expansion Has Germany on the Defensive'. *Der Spiegel,* May 24, 2018, retrieved 01.06.2018, from <https://www.spiegel.de/international/business/chinese-economic-expansion-has-germany-worried-a-1209325.html>.

Hage, Simon et al.: 'German Companies Ignore Major Risks in China'. *Der Spiegel,* January 01, 2022, retrieved 04.11.2022, from <https://www.spiegel.de/international/business/business-as-usual-german-companies-ignore-major-risks-in-china-a-27b66d20-f228-47d0-b2bf-95f3cc976e6c>.

Hinshaw, Drew / Woo, Stu: 'U.S. Campaign Against Huawei Faces Challenge in Eastern Europe'. *Wall Street Journal,* February 10, 2019, retrieved 11.02.2023, from <https://www.wsj.com/

articles/u-s-campaign-against-huawei-faces-challenge-in-eastern-europe-11549833381>.

Hinshaw, Drew: 'Allies Wary of U.S. Stance on Huawei and 5G'. *Wall Street Journal,* April 09, 2020, retrieved 13.06.2023, from <https://www.wsj.com/articles/allies-wary-of-u-s-stance-on-huawei-and-5g-11586460582?mod=ig_fivegtchnologyreport>.

Hong, Yelin: 'The AIIB Is Seen Very Differently in the US, Europe, and China'. *The Diplomat,* May 08, 2015, retrieved 03.04.2023, from <https://thediplomat.com/2015/05/the-aiib-is-seen-very-differently-in-the-us-europe-and-china/.Janke>.

Igor / Bielecki, Jędrzej: 'Prezydent Francji podważa rolę USA. Znaczenie wizyty Macrona w Chinach dla Europy - Jędrzej Bielecki'. *Układ Otwarty,* April 04, 2023, minutes: 8:00-9:00, retrieved 20.04.2023, from <https://www.youtube.com/watch?v=45TvjpOLf-4>.

Kaczmarski, Marcin: 'The UK shows its openness to China'. *Centre for Eastern Studies,* October 28, 2015, retrieved 29.05.2023, from <https://www.osw.waw.pl/en/publikacje/analyses/2015-10-28/uk-shows-its-openness-to-china>.

'Kłótnia w rodzinie z Huawei w tle'. *Gazeta Finansowa,* May 28, 2020, retrieved 10.06.2023, from <https://www.gf24.pl/wydarzenia/swiat/item/2734-klotnia-w-rodzinie-z-huawei-w-tle>.

Kolarz, Stefania: 'EU Targets Insufficient Monitoring of Foreign Investment'. *PISM Bulletin,* 2664(43), April 13, 2023, p. 1, retrieved 04.05.2023, from <https://www.pism.pl/publications/eu-targets-insufficient-monitoring-of-foreign-investment>.

Legorano, Giovanni: 'Italy Signs Up to China's Global Infrastructure Plan Despite U.S. Ire'. *Wall Street Journal,* March 23, 2019, retrieved 23.05.2023, from <https://www.wsj.com/articles/italy-signs-up-to-chinas-global-infrastructure-plan-despite-u-s-ire-11553341408>.

Norman, Laurence / Mackrael, Kim: 'China Wants to Be at Center of New World Order, Top EU Official Says'. *Wall Street Journal,* March 30, 2023, retrieved 20.4.2023, from <https://www.wsj.com/articles/china-wants-to-be-at-center-of-new-world-order-top-eu-official-says-22987030>.

Norman, Laurence / Mackrael, Kim: 'China Wants to Be at Center of New World Order, Top EU Official Says'. *Wall Street Journal,* March

30, 2023, retrieved 20.04.2023, from <https://www.wsj.com/articles/china-wants-to-be-at-center-of-new-world-order-top-eu-official-says-22987030>.

Popławski, Konrad: 'Capital does have nationality: Germany's fears of Chinese investments'. *Komentarze OSW,* 230, January 25, 2017, retrieved 04.06.2023 from <https://www.osw.waw.pl/en/publikacje/osw-commentary/2017-01-25/capital-does-have-nationality-germanys-fears-chinese>.

Popławski, Konrad: 'Globalne starcie o elektromobilność zagrożeniem dla Europy Środkowej?'. *Komentarze OSW,* 504, 30.3.2023, p. 3.

Przychodniak, Marcin: 'Regression and Pro-Russia Rhetoric. China's Reaction to Lithuania's Change of Policy'. *PISM Bulletin,* 2389(19), November 16, 2021, retrieved 04.05.2023, from <https://www.pism.pl/publications/regression-and-pro-russia-rhetoric-chinas-reaction-to-lithuanias-change-of-policy>.

Ramzy, Austin: 'China's Xi Jinping Seeks to Shake Trans-Atlantic Solidarity With Flurry of Diplomacy'. *Wall Street Journal,* April 17, 2023, retrieved 19.04.2023, from <https://www.wsj.com/articles/chinas-xi-jinping-seeks-to-shake-trans-atlantic-solidarity-with-flurry-of-diplomacy-b671c6af?mod=world_major_1_pos1>.

Rawicz, Marta / Mazurek, Robert: 'Sławomir Dębski: To od USA zależy pokój w Europie'. *Poranna rozmowa w RMF FM,* April 12, 2023, retrieved 21.04.2023, from <https://www.rmf24.pl/tylko-w-rmf24/poranna-rozmowa/news-slawomir-debski-to-od-usa-zalezy-pokoj-w-europie,nId,6711044?utm_source=www.rmf24.pl&utm_medium=link&utm_campaign=rozmowa_kolumna#crp_state=1>.

'The conundrum of Germany's business ties with China'. *The Economist,* April 27, 2023, retrieved 04.05.2023 2023, from <https://www.economist.com/business/2023/04/27/the-conundrum-of-germanys-business-ties-with-china>.

'The Future of Chinese Investment in Europe'. *Stratfor,* February 25, 2021, retrieved 02.04.2023, from <https://webcache.googleusercontent.com/search?q=cache>:-bX8ATMT8NMJ:<https://worldview.stratfor.com/article/future-chinese-investment-europe+&cd=1&hl=pl&ct=clnk&gl=pl>.

'The U.S., Japan and the Netherlands Mull New Restrictions on China's Tech Sector'. *Stratfor.com*, June, 02, 2023, retrieved 11.02.2023, from <https://cc.bingj.com/cache.aspx?q=%22The+U.S.%2c+Japan+and+the+Netherlands+Mull+New+Restrictions+on+China%27s+Tech+Sector%22&d=4351532448908&mkt=pl-PL&setlang=pl-PL&w=oLTWziHDbtZ70fdhCFB6Uhf2_csCzzoQ>.

Wong, Audrye: 'China's Economic Statecraft: Lessons Learned from Ukraine', *The Washington Quarterly*, 46(1), 2023, pp. 122–123.

Woo, Stu: 'Beijing Shuns Ericsson, Nokia as the West Curbs Huawei'. *Wall Street Journal*, August 03, 2021, retrieved 03.08.2023, from <https://www.wsj.com/articles/beijing-shuns-ericsson-nokia-as-the-west-curbs-huawei-11627982882?mod=hp_lista_pos1>.

Business as Usual? Europe as an Economic Partner of the US and China

Łukasz Stach

China Shakes the World: A Titan's Rise and Troubled Future – and the Challenge for America – the title of journalist James Kynge's book published in 2006 was quite prophetic. Since 2006, China has significantly increased its economic and military potential, and the US-PRC relations deteriorated, as rivalry between both great powers arose. The turning point came in 1979, when Deng Xiaoping – China's new supreme the PRC leader – announced the 'Four Modernisations' and China's economy was transformed from a planned economy based on Maoist ideology to one adopting capitalist growth strategies and market forces, as well as opening to Western technologies and investments (interestingly, Singapore was the model for Chinese modernisation).[1] The results are astonishing. In 2019 the Congressional Research Service noticed: 'Since opening up to foreign trade and investment and implementing free-market reforms in 1979, China has been among the world's fastest-growing economies, with real annual gross domestic product (GDP) growth averaging 9.5% through 2018, a pace described by the World Bank as 'the fastest sustained expansion by a major economy in history'. Such growth has enabled China, on average, to double its GDP every eight years and helped raise an estimated 800 million people out of poverty. China has become the world's largest economy (on a Purchasing Power Parity basis), manufacturer, merchandise trader, and holder of foreign exchange reserves. This in turn has made China a major commercial partner of the United States. China is the USA's largest merchandise trading partner, biggest source of imports, and third-largest export market. China is also the largest foreign holder of US Treasury securities, which help fund the federal debt and keep US interest rates low'.[2] The report clearly explained how significant China's economic growth was, as well as its importance and challenge for the US. Provider of marketing and consumer data,

Statista underlines that China developed from the world's workbench to an economic superpower. The PRC's technological capabilities are growing, and China advances in sophisticated technologies like artificial intelligence and 5G. In short, China became a great power and has evolved from a poor, stagnant, and centrally controlled economy to a global one. China's growing economic power has led Beijing to achieve a global power status, which also has significant political consequences. Tensions between China and the developed countries are rising and the PRC is increasingly challenging the economic world order, led by the US.[3] In fact, China has challenged the U.S, and some argue that China is a 'revisionist' power.[4]

Although the Sino-American rivalry has attracted the most attention, its implications are significant for Europe as well. The European Union (as a single market comprising the 27 member states) is the third world economy, both in nominal and PPP terms. Currently, the EU, the PRC, and the US are the three biggest global economies, so economic relations between these three powers have global implications. However, there is one fundamental difference between the PRC, the US and the European Union. Both the US and China are states, while the EU is a supranational and political union of 27 member states. In 2019 Jan Zielonka wrote that Europe is a complicated maze with many fault lines that defy any simple categorisation.[5] Furthermore, its decision-making process is complicated, and '[...] achieving a consensus is often cumbersome and requires complex negotiations and 'lateral progress'.[6] As a result, the European Union has some difficulty in taking quick and effective actions, especially during any crisis, when a swift response is essential. So far, European integration has progressed furthest in the field of economics (Economic and Monetary Union, single common market, introduction of the Euro as a common currency) and the EU is an economic giant. However, despite the achievements and benefits of European integration, there are problems which may threaten the EU's future, as well as its position in the turbulent times of a China-US rivalry.

After the end of the Cold War, European integration gained steam. In 1993 the Maastricht Treaty formally established the European Union, in 1995 enlargement saw Austria, Finland, and Sweden join the EU. Nine years later, in 2004, the European Union expanded to include 10 more countries, 8 of which were from the former Soviet sphere of influence. European economy was growing, and the future of the European project was viewed through rose-tinted glasses. For example, the introduction of the euro was presented as a symbols of the EU's integration success, despite some doubts pointed out by some economists, especially American ones. Milton Friedman, Martin Feldstein, Thomas Willett, James Tobin, Paul Krugman, amongst many other, were sceptical of the euro as a common currency.[7] In retrospect, including the European debt crisis, it has become obvious that the sceptical voices were justified. As Joseph Stiglitz noticed, the Eurozone is a political project not an economic one – it aimed to not only strengthen economic stability, but also to enhance the EU's political integration.[8] However, the euro failed to achieve its principal goals – prosperity and political integration.[9] Paul de Grauwe underlines the design failures of the Eurozone and the fact, that it is not an optimal currency area.[10] It may lead to divergent economic development between countries. The European sovereign debt crisis has shown the fragility of the euro and the risk of a disintegration of the whole EMU system. Such a scenario did not materialise; however, the risk of a new crisis in the Eurozone still exists.[11] Overall, the Eurozone is the embodiment of the European political and economic ambitions, but it has not lived up to expectations, and its design flaws still exist. The problem is that the EU has a tendency to implement public policies, the results of which are far from expected. The Lisbon Strategy is another example of such an approach. Proposed in 2000, it aimed to transform the European Union by 2010 into the most competitive and knowledge-based economy in the world, capable of sustainable economic growth with greater social cohesion and better jobs.[12] In 2005 it was revised and narrowly focused on growth, employment and preservation of the European model – its ambitions became modest.[13] Finally, the Lisbon Strategy disappeared from public consciousness altogether.

These two examples (the Euro and the Lisbon Strategy) illustrate Europe's problem – ambitious goals versus modest results. The European Union has a problem with efficient implementation of its policies. It was not a significant problem when the world order was relatively stable and Europe did not face any significant external threats. However, in turbulent times, when world politics have been shaped by raw power and the systemic China-US rivalry is growing, Europe suddenly has to adapt to an international environment where China has become both an economic and military great power, and the US wants to preserve its status as the sole superpower. It should be noted that it is China's rapid economic growth that has enabled Beijing to compete effectively with the US, although the PRC's position was strengthened by the misguided policy of Western states and concerns that prioritised economic gains over policy issues.

Indicators such as GDP growth and value, China's share in the world economy, and the value of its exports and imports can be used to analyse the dynamics of Beijing's economic growth. Analysing these figures over the last few decades helps to illustrate the rate at which the Chinese economy has grown compared to the EU and the US. During the last decades economic growth in the People's Republic of China was rapid and much higher than in the EU and the US. Figure 1 illustrates that the average economic growth for the period 1990–2021 in the European Union was 1.69%, in the US 2.5%, while the PRC recorded a rate of more than 9% per year (Table 1). Even during the 2007–2008 Financial Crisis and COVID 19 recession, its economy – despite a slowdown – achieved growth, while the EU and US economies had negative growth.

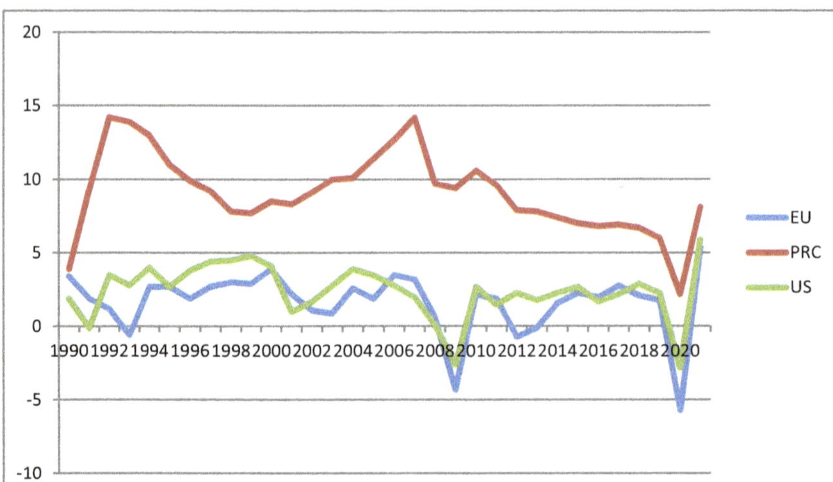

Figure 1. GDP growth in the EU, the PRC and the US (annual %), (1990–2021)

Source: World Bank

Thanks to its fast economic growth, China's GDP (both in terms of current the USD and Purchasing Power Parity) has grown significantly (Figure 2 and Figure 3). At the beginning of the 1990s the PRC's economy was significantly smaller than that of the US and the EU but after three decades of growth, the International Monetary Fund estimates that Chinese economy in terms of PPP is already 23% larger than that of the US, and the World Bank estimates the Chinese economy to be over 18% larger than American.[14] European Union's GDP is smaller than China's, even taking into account GDP expressed in current USD.

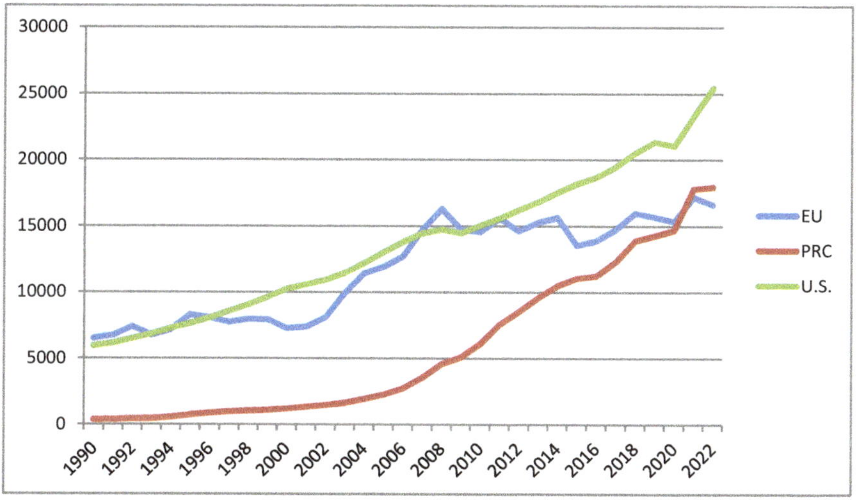

Figure 2. GPD, current USD (June 2023), in USD billions (1990–2021)

Source: World Bank

The fact that the Chinese economy has outgrown the European one is not surprising. It is, however, symptomatic that the total GDP of EU countries has not grown significantly since the Eurozone crisis. In 2008 it was 16.3 trillion USD, in 2021 16.64 trillion. Brexit has definitely had an impact on the EU economy's total GDP (in 2021 the United Kingdom's GDP was 3.07 trillion USD), but the EU's economy has slowed down and the COVID 19 pandemic only deteriorated the overall situation.

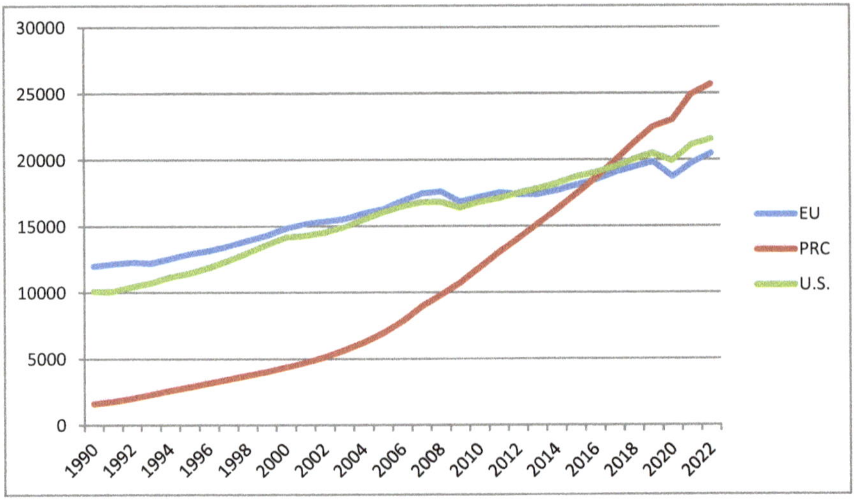

Figure 3. GDP (PPP), constant 2017 international USD, in billions USD (1990–2021)

Source: World Bank

Table 1. Chosen EU, PRC and US economic indicators 1990 to 2021 comparison.

	EU		**PRC**		**U.S.**	
	1990	**2021**	**1990**	**2021**	**1990**	**2021**
GDP (current USD)	6,500	17,180	361	17,730	5,960	23,320
GDP PPP (current USD)	6,230	21,680	1,110	27,310	5,960	23,320
Average GDP growth (1990–2021)	1.65%		9.54%		2.48%	
Export of goods and services (current US$)	1.65 trillion	8.65 trillion	43.94 billion	3.55 trillion	551.87 billion	2.54 trillion

Source: World Bank

The consequence of China's economic success story has been an increase in the PRC's share of the global economy. During the Cold War, as well as in the 1990s and early twenty-first century, the economic dominance of the West was undisputed. However, the last two decades have seen the rise of China in the global economy. The US has been able to maintain its position from the early 1990s, while the EU's share in the world's economy has declined gradually. China's share in the world economy became similar to that of the EU, and just 6% lower than that of the US (Figure 4).

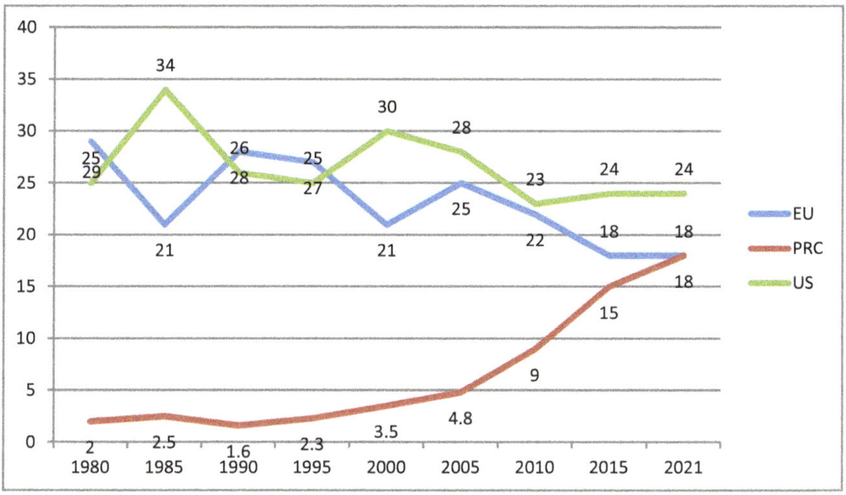

Figure 4. EU, PRC and US share of World Economy (in percentage)

Source: World Bank

China has also become the world's manufacturing superpower. The United Nations Industrial Development Organisation clearly indicates that in the 1990s the world's manufacturing centres were located in the Americas and Europe.[15] However, during the last decades, global production has moved away to Asia, which currently accounts for 54.1% of world manufacturing. The PRC achieved staggering results, in 1990 it held a 3.5% share in world manufacturing and in 2021 it reached 30.5%. The US is the second world manufacturer (16.8%), followed by Japan (7.0%), Germany (4.8%) and India (3.2%). China became a world's factory thanks to expansion of its manufacturing capabilities and output. The strategy of exporting cheaply made goods and components enabled the PRC to achieve double digit GDP growth for three decades.[16] Since 1990, the value of the PRC's export and import has grown enormously, in terms of exports, China surpassed the US and Germany and has been the world's largest exporter. As a whole, the European Union's export and import value (especially in services) is still bigger than the PRC's, but the EU consists of 27 states, many of which (mostly from Western Europe) are highly developed. Figure 5 and Figure 6 show the value of EU, PRC, US and German export of goods and services, which illustrate Beijing's growing significance in these fields. In 1990 China's share in the global export and import was marginal, nowadays the PRC is a key player.

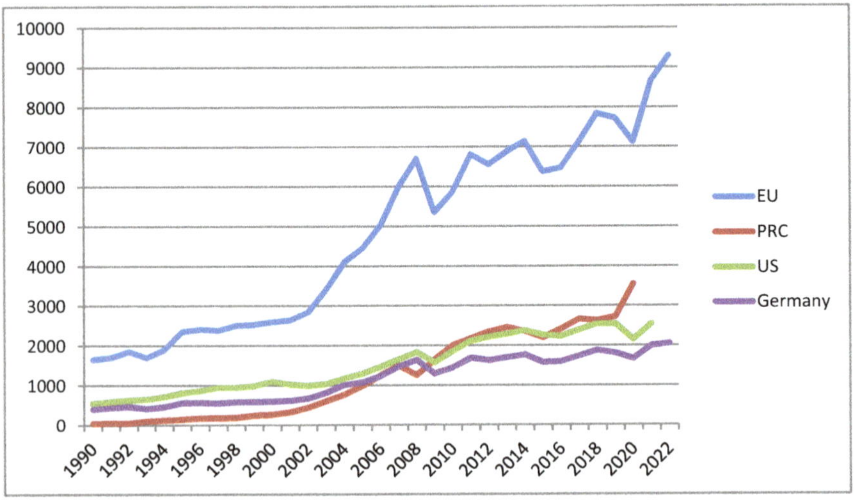

Figure 5. Export of goods and services (current the USD: June 2023): EU, PRC, US, Germany.

Source: World Bank

There were many keys to such outstanding economic success, like economic reforms under Deng Xiaoping, high rate of savings, productivity gains, cheap labour, foreign direct investment, etc. Trade liberalisation was also a key factor in the PRC's economic success.[17] Trade barriers were removed; China boosted its export and transformed itself into a global manufacturing hub. The process accelerated in 2001 when the PRC was admitted to the World Trade Organisation. China's WTO accession was an American-supported process and helped turn the PRC into the world's workshop.[18] The PRC is one of the winners of globalisation, but despite the fact that its share in the world economy has grown from 2% in 1980 to 18% in 2021, China's economic success has not meant the marginalisation of Western economies. In fact, Western governments and companies have been doing great business with Beijing. From the end of the Cold War till 2008, the global economy has grown from 22.86 trillion USD to 64.14 trillion USD and the US, and the EU also took part in this process. The West profited by gaining access to the Chinese consumer market, while China's low labour costs enabled many Western companies to produce for less. Moreover, Western countries nurtured the hope that China's economic success would bring political liberalisation.[19] However, China's political development would not mirror the West and Beijing's economic liberalisation has not brought a similar process in politics, so far. Moreover, the PRC became a global power and an economic and political competitor to the West in political and economic fields, including hi-tech.

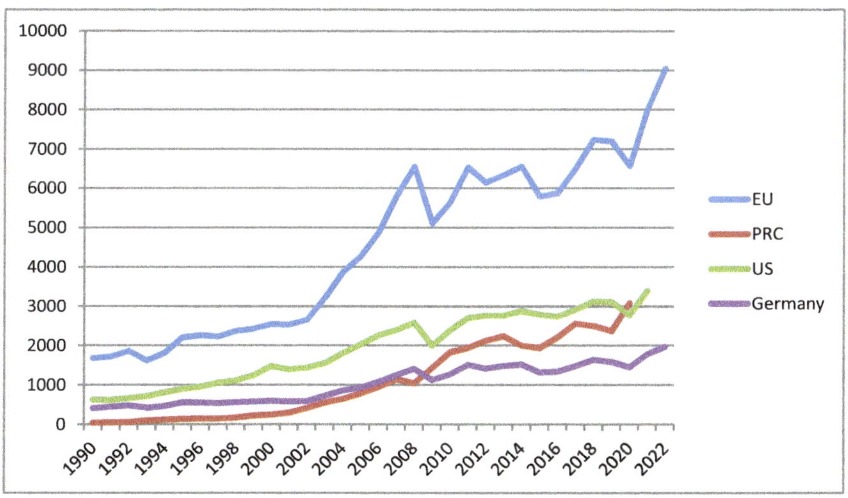

Figure 6. Import of goods and services (current the USD: June 2023): EU, PRC, US, Germany

Source: World Bank

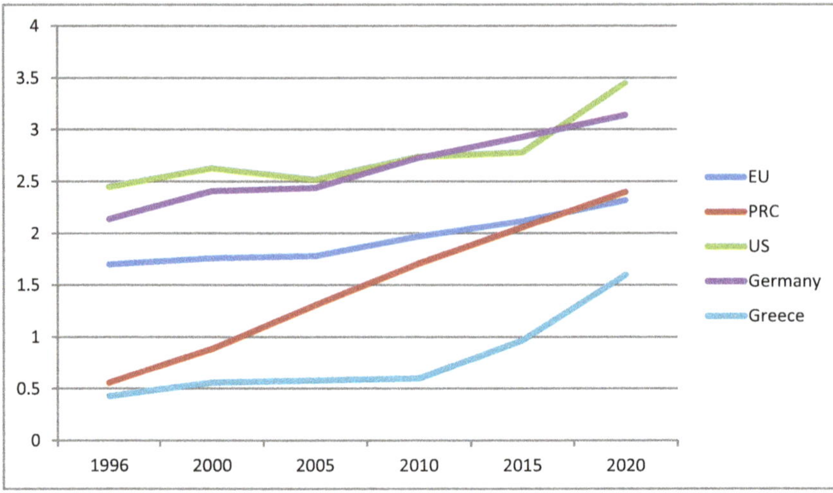

Figure 7. Research and development expenditure (% of GDP) – EU, PRC, US, Germany and Greece.

Source: World Bank
In the case of the EU, total expenditure as a percentage of GDP is shown, as well as that of Germany, the EU largest economy, and Greece, which has been hit by the debt crisis. The example of these two countries shows that different EU countries have different approaches to R&D spending, resulting in uneven R&D spending and an innovation gap between some EU countries.

China has maintained its growth and is becoming a centre for new technologies and innovations. China expanded not only in manufacturing products like textiles or rubber and plastics. By 2020 China had become the world's manufacturing leader in such industries as: computers, electronics, and optics (growth from 15.7% in 2000 to 41.5%); electrical equipment (11.8% to 41.5%); machinery and other equipment (7.7% to 38%); motor vehicles, trailers and semi-trailers (5.6% to 32.5%); or pharmaceuticals, medicinal chemicals (4.7% to 21.8%).[20] China also increased its expenditures in the research and development sector, which helped Beijing transform its economy into a knowledge-based one. Research and development (R&D) plays a crucial role in advanced economies, so governments, companies and other stakeholders have made substantial investments in this area. In last two decades, global

R&D expenditures have tripled, from 675 billion USD (2000) to 2.4 trillion USD (2020). Leadership in science and technology significantly helps the United States to maintain its supremacy in economy and the military and the US still funds more R&D than any other country.[21] Currently, the US spends almost 3.5% of its GDP on research and development. On average, the European Union spends more than 2% of its GDP in this field, although R&D expenditure varies widely among member countries. For instance, Germany is almost equal to the US, while Greece significantly lags behind. Since the mid-1990s the PRC has significantly increased the percentage of GDP spent on research, from about 0.5% to almost 2.5% (more than the EU average) (Figure 7).

R&D expenditures in terms of PPP USD seems more favourable for the US and the PRC than in percentage of GDP. In 2020 the US spent almost 730 billion USD and China, ranked second, 582.8 billion USD (Chinese expenditures were bigger than the next four countries combined). The third place belongs to Japan (174.1 billion USD), fourth to Germany (143.4 billion USD). In the first 'top 10', there were also two EU member states: France (6th place with 74.6 billion USD) and Italy (10th place with 38.2 billion USD). It is worth pointing out that in 2020 the 10 largest R&D-funding countries accounted for $1.999 trillion in R&D expenditures (85.0% of the global total). The top 20 R&D-funding countries accounted for $2.225 trillion (94.6% of the global total).[22] In general, there are two leaders of R&D expenditures (United States and China) – plus some technologically advanced economies. As for the European Union – amongst the 20 leading R&D-funding countries there are 8 EU member states (Germany, France, Italy, Spain, Netherlands, Belgium, Sweden and Poland) which together spend 364.5 billion USD in PPP. It is around 50% of the USA's and 63% of the PRC's R&D spending. Similarly to military expenditures, the European Union's total R&D spending looks impressive. However, they are not combined but dispersed between 27 member states. Moreover, research efforts are also dispersed – despite the increasing internationalisation of science, research efforts are duplicated in many UE states. In fact, the EU is falling behind in general and digital innovations. Europe's R&D is concentrated in the automotive industry, rather than in electronics, software and computer services or technology.[23] The EU's technological backwardness compared to the US or China is starting to become apparent in Artificial Intelligence (AI), for example. In the field of AI, the EU is losing distance to both the PRC and the US. The Center for Data Innovation estimates that currently the US is leading the AI race, although the PRC is catching up quickly and the EU is behind both. According to the report, the EU has many AI researchers but there is a disconnect between the significant number of people involved in AI research and commercial AI adoption and funding. It reduces the EU's ability to gain maximum social and economic benefits from AI.[24] 'Brain drain' is also a problem, as many European AI talents migrate to the US. The EU should focus on encouraging researchers to stay in Europe and help convert research into business applications.[25] The European Commission prepared papers like 'Coordinated Plan on Artificial Intelligence' and 'Artificial Intelligence for Europe', and the EU has ambitions to become the world-leading region for developing and deploying AI.[26] Its scientific and industrial base, however, without investments, public-private sector cooperation, combining EU member states' efforts, etc. Europe will continue to lag behind the US and China in AI technology. In November 2022 Future of Life Institute noticed that European companies are not developing AI systems due to their relative competitive disadvantage vis-à-vis American and Chinese companies. So far, small European AI players are unable to compete with large companies from the US and the PRC. As it is, the largest players attract capital, researchers, etc. As a results, European companies depend in AI technologies on American and Chinese solutions.[27]

Some European countries (like Germany, Ireland or the Netherlands) are positioned as competitive industrial economies but Beijing has also significantly improved its position in this ranking. According to the Competitive Industrial Performance (CIP) index, since 2016 China is has ranked as second in the world amongst the most competitive industrial economies. For over a decade, Germany occupied the first place, while the US placed sixth in 2020. Amongst the top 10 world's most competitive industrial economies there are also EU economies like: Ireland (3rd place) and the Netherlands (10th place), and during the last decade France and Italy also appeared in this group.[28] Average CIP ranking by geographical region shows that Europe is still the most competitive region, followed by Eastern Asia, where China and Japan are the leaders.[29] So, Europe still has the potential to play a significant role in the world, in terms of high technologies, but competing with China and the US in this field is a major challenge for Europe.

Another sign of China's economic significance is the growing number of big companies. According to *Forbes Global 2000* ranking, amongst the world's 50 largest companies, 18 are from the US, 10 from the PRC (plus one from Hong Kong), and 9 from the European Union.[30] The *2022 Fortune Global 500* (the most valuable companies by market capitalisation) ranking shows that American giants like *Apple*, *Microsoft*, *Amazon*, *Tesla*, *Alphabet* are at the top of the list (*Saudi Arabian Oil Company* is placed at second or even first place in some rankings). Chinese companies like *Tencent*, *Kweichow*, and some banks are gradually improving their positions in the rankings, while EU companies lag behind.

The EU is one of the most outward-oriented economies in the world and import and export are crucial for many EU member states' economies. According to *Eurostat*, in 2021 the EU had a 15% share in the world export of goods, China 19%, and the US 10%. The US was the biggest importer of goods (16% of the world market), China occupied second place (15%) and the EU third (14 %).[31] In 2022, on trade in goods, the EU had a 396 billion euro deficit in trade with China, but in services the EU achieved a 20.5 billion euro surplus. However, overall, the EU-PRC trade in goods is much bigger than in services, so the EU faces a trade deficit with China. During the last five years it has grown significantly, from 154.705 billion euro to the aforementioned 396 billion euro. Import from the PRC has also grown much higher, than export from the EU to China.[32]

Export and import play a vital part in EU economy – Figure 8 and Figure 9 present export and import of goods and services (as a percentage of GDP) in the EU, the PRC, and the US.

It is noticeable that, in the case of the US and the PRC, the value of import and export as a percentage of GDP is lower than in the EU. However, a large majority of EU countries exported and imported more within the EU internal market than with countries outside the EU.[33] In 2022, international trade in goods and services with non-EU states relative to GDP amounted to 25% of the EU's GDP, still higher than China and the US. As a result, the EU

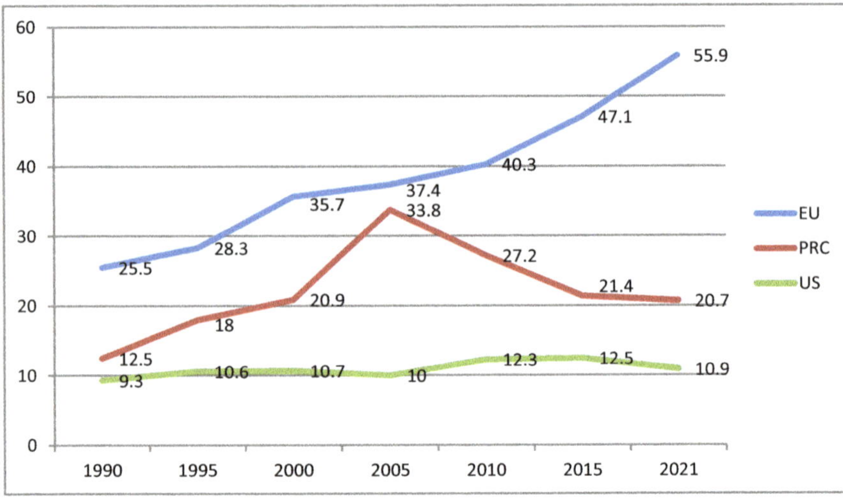

Figure 8. Export of goods and services (% GDP)

Source: World Bank

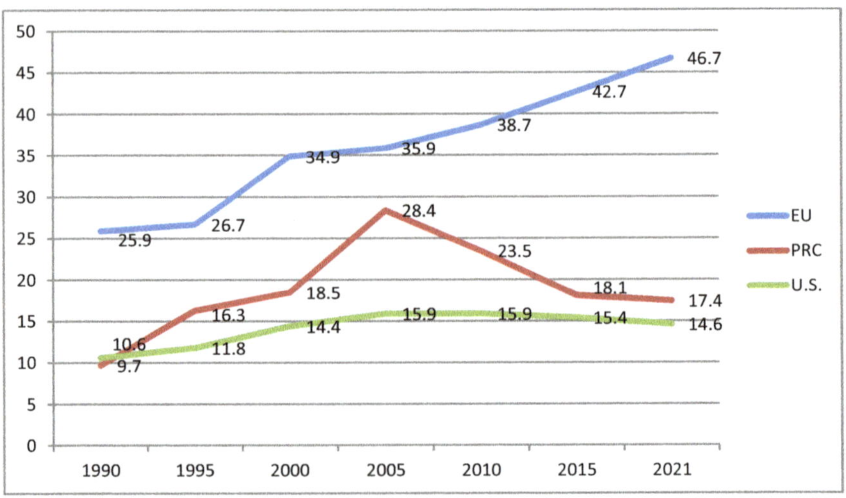

Figure 9. Import of goods and services (% GDP)

Source: World Bank

economy is more dependent on trade, so the growing rivalry between the US and China possess a serious threat to European economic prosperity. The EU's heavy reliance on export leaves Europe vulnerable to market crashes in emerging economies.[34]

The European Commission recognises the risks presented by certain economic linkages and stresses the need to develop a comprehensive approach to assessing and managing risks to the EU's economic security, in such areas as: supply chains (including energy security); physical and cyber security of critical infrastructure; technology security; weaponisation of economic dependencies or economic coercion.[35] The EU correctly identifies the threats but maintaining economic security may be difficult. One of the factors that have contributed to European economic strength is rule-based global trade. Meanwhile, the liberal international economic order has been facing many challenges in recent years.[36] Nowadays, hard power is becoming increasingly important in great power competition and Europe has deficiency in its military strength. The whole system based on free trade and cross-border organisation of production has been disrupted by the COVID-19 pandemic and Russia's attack on Ukraine.[37] It may hit the most globalised economies, like Germany, which is the biggest one in European Union, the hardest. Europe is caught between the US and China – both competing powers are important to the EU economy (especially in trade). However, EU member states differ significantly on this issue. Table 2 illustrates the importance of China and United States for individual EU member states.

Not surprisingly, for most EU member states, China is more important in terms of import, than export. In countries like the Czech Republic, Germany, Greece, Malta, Netherlands, Poland, and Slovenia import from China constitutes over 10% of total import value. For many other EU member states, the PRC is also an important source of import. Meanwhile, as an export partner the PRC is a less significant partner for EU member states, with some exceptions (Denmark, Finland, Germany, Ireland). Meanwhile, United States is an important export destination for many EU countries, including Germany.

Table 2. China and the US as trade partners of the EU economies in terms of export and import (2021)

Country	PRC		USA	
	Import	Export	Import	Export
Austria	3.65% / 7.43 billion	2.99% / 5.91 billion	1.87% / 3.81 billion	6.39% / 12.7 billion
Belgium	5.88% / 26.4 billion	1.76% / 7.08 billion	6.39% / 28.7 billion	6.12% / 24.7 billion
Bulgaria	5.58% / 2.56 billion	3.44% / 1.49 billion	0.71% / 326 million	2.59% / 1.12 billion
Croatia	4.75% / 1.66 billion	1.42% / 323 million	2.44% / 1.66 billion	3.72% / 849 million
Cyprus	6.31% / 934 million	1.23% / 63.5 million	0.95% / 140 million	1.64% / 84.5 million
Czech Republic	10.5% / 20.9 billion	1.43% / 3.22 billion	1.88% / 3.72 billion	2.39% / 5.36 billion
Denmark	8.56% / 10.2 billion	5.85% / 7 billion	3.3% / 3.9 billion	10.5% / 12.5 billion
Estonia	5.93% / 1.55 billion	1.27% / 279 million	1.88% / 492 million	9.29% / 2.03 billion
Finland	7.05% / 5.79 billion	5.83% / 4.84 billion	2.71% / 2.23 billion	7.55% / 6.27 billion
France	6.82% / 47.5 billion	4.9% / 27.8 billion	3.8% / 26.4 billion	7.4% / 42.1 billion
Germany	10% / 134 billion	7.71% / 121 billion	4.8% / 64.2 billion	8.66% / 135 billion
Greece	11.1% / 12.6 billion	1.5% / 1.23 billion	1.72% / 1.95 billion	3.79% / 3.11 billion
Hungary	7.93% / 10.8 billion	1.9% / 2.63 billion	2.11% / 2.87 billion	3.3% / 4.53 billion
Ireland	5.49% / 6.37 billion	6.67% / 14.2 billion	16% / 18.6 billion	28.2% / 59.8 billion
Italy	8% / 45.6 billion	3.21% / 19.1 billion	3.3% / 18.8 billion	9.73% / 58.1 billion
Latvia	4.66% / 1.14 billion	1.09% / 218 million	1.08% / 263 million	2.59% / 518 billion

Table 2. Continued

Country		PRC		USA
Lithuania	5.05% / 2.16 billion	0.77% / 316 million	2.75% / 1.17 billion	5.86% / 2.39 billion
Luxembourg	5.82% / 1.67 billion	2% / 388 million	3.56% / 1.02 billion	2.58% / 501 million
Malta	11.5% / 1.96 billion	3.1% / 156 million	0.64% / 108 million	4.03% / 203 million
Netherlands	13.2% / 88.3 billion	2.53% / 16.3 billion	7.58% / 50.8 billion	4.57% / 29.4 billion
Poland	13% / 45.8 billion	1.17% / 3.76 billion	2.14% / 7.58 billion	2.79% / 9 billion
Portugal	5.17% / 5.06 billion	1.3% / 980 million	2.39% / 2.34 billion	5.95% / 4.49 billion
Romania	6.19% / 6.89 billion	1.73% / 1.57 billion	0.86% / 957 million	2.43% / 2.21 billion
Slovakia	5.54% / 5.6 billion	2.75% / 2.87 billion	0.56% / 564 million	3.51% / 3.67 billion
Slovenia	11.5% / 6.59 billion	0.99% / 464 million	0.89% / 506 million	2.12% / 990 million
Spain	9.4% / 38.5 billion	2.8% / 10.4 billion	4.22% / 17.3 billion	4.78% / 17.8 billion
Sweden	7.13% / 12.4 billion	4.33% / 8.01 billion	2.92% / 5.07 billion	8.24% / 15.2 billion

Source: Observatory of Economic Complexity

Table 3 shows the importance of EU member states for China and the US as a trade partners.

In terms of export, only Germany is a significant partner both for the US and China, but the EU as a whole is an important trade partner for both powers. However, the focus is shifting to Asia. Nowadays, the PRC's largest trading partner is the Association of Southeast Asian Nations (ASEAN), the European Union is the second-largest trading partner, and the US occupies the third place. The value of China's trade with ASEAN and the EU has grown recently, while the value of trade with the US has dropped. However, ASEAN and the EU are multi-state organisations countries. By contrast,

Table 3. EU's member states as a trade partners of China and United States in terms of export and import (2021)

Country	PRC		U.S.	
	Import	Export	Import	Export
Austria	0.3% / 5.91 billion	0.22% / 7.43 billion	0.46% / 12.7 billion	0.23% / 3.81 billion
Belgium	0.35% / 1.08 billion	0.79% / 26.4 billion	0.9% / 24.7 billion	1.76% / 28.7 billion
Bulgaria	0.076% / 1.49 billion	0.077% 2.56 billion	0.041% / 1.12 billion	0.02% / 326 million
Croatia	0.015% / 323 million	0.05% / 1.66 billion	0.03% / 849 million	0.052% / 1.66 billion
Cyprus	0.01% / 63.5 million	0.03% / 934 million	0.01% / 84.5 million	0.01% / 140 million
Czech Republic	0.16% / 3.22 billion	0.63% / 20.9 billion	0.2% / 5.36 billion	0.23% / 3.72 billion
Denmark	0.35% / 7 billion	0.31% / 10.2 billion	0.46% / 12.5 billion	0.24% / 3.9 billion
Estonia	0.013% / 279 million	0.047% / 1.55 billion	0.075% / 2.03 billion	0.03% / 492 million
Finland	0.25% / 4.84 billion	0.17% / 5.79 billion	0.23% / 6.27 billion	0.14% / 2.23 billion
France	1.41% / 27.8 billion	1.42% / 47.5 billion	1.54% / 42.1 billion	1.62% / 26.4 billion
Germany	6.12% / 121 billion	4% / 134 billion	4.96% / 135 billion	3.94% / 64.2 billion
Greece	0.062% / 1.23 billion	0.38% / 12.6 billion	0.11% / 3.11 billion	0.12% / 1.95 billion
Hungary	0.13% / 2.63 billion	0.32% / 10.8 billion	0.17% / 4.53 billion	0.18% / 2.87 billion
Ireland	0.72% / 14.2 billion	0.19% / 6.37 billion	2.19% / 59.8 billion	1.14% / 18.6 billion
Italy	0.97% / 19.1 billion	1.37%/ 45.6 billion	2.13% / 58.1 billion	1.16% / 18.8 billion
Latvia	0.011% / 218 million	0.034% / 1.14 billion	0.019% / 518 billion	0.016% / 263 million

Table 3. Continued

Country	PRC		U.S.	
Lithuania	0.016% / 316 million	0.065% / 2.16 billion	0.09% / 2.39 billion	0.072% / 1.17 billion
Luxembourg	0.02% / 388 million	0.05% / 1.67 billion	0.018% / 501 million	0.063% / 1.02 billion
Malta	0.01% / 156 million	0.059% / 1.96 billion	0.01% / 203 million	0.01% / 108 million
Netherlands	0.83% / 16.3 billion	2.65% / 88.3 billion	1.08% / 29.4 billion	3.12% / 50.8 billion
Poland	0.19% / 3.76 billion	1.37% / 45.8 billion	0.33% / 9 billion	0.47% / 7.58 billion
Portugal	0.05% / 980 million	0.15% / 5.06 billion	0.16% / 4.49 billion	0.14% / 2.34 billion
Romania	0.08% / 1.57 billion	0.21% / 6.89 billion	0.081%/2.21 billion	0.06% / 957 million
Slovakia	0.15% / 2.87 billion	0.17% / 5.6 billion	0.13% / 3.67 billion	0.035% / 564 million
Slovenia	0.024% / 464 million	0.2% / 6.59 billion	0.036% / 990 million	0.031% / 506 million
Spain	0.53% / 10.4 billion	1.15% / 38.5 billion	0.65% / 17.8 billion	1.06% / 17.3 billion
Sweden	0.41% / 8.01 billion	0.37% / 12.4 billion	0.56% / 15.2 billion	0.31% / 5.07 billion
USA	7.65% / 151 billion	15.9% / 530 billion	--	--
PRC	--	--	19.4% / 530 billion	9.26% / 151 billion

Source: Observatory of Economic Complexity

when it comes to individual countries, the United States still remain China's most important trading partner. From the perspective of an export-oriented economy (or in the case of many EU member states), political tensions could negatively affect trade relations, so growing China-the US tensions pose a serious challenge for the European Union. Additionally, there are other risks, which may affect the EU economy.

The first is the growing competitiveness of China's economy and the quality of products produced by its industry. Europe suddenly has to compete with China, for example, in the automotive market or in technologies related to green industries. The EU had a bitter experience when its solar panel industry was decimated by cheaper Chinese imports. The EU's response was to introduce anti-dumping and anti-subsidy duties, but according to Karl-Heinz Remmers it only worsened the situation.[38] The scenario may repeat in the electric vehicles market. Chinese electric vehicle brands are expanding to global markets and the European Commission President Ursula von der Layen announced, that their price is kept artificially low by state subsidies. European Commission imposed punitive tariffs to protect the EU producers against Chinese electric vehicle imports.[39] News organisation *Politico* stresses that the EU risks a trade war with China over electric vehicles.[40] As the green transformation is one of the EU's flagship aims, defeat in this field would be very costly for Europe, in this case for its economically vital car industry. However, imposing punitive tariffs will trigger Chinese retaliation, and Beijing may also use divide-and-conquer tactics and plays the EU countries off against each other.[41] Moreover, the return of protectionism may be dangerous for export-oriented European economies. Christine Lagarde, the president of the European Central Bank, stated: 'As an economy that is very open to trade and deeply integrated into global supply chains, we are vulnerable to geopolitical headwinds. For example, 35% of Europe's manufacturing output is absorbed outside the EU, much more than for the United States or China'.[42] Europe has to respond to the growing protectionist tendencies in the US and the PRC. The biggest challenge, however, is that European industry must quickly develop its competitiveness, and punitive tariffs cannot help it this issue.

Today, the most ambitious EU project is its climate policy. The European Union aims to be climate-neutral by 2050, and this objective is at the heart of the European Green Deal. EU member states will have to drastically reduce their greenhouse gas emissions to reach a net-zero emissions balance. According to the European Council, transition to climate neutrality brings opportunities for: economic growth, markets and jobs, and technological development.[43] The EU has set a target to reduce net greenhouse gas emissions by at least 55% by 2030, and a regulatory package called 'Fit for 55' has been prepared. According to the European Commission: 'The

"Fit for 55" package of legislation makes all sectors of the EU's economy fit to meet this target. It sets the EU on a path to reach its climate targets in a fair, cost-effective and competitive way'.[44] No doubt the programme is ambitious, but the question is whether the benefits will be able to offset its costs? Is Europe really fit for 55?

The costs of the green transition and decarbonisation of the European economy will be high. The Green Deal Investment Plan aims to mobilise at least 1 trillion euro in sustainable investments over the next decade, to reach the EC 2030 climate targets. Regions most affected by the green transition will be supported by the Just Transition Mechanism, which is aimed to alleviate the negative socioeconomic impact of the process.[45] The question is whether the declared funds will be sufficient to finance the costs of the European climate policy, as well as to mitigate its negative effects. It is obvious, that energy-intensive sectors and the fossil-fuel industry could face major disruptions and 'Fit for 55' will have a profound effect on the labour market and households in regions affected by the policy. *Business Europe* stresses the fact that climate ambition must go hand in hand with industrial competitiveness.[46] To prevent the risk of carbon leaking and level up the playing field with the rest of the world on carbon pricing, the European Commission proposed to implement a green tariff on goods entering the EU, called Carbon Border Adjustment Mechanism (CBAM).[47] The European Commission's 'Impact Assessment' indicates that reducing greenhouse gas emissions by as much as 50% to 55% by 2030 is not a risk to the EU economy and its macroeconomic impact will be limited.[48]

Regardless of whether the Union is able to achieve the 'Fit for 55' goals, it should be noted that there are many risks associated with their implementation. According to *Euroactiv* (September 15, 2023), the CBAM mechanism has raised concerns within some WTO member states, including China. China urged the EU to avoid protectionist measures and green trade barriers. The EU Emissions Trading System carbon permit prices are higher than expected, in February 2023 reaching over 100 euros per ton, which increased costs that industry must incur for the emissions.[49] These two examples alone indicate that the European Union's plans to successfully implement the 'Fit for 55' package may face many obstacles that could affect the competitiveness of the European economy and the living standards of its people. Countries not burdened by costly climate policies will have a competitive advantage over Europe. What could bring success to the EU would be a technological leap that would ensure a supply of cheap and clean energy, but in the technological field the EU is lagging behind the US and China. For the time being, the European Union introduced an expensive policy and presents optimism that it can bear the costs and that the benefits will be significant. The less optimistic scenario that the ambitious project will fail or lead to a significant decline in the competitiveness of the European economy is not being considered. More importantly, European climate policy is aimed at EU member states, and it is an open question whether the funds invested in it will contribute to strengthening the EU's economic potential. Meanwhile, Europe has to face significant Chinese activity in the field of business and investment, including the EU's neighbourhood. The PRC's well-known Belt and Road Initiative (BRI) is a global infrastructure strategy, aimed to enhance China's economic and political position not only in Asia, but in the whole world. The BRI is regarded as the most important driver for the PRC's long-term development strategy and a vision expressing its grand ambitions.[50] This project seeks to connect the PRC with Asia, Africa, and Europe via land and maritime routes, which is aimed at improving regional integration, stimulating economic growth, and increasing trade. The BRI is associated with large a programme of investments in infrastructure development, especially in communications infrastructure and telecommunications networks.[51] There are many opinions about this Chinese global project, from perceiving it as a platform of inclusive globalisation and inclusive development,[52] a genuine development project,[53] a new model of international development cooperation,[54] or a revolution in economic geography and the era of win-winism.[55] The Chinese government presents the BRI as a 'helping hand' public policy.[56] On the other hand, there are 'China threat' hypotheses and, as Jeremy Garlick[57] analysed, scholars and analysts are divided in their evaluation of the BRI initiative. Some underline the issue of the PRC's 'debt trap diplomacy',[58] although, there are voices that it is just a myth.[59] It is also no surprise that there is also rhetoric from the US, which warns that the PRC weaponised its capital, and it is not just limited to Africa and Asia, but extends to Europe.[60] The BRI is definitely a part of Beijing's grand strategy, aimed at using its economic strength to pursue political, security, and even cultural goals.[61] Whatever the BRI really is for Beijing, the initiative itself is a challenge for both the US and Europe. It aims to strengthen China's economic and political presence in strategic regions of the world, which is beneficial for Beijing's global policy.

The EU noticed widespread Chinese business and investment activity. The European Commission highlights that the PRC's investments have contributed to the growth of many receiving economies, although, they also have a less favourable face. China's investments frequently neglect financial and socio-economic sustainability and may lead to a high level of debt and the transfer of control over strategic assets and resources. It hampers good social and economic governance, the rule of law, and human rights (European Commission 2019).[62] 'In this light, the EU should continue to promote stability, sustainable economic development, and respect for good governance, in partnership with third countries and with even greater vigour. China's increased international presence can offer major opportunities for trilateral cooperation and positive engagement, when demand-driven and based on mutual interests and understanding, in regions of priority importance for the EU, such as Africa. The EU will encourage China to improve debt transparency and sustainability by implementing the G20 operational guidelines on sustainable financing and support the continued efforts of the Paris Club towards the inclusion of emerging market creditors'.[63] The aforementioned document of the European Commission shows the de facto powerlessness of European institutions, which only have the power to 'encourage' China to play according to Western rules. If the EU desires to promote stability, sustainable economic development, good governance and human rights, it needs something more than rhetoric.

In December 2021 the EU announced the Global Gateway Initiative, its strategy to invest in infrastructure projects and establish economic links. The project aims to mobilise up to 300 billion euros from the EU budget, member states and private initiative.[64] According to *Politico* (September 15, 2021), in September 2021 Ursula von der Layen announced, that: 'We will build Global Gateway partnerships with countries around the world. We want investments in quality infrastructure, connecting goods, people and services around the Word'.[65] The project is perceived as the EU's response to China's Belt and Road programme. However, critics highlight the fact that the initiative does not provide enough funds to compete with China. The programme is vague and financially dubious and duplicates already existing development efforts.[66] There is also a question of values. Tyyne Karjalainen noticed that 'Incapable of competing with China's Belt and

Road Initiative (BRI) in the quantity of investments, the EU's 1-year-old connectivity initiative Global Gateway aims to challenge it with quality, providing more democratic, secure, equal, green, transparent, and sustainable alternatives to lower-income partners'.[67] However, the PRC offers an alternative model of development, which seems to be more attractive for many authoritarian or semi-authoritarian regimes. The European Union is talking about values, meanwhile many potential Global Gateway partners are not interested in values, but in money and investments. Beijing talks less about values and offers investment without worrying about human rights or environmental issues. For many authoritarian regimes the PRC is simply a more attractive partner, especially since Beijing put more money on the table than the EU.

To finance the BRI, China established financial institutions, like the Asian Infrastructure Investment Bank (AIIB) or the Silk Road Fund. AIIB is capitalised at $100 billion, triple A-rated by the major international credit agencies and 109 approved members worldwide,[68] while the Silk Road Fund has a total capital of $40 billion and RMB 100 billion.[69] According to Christoph Nedopil from Green Finance and Development Center, since 2013, BRI engagement amounts to $962 billion ($573 billion in construction contracts, $389 billion in non-financial investments).[70] Such significant funding has resulted in the strengthening of Beijing's economic and political position in many regions of the world, especially Africa, broadening the PRC's economic and political influence. Compared to Beijing's massive investments, the US and EU response looks pale. Critics say that the EU's Global Gateway is a 'drop in the ocean', compared to the BRI.[71] For the moment, China is gaining an advantage over Western countries as a source of capital and investment, especially in the Global South. Through economic diplomacy, Beijing tries to consolidate its influence there. So far, the EU and the US and unable to respond effectively to the challenge caused by the BRI. On the other hand, the issue of the Hambantota port in Sri Lanka is becoming a signal that the PRC would use money to gain political influence, which could be risky for countries receiving Chinese loans and financial aid. Critics of the BRI highlight the fact that China is engaging in 'debt trap diplomacy', offering unsustainable loans to developing countries for infrastructure projects. If there have problems repaying the loans, China can take control of infrastructure placed in strategic locations. This leads to a strengthening of Beijing's position in the global power competition. This is all the more important because China is de facto building an alternative development model to the West that combines economic growth with a non-democratic political system. For many authoritarian regimes, this model is more attractive than that offered by liberal-democratic countries, because it allows for economic growth without liberalising the political system. Moreover, as it was mentioned, the PRC offers investments, credits and loans without asking about democratic values and human rights. On the other hand, the EU likes to portray itself as a promoter of liberal values and human rights but, unlike Beijing, it puts less money on the table, which puts the EU in a losing position in the competition for influence in Africa, for example.

Conclusions

The rise of China's economic power has changed the balance of power in the contemporary world. The rise of China's economic power has changed the balance of power in the modern world. In the early stages of the Chinese economic miracle, China was treated by the West as a potential market for goods and a place to invest because of its cheap labour. However, China has taken on the ambitious challenge of transforming its economy from a manufacturing-heavy economic model to a services-led one. Despite the achieved economic growth, the model of economic development based on the idea of China as the world's factory has some limitations and has led to some negative effect: overinvestment, environmental pollution, and growing debt.[72] In spite of these problems, China has become a challenge for both Europe and the United States. China represents a significant economic and trade challenge to the European Union, mostly due to its state-dominated economy and unfair trade practices. De-industrialisation and declining living standards in some regions of Europe is a problem and there are calls for a more assertive position towards Beijing in terms of trade and investment. On the other hand, European industry and business is still attracted by China's huge domestic market, including the ever-richer Chinese middle class. Such opportunity is very tempting for many European companies, and some of them have moved production to China, to take advantage of lower production costs and global supply chains.[73] Nevertheless, the growing US-China rivalry is a challenge for the European Union. The EU would like to have its cake and eat it – have good relations both with China and the US; however, in the age of growing bilateral power rivalry, it may be difficult to achieve.

Economic competition and even conflicts over trade, economic and financial policies are one of the dimensions of growing rivalry. The US accuses the PRC of unfair competition, and this view is widely shared in Europe. Bilateral US-China trade is no longer a stabiliser which balances out political conflicts.[74] This is bad news for the European Union, which has seen trade as a stabilising factor in international relations, especially as Europe's capacity for hard power is limited. Overall, the prospects for Europe, caught between the US and China, are not good. An ageing society, a high-tech sector falling further and further behind the US and the PRC, high costs of the European Green Deal, loss of competitiveness for European industry, increasing bureaucracy – these are just a few of the challenges currently facing the European economy. The EU must find itself in a world of economic competition between the world's largest economies.

Notes

1 '"Singapore Model" as a path to Chinese modernisation', Nahui, Chen: 'The Construction of the Singapore Model in Mainland China'. *Think China*, September 24, 2019, retrieved: 18.02.2023, from <https://www.thinkchina.sg/construction-singapore-model-mainland-china>.

2 Morrison, M. Wayne: 'China's Economic Rise: History, Trends, Challenges, and Implications for the United States'. *Congressional Research Service*, June 25, 2020, retrieved: 18.02.2023, from <https://sgp.fas.org/crs/row/RL33534.pdf>.

3 'China as a global power'. *Statista*, July 2021, retrieved 21.02.2023, from: <https://www.statista.com/study/88121/china-as-a-global-power/>.

4 Mearscheimer, John: *The Tragedy of Great Powers Politics*. W.W. Norton: New York 2001; Mearscheimer, John: 'The gathering storm: China's challenge to the US power in Asia'. *The Chinese Journal of International Politics* 3(4), 2010, pp. 381–396; Shambaugh, David: 'China or America: Which is Revisionist Power?'. *Survival* 43 (3), 2001, pp. 25–30; Stent, Angela: 'Russia and China: Axis of Revisionists'. *Brookings Institution*, February 2020, retrieved 25.02.2023, from <https://www.brookings.edu/research/russia-and-china-axis-of-revisionists/>; Taylor, Nicholas: 'China as a Status Quo or Revisionist Power? Implications for Australia'. *Security Challenges* 3(1), 2007, pp. 29–45.

5 Lehne, Stefan: 'Europe's East-West Divide: Myth or Reality?', *Carnegie Europe*, April 1, 2019, retrieved 21.02.2023, from <https://carnegieeurope.eu/2019/04/11/europe-s-east-west-divide-myth-or-reality-pub-78847>; Zielonka, Jan. 2019. 'The Mythology of

East-West Divide'. *Eurozine*, March 05, 2019, retrieved 21.02.2023, from <https://www.eurozine.com/mythology-east-west-divide/>.

6 Buti, Marco: 'Lessons from a European journey through two crises'. *Vox.eu*, November 18, 2021, retrieved 23.02.2023, from <https://cepr.org/voxeu/columns/lessons-european-journey-through-two-crises>.

7 Friedman, Milton: 'The Euro: Monetary Unity to political Disunity?' *Project Syndicate*, August 28, 1997, retrieved 03.03.2023, from <https://www.project-syndicate.org/commentary/the-euro--monetary-unity-to-political-disunity>; Feldstein, Martin: 'The Political Economy of the European Economic and Monetary Union: Political Sources of an Economic Liability'. *Journal of Economic Perspectives*, 11(4), 1997, pp. 23–42; Willett, Thomas D.: 'Some political economy aspects of EMU'. *Journal of Policy Modelling* 23(3), 2000, pp. 379–389; Tobin, James: 'Currency unions: Europe vs. United States'. *Policy Option Politiques*, May 1, 2001, retrieved 03.03.2023, from <https://policyoptions.irpp.org/magazines/one-world-one-money/currency-unions-europe-vs-the-united-states/>; Krugman, Paul: 'Beware of what you wish for'. *Massachusetts University of Technology*, 1998, retrieved 21.02.2023, from <https://web.mit.edu/krugman/www/euronote.html>; Krugman, Paul: 'The Euro, Living Dangerously'. *The Unofficial Paul Krugman Archive*, 1999, retrieved 21.02.2023, from <http://www.pkarchive.org/trade/euro.html>.

8 Stiglitz, Joseph: *The Euro: How a Common Currency Threatens the Future of Europe*. Norton: New York, London 2016.

9 Stiglitz, Joseph: 'The problem with Europe is the euro'. *The Guardian*, August 10, 2016, retrieved 25.03.2023, from <https://www.theguardian.com/business/2016/aug/10/joseph-stiglitz-the-problem-with-europe-is-the-euro>.

10 Grauwe, Paul de.: 'Design Failures in the Eurozone - can they be fixed?'. *European Economy. Economic papers* 451, April 2013, retrieved 02.03.2023, from <https://ec.europa.eu/economy_finance/publications/economic_paper/2013/ecp491_en.htm>; Grauwe, Paul de: 'Design Failures of the Eurozone'. *Centre for Economic Policy Research*, September 07, 2015, retrieved 02.03.2023, from <https://cepr.org/voxeu/columns/design-failures-eurozone>.

11 Grauwe, Paul de: 'Towards the New Euro Crisis?'. *Intereconomics. Review of European Economic Policy* 57(5), 2022, pp. 277; Micossi, Stefano: 'What future of Eurozone?'. *Centre for Economic Policy Research*, September 07, 2015, retrieved 03.03.2023, from <https://cepr.org/voxeu/columns/design-failures-eurozone>; Tilford, Simon: 'Is the Eurozone really out of the wood?'. *The Centre for European Reform*, September 22, 2017, retrieved 12.03.2023, from <https://www.cer.eu/insights/eurozone-really-out-woods>.

12 Krcek, Jiri: 'Assessing the EU's 'Lisbon Strategy:' Failures & Successes'. *Inquiries* 4(9), 2013, retrieved 18.02.2023, from <http://www.inquiriesjournal.com/articles/754/assessing-the-eus-lisbon-strategy-failures-successes>.

13 Jones, Erik: 'The Economic Mythology of European Integration'. *Journal of Common Market Studies* 48(1), 2010, pp. 104–105.

14 'The World's Biggest Economy. America or China?'. *Worldeconomics.com*, July 25, 2023, retrieved 18.08.2023, from <https://www.worldeconomics.com/Thoughts/The-Worlds-Biggest-Economy.aspx>.

15 'International Yearbook of Industrial Statistics. Edition 2022'. *United Nations Industrial Development Organization*, 2022, pp. 38–39, retrieved 19.03.2023, from <https://www.unido.org/resources-publications-flagship-publications/international-yearbook-industrial-statistics>.

16 Matsagnon, Elizabeth: 'China's transitioning economy'. *World Finance*, retrieved 23.08.2023, from <https://www.worldfinance.com/markets/chinas-transitioning-economy>.

17 Morrison, M. Wayne: 'China's Economic Rise: History, Trends, Challenges, and Implications for the United States'. *Congressional Research Service*. June 25, 2019, retrieved 18.02.2023 from <https://sgp.fas.org/crs/row/RL33534.pdf>.

18 Hillman, Jenniffer A.: 2022. 'China's Entry into the WTO – A Mistake by the United States?'. Forthcoming chapter in: Henry Gao / Damian Raess, (eds.) *China and the WTO: 20 Years On*. Cambridge University Press. Georgetown Law Faculty Publications and Other Works, 2022, retrieved 17.08.2023, from <http://dx.doi.org/10.2139/ssrn.4094346>.

19 Haas, N. Richard: 'China's homegrown crisis'. *The Strategist. Australian Strategic Policy Institute*, August 22, 2023, retrieved 28.08.2023, from <https://www.aspistrategist.org.au/chinas-homegrown-crisis/>.

20 'International Yearbook of Industrial Statistics. Edition 2022'. *United Nations Industrial Development Organization*, 2022, p. 49, retrieved 19.03.2023, from <https://www.unido.org/resources-publications-flagship-publications/international-yearbook-industrial-statistics>.

21 'Federal Research and Development (R&D) Funding: FY2022'. *Congressional Research Service*, January 19, 2022, retrieved 29.08.2023, from <https://crsreports.congress.gov/product/pdf/R/R46869>.

22 'Federal Research and Development…'.

23 Bughin, James et al.: 'Innovation in Europe. Changing the game to regain a competitive edge'. *McKinsey Global Institute*, 2019, retrieved 27.08.2023, from <https://www.mckinsey.com/~/media/mckinsey/featured%20insights/innovation/reviving%20innovation%20in%20europe/mgi-innovation-in-europe-discussion-paper-oct2019-vf.ashx>.

24 Castro, Daniel / McLaughlin, Michael / Chivot Eline: 'Who is Winning the AI Race: China, the EU or the United States?'. *Centre for Data Innovation*, 2019, pp. 2–3, retrieved 24.08.2023, from <https://datainnovation.org/2019/08/who-is-winning-the-ai-race-china-the-eu-or-the-united-states/#_edn2>.

25 Ibidem. p. 52.

26 'Communication from the Commission to the European Parliament, the European Council, the Council, the European Economic and Social Committee and the Committee of the Regions. Coordinated Plan on Artificial Intelligence'. *European Commission*, December 7, 2019, retrieved 11.06.2023, from <https://eur-lex.europa.eu/resource.html?uri=cellar:22ee84bb-fa04-11e8-a96d-01aa75ed71a1.0002.02/DOC_1&format=PDF>; 'Communication from the Commission to the European Parliament, the European Council, the Council, the European Economic and Social Committee and the Committee of the Regions. Artificial Intelligence for Europe'. *European Commission*, April 25, 2018, retrieved 11.06.2023, from <https://eur-lex.europa.eu/legal-content/EN/TXT/PDF/?uri=CELEX:52018DC0237>.

27 ‘Emerging Non-European Monopolies in the Global Ai Market’. *Future for Life Institute*, 2022, retrieved 18.08.2023, from <https://futureoflife.org/wp-content/uploads/2022/11/Emerging_Non-European_Monopolies_in_the_Global_AI_Market.pdf>.

28 ‘International Yearbook of Industrial Statistics. Edition 2022’. *United Nations Industrial Development Organization*, 2022, pp. 28–29, retrieved 19.03.2023, from <https://www.unido.org/resources-publications-flagship-publications/international-yearbook-industrial-statistics>.

29 Ibidem. p. 30.

30 ‘The Global 2000’. *Forbes*, June 08, 2023, retrieved 18.07.2023, from <https://www.forbes.com/lists/global2000/?sh=3a212ded5ac0>.

31 ‘International trade in goods’. *Eurostat*, September 2022, retrieved 29.08.2023, from <https://ec.europa.eu/eurostat/statistics-explained/index.php?title=International_trade_in_goods#The_three_largest_global_players_of_international_trade:_EU.2C_China_and_the_USA>.

32 ‘European Union. Trade with goods with China’. *European Commission. Directorate-Generale for Trade*, April 19, 2023, retrieved 28.08.2023, from <https://webgate.ec.europa.eu/isdb_results/factsheets/country/details_china_en.pdf>.

33 ‘International trade in goods’. *Eurostat*, September 2022, retrieved 29.08.2023, from <https://ec.europa.eu/eurostat/statistics-explained/index.php?title=International_trade_in_goods#The_three_largest_global_players_of_international_trade:_EU.2C_China_and_the_US A>.

34 Neuman, Jeanette / Horobin, William / Mesco, Manuela: ‘China’s Turbulence Exposes Risk to Europe’s Growth’. *The Wall Street Journal*, August 27, 2015, retrieved 29.08.2023, from <https://www.wsj.com/articles/chinas-turbulence-exposes-risks-to-europes-growth-1440698856>.

35 ‘An EU approach to enhance economic security’. *European Commission*, June 20, 2023, retrieved 30.08.2023, from <https://ec.europa.eu/commission/presscorner/detail/en/ip_23_3358>.

36 Kentikelenis, Alexander / Voeten, Erik: ‘Legitimacy challenges to the liberal world order: Evidence from United Nations speeches, 1970-2018’. *The Review of International Organisations* 16, 2021, pp. 722.

37 Plociennik, Sebastian: ‘Germany and the crisis of globalisation: adjustment strategies’. *Centre for Eastern Studies*, May 17, 2022, retrieved 21.08.2023, from <https://www.osw.waw.pl/pl/publikacje/komentarze-osw/2022-05-17/niemcy-i-kryzys-globalizacji-strategie-dzialania>.

38 Remmers, Karl-Heinz: ‘How solar tariffs destroyed then of thousands of jobs in Germany’. *Pvmagazine.com*, September 22, 2023, retrieved 29.09.2023 from <https://www.pv-magazine.com/2023/09/22/how-solar-tariffs-destroyed-tens-of-thousands-of-jobs-in-germany/>.

39 Blenkinsop, Philip: ‘EU to investigate ‘flood’ of Chinese electric cars, weight tariffs’. *Reuters*, September 13, 2023, retrieved 29.09.2023, from <https://www.reuters.com/world/europe/eu-launches-anti-subsidy-investigation-into-chinese-electric-vehicles-2023-09-13/>.

40 Posander, Joshu / Moens, Barbara / Lau, Stuart: ‘EU risks trade war with China over electric vehicles’. *Politico*, September 13, 2023, retrieved 30.09.2023 from <https://www.politico.eu/article/eu-ursula-von-der-leyen-china-electric-cars-probe-trade-war/>.

41 Moens, Barbara / Gijs, Camille: 'The EU lost a trade war with China 10 years ago. Has it learned?'. *Politico*, September 21, 2023, retrieved 30.09.2023, from <https://www.politico.eu/article/eu-lost-trade-war-china-10-years-ago-has-it-learned-electric-vehicle-subsidies/>.

42 'Speech by Christine Lagarde, President of the ECB, at the Deutsche Börse Annual Reception in Eschborn'. *European Central Bank*, January 23, 2023, retrieved 16.08.2023, from <https://www.ecb.europa.eu/press/key/date/2023/html/ecb.sp230123_1~2d9786eedf.en.html>.

43 'Climate change. What the EU is doing'. *European Council*, 2023, retrieved 15.07.2023 from <https://www.consilium.europa.eu/en/policies/climate-change/>.

44 'Financing the green transition: The European Green Deal Investment Plan and Just Transition Mechanism'. *European Commission*, 2023, retrieved 18.07.2023, from <https://ec.europa.eu/commission/presscorner/detail/en/ip_20_17>.

45 'Impact Assessment'. *European Commission*, September 17, 2020, retrieved 18.07.2023, from <https://eur-lex.europa.eu/resource.html?uri=cellar:749e04bb-f8c5-11ea-991b-01aa75ed71a1.0001.02/DOC_1&format=PDF>.

46 'The "Fit for 55 package" - a BusinessEurope position paper'. *BusinessEurope*, 2023, retrieved 01.10.2023, from <https://www.businesseurope.eu/publications/fit-55-package-businesseurope-position-paper>.

47 Colijn, Bert: 'Just how fit the EU's Fit for 55 climate strategy for Europe's economy?'. *ING*, February 16, 2022, retrieved 18.07.2023, from <https://think.ing.com/articles/just-how-fit-is-the-eus-fit-for-55-climate-strategy-for-europes-economy/>.

48 'Impact Assessment'. *European Commission*, September 17, 2020.

49 'EU Carbon Permits'. *Trading Economics*, 2023, retrieved 02.10.2023, from <https://tradingeconomics.com/commodity/carbon>.

50 'China's new silk route. The long and winding road'. *PwC's Growth Market Centre*, 2016, retrieved 18.09.2023, from <https://www.pwc.com/gx/en/growth-markets-center/assets/pdf/china-new-silk-route.pdf>.

51 'Belt and Road Initiative'. *European Bank for Reconstruction and Development*, retrieved 19.09.2023, from <https://www.ebrd.com/what-we-do/belt-and-road/overview.html>.

52 Weidong Liu: *The Belt and Road Initiative. A Pathway towards Inclusive Globalisation*. Routledge: London, New York, 2019, p. 67.

53 Ahmed, Faisal / Lambert, Alexander: *The Belt and Road Initiative. Geopolitical and Geoeconomic Aspects*. Routledge: London, New York, 2022, pp. 68–69.

54 Lin, Yifu: 'The Belt and Road and a New Model of International Development Cooperation'. In: Wei Liu (eds.): *China's Belt and Road Initiatives: Economic Geography*. Springer: Singapore, 2018 pp. 33–37.

55 Hu, Angang: 'The Belt and Road: Revolution of Economic Geography and the Era of Win-Winism'. In: Wei Liu (eds.): *China's Belt and Road Initiatives: Economic Geography*. Singapore: Springer, pp. 15–32.

56 Wang, Ruping / Pan, Zhen / Yang, Liu: 'The "Debt Trap" or the "Benefit Pie" View of China's Belt and Road Initiative on Host Countries: Evidence from Chinese Enterprises' Outward Foreign Direct Investment'. *Emerging Markets Finance and Trade* 29(7), 2023, p. 2269.

57 Garlick, Jeremy: *The Impact of China's Belt and Road Initiative. From Asia to Europe*. Routledge: London, New York, 2020, pp. 13–19.

58 Balding, Christopher: 'Why Democracies are Turning Against Belt and Road: Corruption, Debt and Blacklash'. *Foreign Affairs*, October 24, 2018, retrieved 23.10.2023, from <https://www.foreignaffairs.com/articles/china/2018-10-24/why-democracies-are-turning-against-belt-and-road>; Chellaney, Brahma: 'China's Debt-Trap Diplomacy'. *Project Syndicate*, January 23, 2017, retrieved 18.09.2023, from <https://www.project-syndicate.org/commentary/china-one-belt-one-road-loans-debt-by-brahma-chellaney-2017-01?barrier=accesspaylog>; Hurley, John / Scott, Morris / Portelance, Gaylin: 'Examining the debt implications of the Belt and Road Initiative from a policy perspective'. *Journal of Infrastructure, Policy and Development* 3(1), 2019, pp. 139–175; Mishra, Mansi / Mishra, Vivek Kumar: 'China's Belt And Road Initiatives: Examining the Debt Trap Diplomacy For Regional Supremacy In The Context Of Sri Lanka'. *World Affairs: The Journal of International Issues* 25 (1), 2021, pp. 122–135.

59 Singh, Ajit: 'The myth of "debt-trap diplomacy" and realities of Chinese development finance'. *Third World Quarterly* 42(2), 2019, pp. 239–253.

60 Grassley, Chuck: 'Grassley, Senators Express Concerns Over China's "Debt Trap" Diplomacy With Developing Countries'. *Grassley.senate.gov*, October 08, 2018, retrieved 12.10.2023, from <https://www.grassley.senate.gov/news/news-releases/grassley-senators-express-concerns-over-china-s-debt-trap-diplomacy-developing>.

61 Callahan, William: 'China's Belt and Road Initiative and the New Euroasian Order'. *Norwegian Institute of International Affairs*, 2016, retrieved 19.09.2023, from <https://css.ethz.ch/content/dam/ethz/special-interest/gess/cis/center-for-securities-studies/resources/docs/NUPI_China%E2%80%99s%20Belt%20and%20Road%20Initiative%20and%20the%20new%20eurasian%20order.pdf>.

62 'EU-China – A strategic outlook'. *European Commission*, March 12, 2019, retrieved 18.02.2023, from <https://ec.europa.eu/info/sites/default/files/communication-eu-china-a-strategic-outlook.pdf>.

63 Ibidem.

64 Barbero, Michele: 'Europe is Trying (and Failing) to Beat China at the Development Game'. *Foreign Policy*, January 10, 2023, retrieved 18.09.2023, from <https://foreignpolicy.com/2023/01/10/europe-china-eu-global-gateway-bri-economic-development/>.

65 Stuart, Lau / Cokelaere, Hanne: 'EU launches 'Global Gateway' to counter China's Belt and Road'. September 15, 2021, retrieved 21.10.2023, from <https://www.politico.eu/article/eu-launches-global-gateway-to-counter-chinas-belt-and-road/>.

66 Portal, Leo: 'The Global Gateway (Part 2): Is it failing its objectives?'. *Blue Europe*, July 31, 2023, retrieved 23.09.2023, from <https://www.blue-europe.eu/analysis-en/full-reports/the-global-gateway-part-2-is-it-failing-its-objectives/>; Bermingham, Finbarr / Nyabiage, Jevans: '1 year on, EU alternative to China's belt and road fails to deliver'. *South China Morning Post*, December 30, 2022, retrieved 19.09.2023, from <https://www.scmp.com/news/china/diplomacy/article/3204431/one-year-eu-alternative-chinas-belt-and-road-fails-deliver>.

67 Karjalainen, Tyyne: 'European Norms Trap? EU Connectivity Policies and the Case of the Global Gateway'. *East Asia* 40, 2023, pp. 293–316.

68 'Members and prospective members of the bank'. Asian Infrastructure Investment Bank. September 28, 2023, retrieved 11.10.2023, from <https://www.aiib.org/en/about-aiib/governance/members-of-bank/index.html>.

69 'Company profile'. *Silk Road Fund*, retrieved 11.10.2023, from <http://www.silkroad-fund.com.cn/enweb/gywm/gsgk/gsjj/index.html>.
70 Nedopil, Christoph: 'China Belt and Road Initiative (BRI) Investment Report 2022'. *Green Finance & Development Center*, FISF Fudan University: Shanghai, retrieved 13.10.2023, from <https://greenfdc.org/wp-content/uploads/2023/02/Nedopil-2023_China-Belt-and-Road-Initiative-BRI-Investment-Report-2022.pdf>.
71 Barbero, Michele: 'Europe is Trying (and Failing) to Beat China at the Development Game'. *Foreign Policy*, January 10, 2023.
72 Matsagnon, Elizabeth: 'China's transitioning economy'. *World Finance*.
73 Casarini, Nicola: 'A European strategic "third way?" The European Union between the traditional transatlantic alliance and the pull of Chinese market'. *China International Strategic Review* 4, 2022, pp. 96.
74 Perthes, Volker: 'Dimensions on rivalry: China, the United States, and Europe'. *China International Strategy Review* 3, 2021, pp. 58.

Bibliography

'An EU approach to enhance economic security'. *European Commission*, June 20, 2023, retrieved 30.08.2023, from <https://ec.europa.eu/commission/presscorner/detail/en/ip_23_3358>.

'Belt and Road Initiative'. *European Bank for Reconstruction and Development*, retrieved 19.09.2023, from <https://www.ebrd.com/what-we-do/belt-and-road/overview.html>.

'China as a global power'. *Statista*, July 2021, retrieved 21.02.2023, from: <https://www.statista.com/study/88121/china-as-a-global-power/>.

'China's new silk route. The long and winding road'. *PwC's Growth Market Centre*, 2016, retrieved 18.09.2023, from <https://www.pwc.com/gx/en/growth-markets-center/assets/pdf/china-new-silk-route.pdf>.

'Communication from the Commission to the European Parliament, the European Council, the Council, the European Economic and Social Committee and the Committee of the Regions. Artificial Intelligence for Europe'. *European Commission*, April 25, 2018, retrieved 11.06.2023, from <https://eur-lex.europa.eu/legal-content/EN/TXT/PDF/?uri=CELEX>:52018DC0237.

'Communication from the Commission to the European Parliament, the European Council, the Council, the European Economic and Social Committee and the Committee of the Regions. Coordinated Plan on Artificial Intelligence'. *European Commission*, December 7, 2019, retrieved 11.06.2023, from <https://eur-lex.europa.eu/resource.

html?uri=cellar>:22ee84bb-fa04-11e8-a96d-01aa75ed71a1.0002.02/DOC_1&format=PDF.

'Company profile'. *Silk Road Fund*, retrieved 11.10.2023, from <http://www.silkroadfund.com.cn/enweb/gywm/gsgk/gsjj/index.html>.

'Emerging Non-European Monopolies in the Global Ai Market'. *Future for Life Institute*, 2022, retrieved 18.08.2023, from <https://futureoflife.org/wp-content/uploads/2022/11/Emerging_Non-European_Monopolies_in_the_Global_AI_Market.pdf>.

'EU Carbon Permits'. *Trading Economics*, 2023, retrieved 02.10.2023, from <https://tradingeconomics.com/commodity/carbon>.

'EU-China – A strategic outlook'. *European Commission*, March 12, 2019, retrieved 18.02.2023, from <https://ec.europa.eu/info/sites/default/files/communication-eu-china-a-strategic-outlook.pdf>.

'European Union. Trade with goods with China'. *European Commission. Directorate-Generale for Trade*, April 19, 2023, retrieved 28.08.2023, from <https://webgate.ec.europa.eu/isdb_results/factsheets/country/details_china_en.pdf>.

'Federal Research and Development (R&D) Funding: FY2022'. *Congressional Research Service*, January 19, 2022, retrieved 29.08.2023, from <https://crsreports.congress.gov/product/pdf/R/R46869>.

'Financing the green transition: The European Green Deal Investment Plan and Just Transition Mechanism'. *European Commission*, 2023, retrieved 18.07.2023, from <https://ec.europa.eu/commission/presscorner/detail/en/ip_20_17>.

'Impact Assessment'. *European Commission*, September 17, 2020, retrieved 18.07.2023, from <https://eur-lex.europa.eu/resource.html?uri=cellar>:749e04bb-f8c5-11ea-991b-01aa75ed71a1.0001.02/DOC_1&format=PDF.

'International trade in goods'. *Eurostat*, September 2022, retrieved 29.08.2023, from <https://ec.europa.eu/eurostat/statistics-explained/index.php?title=International_trade_in_goods#The_three_largest_global_players_of_international_trade>:_EU.2C_China_and_the_USA.

'International Yearbook of Industrial Statistics. Edition 2022'. *United Nations Industrial Development Organization*, 2022, retrieved 19.03.2023, from

<https://www.unido.org/resources-publications-flagship-publications/international-yearbook-industrial-statistics>.

'Members and prospective members of the bank'. Asian Infrastructure Investment Bank. September 28, 2023, retrieved 11.10.2023, from <https://www.aiib.org/en/about-aiib/governance/members-of-bank/index.html>.

'Speech by Christine Lagarde, President of the ECB, at the Deutsche Börse Annual Reception in Eschborn'. *European Central Bank*, January 23, 2023, retrieved 16.08.2023, from <https://www.ecb.europa.eu/press/key/date/2023/html/ecb.sp230123_1~2d9786eedf.en.html>.

'The 'Fit for 55 package' - a BusinessEurope position paper'. *BusinessEurope*, 2023, retrieved 01.10.2023, from <https://www.businesseurope.eu/publications/fit-55-package-businesseurope-position-paper>.

'The Global 2000'. *Forbes*, June 08, 2023, retrieved 18.07.2023, from <https://www.forbes.com/lists/global2000/?sh=3a212ded5ac0>.

'The World's Biggest Economy. America or China?'. *Worldeconomics.com*, July 25, 2023, retrieved 18.08.2023, from <www.worldeconomics.com/Thoughts/The-Worlds-Biggest-Economy.aspx>.

Ahmed, Faisal / Lambert, Alexander: *The Belt and Road Initiative. Geopolitical and Geoeconomic Aspects*. Routledge: London, New York, 2022.

Balding, Christopher: 'Why Democracies are Turning Against Belt and Road: Corruption, Debt and Blacklash'. *Foreign Affairs*, October 24, 2018, retrieved 23.10.2023, from <https://www.foreignaffairs.com/articles/china/2018-10-24/why-democracies-are-turning-against-belt-and-road>.

Barbero, Michele: 'Europe is Trying (and Failing) to Beat China at the Development Game'. *Foreign Policy*, January 10, 2023, retrieved 18.09.2023, from <https://foreignpolicy.com/2023/01/10/europe-china-eu-global-gateway-bri-economic-development/>.

Bermingham, Finbarr / Nyabiage, Jevans: '1 year on, EU alternative to China's belt and road fails to deliver'. *South China Morning Post*, December 30, 2022, retrieved 19.09.2023, from <https://www.scmp.com/news/china/diplomacy/article/3204431/one-year-eu-alternative-chinas-belt-and-road-fails-deliver>.

Blenkinsop, Philip: 'EU to investigate 'flood' of Chinese electric cars, weight tariffs'. *Reuters*, September 13, 2023, retrieved 29.09.2023, from <https://www.reuters.com/world/europe/eu-launches-anti-subsidy-investigation-into-chinese-electric-vehicles-2023-09-13/>.

Bughin, James et al.: 'Innovation in Europe. Changing the game to regain a competitive edge'. *McKinsey Global Institute*, 2019, retrieved 27.08.2023, from <https://www.mckinsey.com/~/media/mckinsey/featured%20insights/innovation/reviving%20innovation%20in%20europe/mgi-innovation-in-europe-discussion-paper-oct2019-vf.ashx>.

Buti, Marco: 'Lessons from a European journey through two crises'. *Vox.eu*, November 18, 2021, retrieved 23.02.2023, from <https://cepr.org/voxeu/columns/lessons-european-journey-through-two-crises>.

Callahan, William: 'China's Belt and Road Initiative and the New Euroasian Order'. *Norwegian Institute of International Affairs*, 2016, retrieved 19.09.2023, from <https://css.ethz.ch/content/dam/ethz/special-interest/gess/cis/center-for-securities-studies/resources/docs/NUPI_China%E2%80%99s%20Belt%20and%20Road%20Initiative%20and%20the%20new%20eurasian%20order.pdf>.

Casarini, Nicola: 'A European strategic 'third way?' The European Union between the traditional transatlantic alliance and the pull of Chinese market'. *China International Strategic Review* 4, 2022, pp. 91–107.

Castro, Daniel / McLaughlin, Michael / Chivot Eline: 'Who is Winning the AI Race: China, the EU or the United States?'. *Centre for Data Innovation*, 2019, retrieved 24.08.2023, from <https://datainnovation.org/2019/08/who-is-winning-the-ai-race-china-the-eu-or-the-united-states/#_edn2>.

Chellaney, Brahma: 'China's Debt-Trap Diplomacy'. *Project Syndicate*, January 23, 2017, retrieved 18.09.2023, from <https://www.project-syndicate.org/commentary/china-one-belt-one-road-loans-debt-by-brahma-chellaney-2017-01?barrier=accesspaylog>.

Colijn, Bert: 'Just how fit the EU's Fit for 55 climate strategy for Europe's economy?'. *ING*, February 16, 2022, retrieved 18.07.2023, from <https://think.ing.com/articles/just-how-fit-is-the-eus-fit-for-55-climate-strategy-for-europes-economy/>.

European Council. 2023. 'Climate change. What the EU is doing'. Accessed 15 July 2023.<https://www.consilium.europa.eu/en/policies/climate-change/>.

Feldstein, Martin: 'The Political Economy of the European Economic and Monetary Union: Political Sources of an Economic Liability'. *Journal of Economic Perspectives*, 11(4), 1997, pp. 23–42.

Frayer, Janis Mackey and Larissa Gao. 2023. 'Chinese electric vehicles makers lead the world, rivalling U.S. pioneers'. *NBC News*, July 18. Accessed 22 August 2023. <https://www.nbcnews.com/news/world/chinese-electric-vehicle-makers-lead-world-rivaling-us-pioneers-rcna88990>

Friedman, Milton: 'The Euro: Monetary Unity to political Disunity?' *Project Syndicate*, August 28, 1997, retrieved 03.03.2023, from <https://www.project-syndicate.org/commentary/the-euro--monetary-unity-to-political-disunity>.

Garlick, Jeremy: *The Impact of China's Belt and Road Initiative. From Asia to Europe*. Routledge: London, New York, 2020.

Grassley, Chuck: 'Grassley, Senators Express Concerns Over China's 'Debt Trap' Diplomacy with Developing Countries'. *Grassley.senate.gov*, October 08, 2018, retrieved 12.10.2023, from <www.grassley.senate.gov/news/news-releases/grassley-senators-express-concerns-over-china-s-debt-trap-diplomacy-developing>.

Grauwe, Paul de.: 'Design Failures in the Eurozone - can they be fixed?'. *European Economy. Economic papers* 451, April 2013, retrieved 02.03.2023, from <https://ec.europa.eu/economy_finance/publications/economic_paper/2013/ecp491_en.htm>.

Grauwe, Paul de: 'Design Failures of the Eurozone'. *Centre for Economic Policy Research*, September 07, 2015, retrieved 02.03.2023, from <https://cepr.org/voxeu/columns/design-failures-eurozone>.

Grauwe, Paul de: 'Towards the New Euro Crisis?'. *Intereconomics. Review of European Economic Policy* 57(5), 2022, pp. 273–277.

Haas, N. Richard: 'China's homegrown crisis'. *The Strategist. Australian Strategic Policy Institute,* August 22, 2023, retrieved 28.08.2023, from <https://www.aspistrategist.org.au/chinas-homegrown-crisis/>.

Hillman, Jenniffer A.: 2022. 'China's Entry into the WTO – A Mistake by the United States?'. Forthcoming chapter in: Henry Gao / Damian Raess, (eds.) *China and the WTO: 20 Years On*. Cambridge University Press. Georgetown Law Faculty Publications and Other Works, 2022, retrieved 17.08.2023, from <http://dx.doi.org/10.2139/ssrn.4094346>.

Hu, Angang: 'The Belt and Road: Revolution of Economic Geography and the Era of Win-Winism'. In: Wei Liu (eds.): *China's Belt and Road Initiatives: Economic Geography*. Singapore: Springer, pp. 15–32.

Hurley, John / Scott, Morris / Portelance, Gaylin: 'Examining the debt implications of the Belt and Road Initiative from a policy perspective'. *Journal of Infrastructure, Policy and Development* 3(1), 2019, pp. 139–175.

Jones, Erik: 'The Economic Mythology of European Integration'. *Journal of Common Market Studies* 48(1), 2010, pp. 89–109.

Karjalainen, Tyyne: 'European Norms Trap? EU Connectivity Policies and the Case of the Global Gateway'. *East Asia* 40, 2023, pp. 293–316.

Kentikelenis, Alexander / Voeten, Erik: 'Legitimacy challenges to the liberal world order: Evidence from United Nations speeches, 1970-2018'. *The Review of International Organisations* 16, 2021, pp. 721–754.

Krcek, Jiri: 'Assessing the EU's 'Lisbon Strategy:' Failures & Successes'. *Inquiries* 4(9), 2013, retrieved 18.02.2023, from <http://www.inquiriesjournal.com/articles/754/assessing-the-eus-lisbon-strategy-failures-successes>.

Krugman, Paul: 'Beware of what you wish for'. *Massachusetts University of Technology*, 1998, retrieved 21.02.2023, from <https://web.mit.edu/krugman/www/euronote.html>.

Krugman, Paul: 'The Euro, Living Dangerously'. *The Unofficial Paul Krugman Archive*, 1999, retrieved 21.02.2023, from <http://www.pkarchive.org/trade/euro.html>.

Kynge, James. 2006. China Shakes the World: A Titan's Rise and Troubled Future - and the Challenge for America. Boston: Houghton Mifflin Harcourt.

Lehne, Stefan: 'Europe's East-West Divide: Myth or Reality?', *Carnegie Europe*, April 1, 2019, retrieved 21.02.2023, from <https://carnegieeurope.eu/2019/04/11/europe-s-east-west-divide-myth-or-reality-pub-78847>.

Lin, Yifu: 'The Belt and Road and a New Model of International Development Cooperation'. In: Wei Liu (eds.): *China's Belt and Road Initiatives: Economic Geography*. Springer: Singapore, 2018 pp. 33–37.

Matsagnon, Elizabeth: 'China's transitioning economy'. *World Finance*, retrieved 23.08.2023, from <https://www.worldfinance.com/markets/chinas-transitioning-economy>.

Mearscheimer, John: 'The gathering storm: China's challenge to US power in Asia'. *The Chinese Journal of International Politics* 3(4), 2010, pp. 381–396.

Mearscheimer, John: *The Tragedy of Great Powers Politics*. W.W. Norton: New York 2001

Micossi, Stefano: 'What future of Eurozone?'. *Centre for Economic Policy Research*, September 07, 2015, retrieved 03.03.2023, from <https://cepr.org/voxeu/columns/design-failures-eurozone>.

Mishra, Mansi / Mishra, Vivek Kumar: 'China's Belt And Road Initiatives: Examining the Debt Trap Diplomacy For Regional Supremacy In The Context Of Sri Lanka'. *World Affairs: The Journal of International Issues* 25 (1), 2021, pp. 122–135.

Moens, Barbara / Gijs, Camille: 'The EU lost a trade war with China 10 years ago. Has it learned?'. *Politico*, September 21, 2023, retrieved 30.09.2023, from <https://www.politico.eu/article/eu-lost-trade-war-china-10-years-ago-has-it-learned-electric-vehicle-subsidies/>.

Morrison, M. Wayne: 'China's Economic Rise: History, Trends, Challenges, and Implications for the United States'. *Congressional Research Service*. June 25, 2019, retrieved 18.02.2023 from <https://sgp.fas.org/crs/row/RL33534.pdf>.

Nahui, Chen. 2019. 'The Construction of the Singapore Model in Mainland China'. *ThinkChina*, September 24. Accessed: 18 February 2023. <https://www.thinkchina.sg/construction-singapore-model-mainland-china>.

Nedopil, Christoph: 'China Belt and Road Initiative (BRI) Investment Report 2022'. *Green Finance & Development Center*, FISF Fudan University: Shanghai, retrieved 13.10.2023, from <https://greenfdc.org/wp-content/uploads/2023/02/Nedopil-2023_China-Belt-and-Road-Initiative-BRI-Investment-Report-2022.pdf>.

Neuman, Jeanette / Horobin, William / Mesco, Manuela: 'China's Turbulence Exposes Risk to Europe's Growth'. *The Wall Street Journal*, August 27, 2015, retrieved 29.08.2023, from <https://www.wsj.com/articles/chinas-turbulence-exposes-risks-to-europes-growth-1440698856>.

Perthes, Volker. 2021. 'Dimensions on rivalry: China, the United States, and Europe'. *China International Strategy Review* 3, pp. 56–65.

Plociennik, Sebastian: 'Germany and the crisis of globalisation: adjustment strategies'. *Centre for Eastern Studies*, May 17, 2022, retrieved 21.08.2023, from <https://www.osw.waw.pl/pl/publikacje/komentarze-osw/2022-05-17/niemcy-i-kryzys-globalizacji-strategie-dzialania>.

Portal, Leo: 'The Global Gateway (Part 2): Is it failing its objectives?'. *Blue Europe*, July 31, 2023, retrieved 23.09.2023, from <https://www.blue-europe.eu/analysis-en/full-reports/the-global-gateway-part-2-is-it-failing-its-objectives/>.

Posander, Joshu / Moens, Barbara / Lau, Stuart: 'EU risks trade war with China over electric vehicles'. *Politico*, September 13, 2023, retrieved 30.09.2023 from <https://www.politico.eu/article/eu-ursula-von-der-leyen-china-electric-cars-probe-trade-war/>.

Remmers, Karl-Heinz: 'How solar tariffs destroyed then of thousands of jobs in Germany'. *Pvmagazine.com,* September 22, 2023, retrieved 29.09.2023, from <www.pv-magazine.com/2023/09/22/how-solar-tariffs-destroyed-tens-of-thousands-of-jobs-in-germany/>.

Shambaugh, David: 'China or America: Which is Revisionist Power?'. *Survival* 43 (3), 2001, pp. 25–30.

Singh, Ajit: 'The myth of 'debt-trap diplomacy' and realities of Chinese development finance'. *Third World Quarterly* 42(2), 2019, pp. 239–253.

Stent, Angela: 'Russia and China: Axis of Revisionists'. *Brookings Institution*, February 2020, retrieved 25.02.2023, from <https://www.brookings.edu/research/russia-and-china-axis-of-revisionists/>.

Stiglitz, Joseph: 'The problem with Europe is the euro'. *The Guardian*, August 10, 2016, retrieved 25.03.2023, from <https://www.theguardian.com/business/2016/aug/10/joseph-stiglitz-the-problem-with-europe-is-the-euro>.

Stiglitz, Joseph: *The Euro: How a Common Currency Threatens the Future of Europe*. Norton: New York, London 2016.

Stuart, Lau / Cokelaere, Hanne: 'EU launches 'Global Gateway' to counter China's Belt and Road'. September 15, 2021, retrieved 21.10.2023, from <https://www.politico.eu/article/eu-launches-global-gateway-to-counter-chinas-belt-and-road/>.

Taylor, Nicholas: 'China as a Status Quo or Revisionist Power? Implications for Australia'. *Security Challenges* 3(1), 2007, pp. 29–45.

Tilford, Simon: 'Is the Eurozone really out of the wood?'. *The Centre for European Reform*, September 22, 2017, retrieved 12.03.2023, from <https://www.cer.eu/insights/eurozone-really-out-woods>.

Tobin, James: 'Currency unions: Europe vs. United States'. *Policy Option Politiques*, May 1, 2001, retrieved 03.03.2023, from <https://policyoptions.irpp.org/magazines/one-world-one-money/currency-unions-europe-vs-the-united-states/>.

Wang, Ruping / Pan, Zhen / Yang, Liu: 'The 'Debt Trap' or the 'Benefit Pie' View of China's Belt and Road Initiative on Host Countries: Evidence from Chinese Enterprises' Outward Foreign Direct Investment'. *Emerging Markets Finance and Trade* 29(7), 2023, p. 2269–2282.

Weidong Liu: *The Belt and Road Initiative. A Pathway towards Inclusive Globalisation*. Routledge: London, New York, 2019.

Willett, Thomas D.: 'Some political economy aspects of EMU'. *Journal of Policy Modelling* 23(3), 2000, pp. 379–389.

Zielonka, Jan. 2019. 'The Mythology of East-West Divide'. *Eurozine*, March 05, 2019, retrieved 21.02.2023, from <https://www.eurozine.com/mythology-east-west-divide/>.

US, China and European Security: Great Power Competition or Cold War 2.0?

Łukasz Stach

Great powers seek more power

'Winter is coming' is the motto of House Stark in the famous television series 'Game of Thrones'. It means, that hard times can come suddenly, and everyone should be prepared to face them. Although the phrase 'winter is coming' has become a part of pop-culture, its meaning also applies to the world of international politics. Turbulent times can come surprisingly quickly, and Europe is experiencing them right now. History is not over.

After the collapse of the Soviet Union, Europe was perceived as a safe and prosperous place, far away from any serious regional or international turmoil. In fact, there have always been regions with ongoing armed conflicts, plagued by crises and instability, or descending into anarchy. Since 1991, however, Europe has become more united and despite its relative weakness in military matters, has made significant progress towards becoming a global player. As Mark Eyskens, former Belgian foreign affairs minister, said in 1991, Europe is 'an economic giant, a political dwarf, and a military worm'.[1] However, being a 'military worm' was not a problem for Europe at the time. The collapse of the Soviet Union almost completely reduced the risk of a full-scale, high-intensity war in Europe. Gradually, the European Community became the European Union, and it expanded – mainly eastwards. Many academics, analysts or scholars called the EU an emerging superpower.[2] The EU was transformed into a supranational organisation and – despite all its weaknesses – seemed to be a clear-cut success story. Integration has progressed disparately at different levels – it has gone the furthest in the economic sphere, but the situation is different in matters of defence policy. 'In the short space of just over 30 years, we have seen the creation of a European Union that increasingly resembles a federal state. It has a complex, multi-layered institutional structure, far-reaching policy competences in some of the most sensitive national policy areas, such as home affairs, trade policy and monetary policy, but also foreign policy and defence policy, which are still intergovernmental'.[3] In general, the integration process has progressed gradually, but since the end of the 2000s it has been hit by increasing turbulence. The Eurozone crisis, the European migration crisis of 2015, conflicts in the close neighbourhood of the EU (Arab Spring, civil war in Libya, Syria, annexation of the Crimean Peninsula and the Donbass war) have undermined the belief in a safe, peaceful and secure future, and revealed the divisions among the EU member states. Moreover, Europe has begun to face a new challenge – great power rivalry. Russia (the EU's main supplier of crude oil and natural gas) and the People's Republic of China (one of the EU's most important trading partners) are openly seeking to reshape the international order and challenge Western (mainly American) dominance. Both Russia and China have increased their military spending and made significant efforts to modernise their armed forces. Meanwhile, the EU's policy towards Beijing and Moscow has been based on economic cooperation and the belief that economic ties would prevent any military conflict. Opinions that both the PRC and Russia were building military capabilities that posed a threat to the West were scorned, especially in Western Europe. In general, the EU was sharply divided over its policy towards Russia. The Baltic states and Poland were reluctant to supports projects such as *Nord Stream 1* (and later *Nord Stream 2*), stressing their negative security implications, especially for Eastern Europe.[4] Meanwhile, Germany argued that these gas pipelines were mostly commercial projects. In fact, Berlin consistently pursued economic and political relations with Russia (and also the PRC) and this approach was based on national, not European, interests.[5] Whether the policy towards Russia was naively based on the illusion that close economic cooperation would bring stability, or whether it was simply a matter of calculating losses and profits, Western Europe (especially Germany) ignored the signals pointing to Moscow's revisionism. Meanwhile, for Vladimir Putin's regime, the formation of a multipolar world with Russia as a global player became a top-priority. In the early 2000s, Russia pacified Chechnya, defeated Georgia in August 2008, annexed the Crimean Peninsula in 2014 and supported so-called 'separatists' in Eastern Ukraine, leading to the war in Donbass. Finally, in February 2022 Russia launched a full-scale invasion of Ukraine, which is seen as a significant threat to the security of the EU member states in Central and Eastern Europe.

The People's Republic of China has also changed its policy. Under Xi Jinping's regime, Beijing's growing assertiveness in foreign relations has raised many concerns, not only in East Asia. The US perceives China as a threat at the economic, military, and political levels. For example, the US National Defence Strategy stresses that 'the most comprehensive and serious challenge to the U.S. national security is the PRC's coercive and increasingly aggressive efforts to reshape the Indo-Pacific region and the international system to suit its interests and authoritarian preferences'.[6] FBI Director Christopher Wray announced that counterintelligence and economic espionage is the greatest long-term threat to USA's economic vitality, information and intellectual property. An official FBI website highlights the 'China Threat' stating that 'counterintelligence and economic espionage efforts emanating from the Government of China and the Chinese Communist Party pose a grave threat to the economic well-being and democratic values of the United States'.[7] The aforementioned statements are just a few examples of the 'China threat' rhetoric, perpetuated by many US officials, analysts, newspapers, etc. Meanwhile, the PRC rejects the USA's approach to China, calling it deceptive, hypocritical and dangerous.[8] It is not just the tough rhetoric that shapes the relationship. Since 2018 there has been an ongoing economic conflict (often referred to as a 'trade war') between the two powers, and in October 2022, Joe Biden's administration imposed new restrictions on the sale of advanced semiconductors to China, aimed at slowing down Beijing's technological advances, including in the military field.

Tensions between the two powers have risen and the question of the risk of military conflict has appeared. The PRC and the US are beginning to perceive each other as military rivals, and both sides no longer hide the fact that their armies must be ready for full-scale war. The 2018 US National Defence Strategy underlines the fact that interstate strategic competition is now the main concern in US national security and the main strategic competitor is China. The 2017 National Security Strategy also shares this view pointing out that China and Russia (described as revisionist powers) are challenging

American power, influence and interests. As a result, the US Army must shift from counterinsurgency operations to large-scale conventional warfare. 'We must cognitively get east of the Vistula and north of the Han, ready for the potential of large-scale, conventional war in Eastern Europe of the Pacific region'.[9] The Chinese are not afraid of strong rhetoric either. In November 2022, Xi Jinping said that China must be prepared for war in such an unstable and uncertain security situation, and this statement was widely reported in the media. Some experts – including in China – said, that the risk of a military conflict between the PRC and the US was higher than ever, partly due to the fact that communication channels between the countries' armed forces had largely fallen silent.[10] In October 2022 *South China Morning Post* reported that China's top military officials have vowed to be prepared for war as China faces a growing risk of military confrontation with the United States.[11] Moreover, some analysts have highlighted the risk of the so-called Thucydides trap. The Harvard Thucydides Trap project has identified 16 cases in which a major rising power threatened to displace a major ruling power. In 12 out of the 16 cases, the result was war.[12] Graham Allison highlights the fact that 'based on the current trajectory, war between the United States and China in the decades ahead is not just possible, but much more likely than recognised at the moment. Indeed, judging by the historical record, war is more likely than not. Moreover, current underestimations and misapprehensions of the hazards inherent in the US-China relations contribute greatly to those hazards. A risk associated with Thucydides' Trap is that business as usual – not just an unexpected, extraordinary event – can trigger large-scale conflict. When a rising power is threatening to displace a ruling power, standard crises that would otherwise be contained, like the assassination of an archduke in 1914, can initiate a cascade of reactions that, in turn, produce outcomes none of the parties would otherwise have chosen'.[13] The current situation (particularly around Taiwan and the South China Sea) is causing much concern not only in the region, but also around the world. Tensions are rising and even one incident could lead to an escalation with unpredictable consequences. Both superpowers have built-up (or are planning to build up) their military capabilities, especially in the air, cyber, maritime, and space domains. The rapid development of the Chinese armed forces (especially air and naval forces, including amphibious capabilities) is causing concern in the US, Taiwan, Japan, the Philippines, and many other states and organisations, including the European Union. In general, the growing Sino-American rivalry is shaping contemporary world's politics, with significant implications for European security. This does not mean that the competition between Beijing and Washington determines all international issues, including European ones. Sino-American competition provides the framework through which actors view important events and developments.[14] A potential Sino-American conflict in the Far East would have disastrous consequences for Europe's highly globalised economy, especially as the European Union is currently facing many serious challenges, including military ones (e.g. a full-scale Russian invasion of Ukraine). Meanwhile – as Mark Leonard noted 'the Ukraine crisis shows that the European Union has a hard power deficit'.[15] In fact, the EU's military potential is very limited; in foreign policy Europe relies on soft power and economic instruments. In 'The European Dream' Jeremy Rifkin highlighted the fact that the EU relies mostly on soft power (humanitarian aid, diplomacy, trade, economics), in contrast to the US, which prefers military strength and economic dominance. Robert Kagan also highlighted this difference with his famous phrase 'Americans are from Mars and Europeans are from Venus'.[16] The US is the superpower and the world's leading military power, and Washington is much more willing to use military force than the militarily weak EU. However, as John McCormick pointed out, the view that the Americans use military power because they can, and the Europeans use diplomacy because it is all they have does not fully explain the more complex reality.[17] 'The EU has made a conscious decision to pursue non-military options and the nature of the international system today is more suited to a new model of superpower, one that prefers to avoid military solutions of the problems'. In this view, not using military force is a deliberate choice, not a necessity caused by military weakness. However, if this fits with the idea of a 'liberal empire', as the European Union is sometimes described,[18] it is debatable whether the EU can be understood as a form of empire.[19] In sum, the vision of Europe as a soft power liberal empire, quite different from other 'empires', in which military power plays an important role, is tempting and well-suited to peaceful and stable times. But turbulent times and hard power have returned. Europe must find itself at a time when a new world order is taking shape.

The EU has a problem with the Sino-American rivalry. This conflict affects Europe, whether the EU wants to stand aside or get involved, because the EU has strong ties with both the PRC and the US. The competing superpowers are the EU's main trading partners. According to *Eurostat*, China became the EU's largest trading partner in 2020, overtaking the US.[20] The US is important both economically and militarily, although 'the end of the Cold War has reduced Western Europe's dependence on the American security umbrella'.[21] However, the intervention in Libya in 2011 showed that Europe is doing poorly without US military support. In general, Europe and the US are closely linked in economic, security, and political terms. On the other hand, some factors suggest that the transatlantic relationship is under more pressure today than in the past.[22] Under the first presidency of Donald Trump the US-EU relationship deteriorated,[23] but – despite the crisis – it was not a terminal decline.[24] Joe Biden's presidency was perceived as a new beginning for transatlantic relations,[25] but there were still areas of diplomatic tension between the US and the EU, most notably on trade, climate, and China.[26] 'The Military Balance' also noted that despite the unifying rhetoric, there are structural factors that create divisions in transatlantic relations.[27] The deterioration in Sino-American relations is clearly visible, and it is not just hawkish rhetoric. In August 2022, Nancy Pelosi, the Speaker of the US House of Representatives, visited Taiwan, which infuriated Beijing. In October 2022, the Biden administration banned the export of semiconductors to China, seen as the most serious attempt to undermine China's military modernisation.[28] Washington seeks to strengthen its position through US-led informal or formal alliance systems, such as AUKUS (Australia, UK, US) or the Quadrilateral Security Dialogue (QUAD: Australia, India, Japan, US). On the other hand, China is developing its military capabilities, militarising the South China Sea region (e.g. by building 'artificial islands'), and strengthening its regional and global position through initiatives such as the Belt and Road Initiative, economic diplomacy or military presence, for example, in Africa.

In such turbulent times, the EU is trying to navigate between the US Eagle and the Chinese Dragon. Despite transatlantic partnerships, there are voices from the EU that Europe prefers a different approach to China than the US. In November 2022, the EU High Representative for Foreign Affairs and Security Policy, Joseph Borrel said: 'Certainly, the United States is our most important ally, but, in some cases, we will not be in the same position or on the same approach towards China'.[29] The EU Indo-Pacific strategy published in September 2021 is clearly not framed in anti-China terms and differs from the American approach.[30] Chinese leader Xi Jinping also calls on the EU to act independently of the US in foreign policy.[31] Some European leaders (such as the German Chancellor Olaf Scholz or the EU Council President Charles Michel) visited the PRC in the second half of 2022, showing that Europe wants to secure economic ties with Beijing.[32] For Beijing, the development of China-EU relations is a chance to drive a wedge into transatlantic relations and weaken the US's power. This is why Chinese leaders support Europe's integration process and the concept of 'strategic autonomy'.[33]

Even if Europe does not want to follow all US policies towards China, it is bound to feel pressured by Washington to toughen its stance towards the PRC.[34] The problem is that the EU has little, if any, influence on Washington's policy towards Beijing and the European approach to China is different from that of the US. Europe is likely to see China both as a partner and a competitor, so the idea of 'decoupling' from China is not an option.[35] In 'EU-China – A strategic outlook paper', the EU defined the PRC as a cooperation partner, a negotiating partner, an economic competitor, and a systemic rival (promoting alternative models of governance). The European Commission emphasised that this requires a flexible and pragmatic EU-wide approach.[36] Moreover, according to the EU, China has the capacity to play an important role in addressing regional security challenges (e.g. JCPOA Iran, counter-piracy in the Horn of Africa, peace process in Afghanistan). However, the PRC's maritime claims in the South China Sea and its refusal to accept the arbitration ruling issued under the UN Convention on the Law of the Sea affect the international order and increase tensions in the sea lanes, which are vital for the EU economy. Similarly, China's growing military capabilities and further ambitions to develop its armed forces pose security challenges for the EU, and large-scale military exercises and cross-sectoral hybrid threats challenge EU's security and undermine mutual trust. In general, the EU sees the PRC both as an opportunity and a challenge, but its approach to China has changed. In the not-too-distant past, China was seen as an attractive economic partner, but today Beijing's rising power and growing assertiveness is causing concern in the EU, and the view of China is becoming more critical. Europe has found itself in a situation of rivalry between two global powers and is closely involved in the process. Both the US and the PRC are key economic partners, and so far the US has also been important to Europe politically and militarily. Any major conflict between China and the United States will affect European stability, and the European Union in particular has some problems in responding quickly to a crisis, especially when 'hard security' threats arise. The EU's main strength is its economic clout, but this is not always strong enough to prevent or effectively manage a crisis. Money is important but, according to many researchers, politicians, and commentators, the EU has very little to bring to the table when it comes to hard security issues and military matters.[37] Moreover, post-Brexit, the EU's potential military capabilities have decreased, as UK armed forces are modern, especially in the air and maritime domains. The UK also has nuclear deterrence and power projection capabilities.

Europe, navigating in an increasingly complex international environment, is trying to find a response to global challenges, in particular the return of war to the European continent with Russia's invasion of Ukraine. This response is called 'strategic autonomy'.[38] In 'Shared Vision, Common Action: A Stronger Europe. A Global Strategy for the European Union's Foreign And Security Policy', the phrase 'strategic autonomy' appears five times and the need for strengthening the EU as a security community is clearly expressed.[39] It should enable the EU to act autonomously or in cooperation with NATO and it is important for Europe's ability to promote peace and stability within and beyond its borders. However, 'strategic autonomy' is a broad heading rather than a coherent concept. Under this heading the debate on the future course of the EU's international affairs is being conducted, and 'strategic autonomy' is being included in the discussions on climate change, health security, and WTO reform. It thus goes beyond the framework of hard security and many EU officials interpret the term beyond the traditional framework of defence alliances.[40] Nevertheless, strategic autonomy is analysed mainly from the perspective of defence issues, and the EU-NATO relationship, as well as in the discussion of the EU's role as an international actor.[41] However, achieving 'strategic autonomy' could be challenging for the EU, due to its lack of hard power. Despite all the rhetoric[42] about military security, Europe relies on the strength of the United States and NATO. Meanwhile, without military assets, 'strategic autonomy' remains just a slogan. Admittedly, despite some tensions, there is no risk of a military conflict between China and Europe. However, such a risk exists in the case of the PRC and the US. A strong US military engagement in the Pacific may leave Europe with reduced or only symbolic military support from the US, which means a significant decrease in European security, especially as military conflicts are present in the EU's neighbourhood and its surroundings are far less stable than a decade or two ago. A cold war, a hot war, or a proxy war between the US and China are all unwelcome scenarios for the European Union that could shake its foundations. First of all, a conflict between the US and China could have a devastating impact on EU economy, which is highly globalised and (according to the World Bank) exports around 50% of its GDP in goods and services. Supply chain disruptions, potential embargoes, trade wars, market uncertainty and instability would hamper the EU's economic progress and hit its economy hard. This would be all the more risky as the European economy has recently experienced several turbulences such as the European debt crisis (Eurozone crisis), or the economic downturn caused by the COVID-19 pandemic. In addition, the EU has adopted an ambitious climate policy, which aims to reduce its greenhouse gas emissions by at least 55% by 2030. It is currently difficult to estimate the long-term impact of EU climate policy on the European economy, but one thing is certain – it is expensive. The question is whether the result will be satisfactory, or whether climate policy will be a costly fiasco that will reduce the competitiveness of the EU economy. Secondly, the European Union, with its severely limited military capabilities, would not be able to provide military security for its member states, and European countries would have to rely on their own military assets. In a worst-case scenario, the combination of all these factors would lead to a significant disruption within the EU, perhaps even to its collapse. An international organisation that cannot effectively manage crises and does not provide security for its member states in turbulent times becomes redundant.

The EU is currently in a difficult position. Its economy is weakened, its goals are ambitious but erratic and, last but not least, tensions have arisen between the EU's two main economic partners. Whether Europe remains neutral or takes sides in the Sino-American conflict – the results could prove very painful for the EU. It is also difficult to expect Europe to develop a common policy towards the China-US conflict, given that the EU is deeply divided, for example over its attitude towards the United States. The overall picture is rather pessimistic – the EU as a whole is divided, its economy is heading for recession (as of the end of 2024), and the future is uncertain, due to rising tensions in international politics. During the period of stability and prosperity, when the liberal international order was ensured by US primacy, the EU's military weakness was not a major problem. Times have changed, however, and the European Union is facing a challenge: in the post-Cold War era Europeans have been free riders on American security and those days are coming to an end. EU officials stress that the EU should act as a global player and security provider, so Europe needs to strengthen its range of external actions with efficient and flexible instruments, including military ones.[43] The solution is simple – the EU must take more responsibility for its own security and strengthen its military capabilities – but the devil is in the details.

At first glance, the creation of an EU army would increase Europe's security autonomy, not only militarily, but also politically – the EU would be less dependent on Washington.[44] However, there are many obstacles that could hinder the creation of a reliable European army. Paradoxically, NATO, the alliance that has protected Europe since the end of the Second World War, may be the biggest. Opposition comes from the US, which is interested in preserving a framework that allows Washington to put its interests first. NATO leaders are also keen to protect their own institutional turf and are reluctant to embrace a still hypothetical EU army. Arguments such as avoiding 'duplication' and calls for 'complementary' capabilities are a smokescreen behind which US and NATO leaders continue to resist the EU ever developing the command and control capabilities that would allow it to operate outside the existing NATO umbrella.[45] Moreover, some European states (e.g. Poland) see NATO (and especially the US) as the main pillar of their security. Dependence on the US is also evident in the equipment used by many European armed forces. For example, military aviation in many EU countries relies on US-made aircrafts such as the *F-16* or *F-35*. Recently it has become clear that the *F-35* would be an important part of many European air forces. Despite calls from French leaders to 'buy European', the *F-35* has been chosen by EU member states such as Belgium, Finland, and Poland. Denmark, Italy, and the Netherlands have also joined the programme. Even

Germany is set to buy *F-35s* to replace its ageing nuclear-armed *Tornado* jets.[46] The list of challenges is much longer. Building a European army would require substantial funding, and increasing arms spending may be difficult. In 2006, for example, NATO members agreed to spend 2% of their gross domestic product on defence, but many countries still fall short. It is only since 24 February 2022 that many NATO members have committed to spending more on defence.[47] Thus, NATO countries that are also members of the EU would suddenly be faced with additional military spending if the euro-army project were to become a reality. A common European defence budget will require an increase in EU membership contributions or a cut in social, development, and investment spending. On the other hand, if Europe is to have armed forces with technologically advanced capabilities and meaningful operational autonomy, it will need to continue and deepen cooperation, including industrial cooperation. In fact, the list of challenges and issues to be resolved is much longer. Financing, command, equipment, training – the problems are many and the solutions are not so easy to put into practice.

For now, European defence and military capabilities should be considered at two levels – national and supranational. The total military expenditure of the 27 EU member states is high – even without the UK, the EU ranks second in the world (see Table 4).

Table 4. Military expenditure by US, PRC, Russia and selected European countries in constant (2019) USD. In brackets – military expenditure by country as a percentage of GDP.

	1990	1995	2000	2005	2010	2015	2020
US	636.176 (5.6)	496.360 (3.9)	475.217 (3.1)	698.019 (4.1)	865.268 (4.9)	683.678 (3.5)	766.583 (3.9)
PRC	21.282 (2.5)	25.282 (1.7)	41.167 (1.8)	73.390 (1.9)	129.359 (1.7)	192.843 (1.8)	244.934 (1.7)
Russia (till 1991 USSR)	220.50 (--)	25.64 (3.8)	23.584 (3.3)	35.165 (3.3)	49.834 (3.6)	74.649 (4.9)	66.838 (4.3)
UK	60.892 (4.0)	50.080 (2.9)	48.701 (2.4)	58.716 (2.4)	63.177 (2.6)	53.996 (2.0)	58.485 (2.2)
France	51.395 (2.8)	47.337 (2.5)	45.010 (2.1)	47.469 (2.0)	48.415 (2.0)	48.033 (1.9)	51.572 (2.1)

Table 4. Continued

	1990	1995	2000	2005	2010	2015	2020
Germany	61.408 (2.5)	44.568 (2.5)	42.403 (1.4)	33.323 (1.1)	41.046 (1.3)	40.566 (1.1)	51.570 (1.4)
Italy	28.373 (1.9)	25.025 (1.5)	33.109 (1.7)	32.555 (1.6)	29.944 (1.5)	23.043 (1.2)	28.370 (1.6)
Netherlands	12.347 (2.4)	10.276 (1.8)	10.264 (1.4)	10.772 (1.4)	10.994 (1.3)	9.289 (1.1)	12.211 (1.4)
Spain	17.159 (2.3)	15.963 (1.9)	18.245 (1.7)	17.963 (1.4)	18.488 (1.4)	15.972 (1.3)	17.160 (1.4)
Poland	6.215 (2.6)	4.668 (2.0)	5.350 (1.8)	6.534 (1.9)	7.887 (1.8)	10.594 (2.1)	12.815 (2.2)
EU (total)	253.410	224.455	231.894	249.715	263.394	241.731	286.327

Source: SIPRI

With the end of the Cold War, European military spending declined in both Western and Eastern Europe. At the beginning of the 1990s, the Central and Eastern European countries experienced a transition crisis, while Western Europe reaped a 'peace dividend'. Even in 1995, when Austria, Finland and Sweden joined the EU, total military expenditure was lower than in 1990. The 8 CEE countries (plus Malta and Cyprus) that joined the EU in 2004 also contributed little to military expenditure. In the following decade, European military expenditure remained at a similar level, until the end of the 2010s. At the beginning of the 2020s, Europe decided to spend more on defence, but the shortcomings of the previous decades are difficult to overcome in such a short time.

Looking at the statistics, the combined military expenditure of the EU member states exceeds that of China, overtakes that of Russia, and is second only to the US military budget (Figure 10).

In terms of soldiers, tanks, combat vehicles, artillery pieces, planes, helicopters etc. Europe should also be treated as one of the strongest militaries in the world. However, Europe's military potential is much weaker than the sum of its parts, as each EU member state has its own national military.[48] In

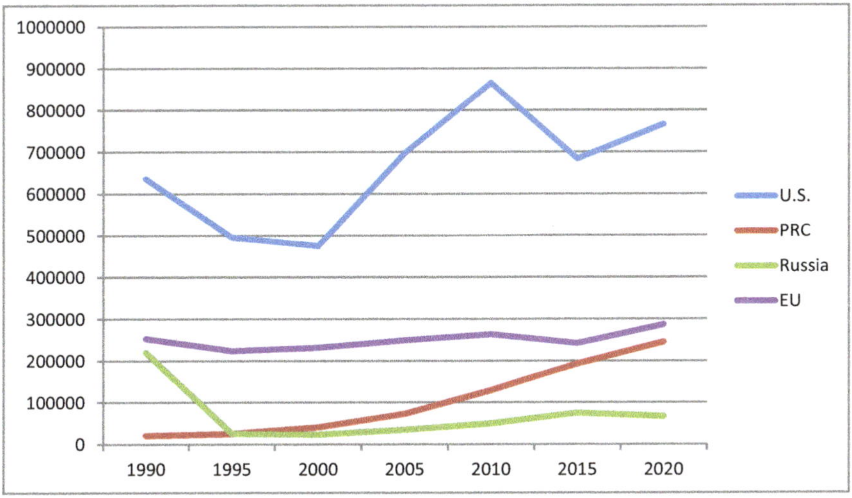

Figure 10. Comparison of the PRC, EU, Russia, and US military expenditure

Source: SIPRI

short, Europe is a global military power in theory, but the reality is different. Certainly, EU countries such as France, Italy, and Germany have significant military potential, but it is fragmented and does not function as an integrated system. Moreover, past experience in building a European defence community is not encouraging.

So far, despite many initiatives, none of the efforts to strengthen European defence capabilities has been successful. In 1952, the Treaty of Paris established the European Defence Community, which aimed to create a pan-European military with a common budget, weapons, centralised military procurement and institutions, but divided into national components. However, this initiative failed, and the treaty never came into force.[49] The Western European Union (which succeeded the Western Union in 1954) had a longer lifespan (it ceased to exist in 2011), but its real significance was modest. During the Cold War, European military security relied on the North Atlantic Treaty Organization and US military power, but Western European countries retained relatively significant military potential. In the post-Cold War era, the process of European integration entered a new phase, and the Maastricht Treaty (signed in 1992) established the European Union. The

Common Foreign and Security Policy became the third 'pillar' of the EU, but foreign and defence policies remained at the level of individual member states. The Treaty of Amsterdam (1997) established the office of High Representative for the Common Foreign and Security Policy to coordinate the EU's efforts in these areas. Finally, the Treaty of Lisbon (2009) created a High Representative of the Union for Foreign Affairs and Security Policy and a European External Action Service (established in 2010). An important component of the Common Foreign and Security Policy is the Common Security and Defence Policy, which enables the EU to take a role in peacekeeping operations, conflict prevention, and strengthening international security.[50] The common Security and Defence Policy comprises directorates and agencies (including the European Defence Agency), thus creating a wide range of bureaucratic bodies[51] Unfortunately, even the best administration and clerks cannot do much unless there is real power behind them. The European Union now has many institutions supported by a well-paid bureaucracy, but the problem is that the EU's real military capabilities are severely limited. At the level of EU member states, the situation is somewhat different, although decades of neglect are evident here. As Bruno Angelet observes: 'After the end of the Cold War, Europe's harvesting of the peace dividend was fed by wrong assumptions and led to a persistent underinvestment in defence. Today, problems are three-fold: too small stockpile, inadequate, and insufficient capabilities, and very low industrial production capacity'.[52] For example, when the Soviet Union collapsed in 1991, the French armed forces consisted of over 450,000 active personnel, over 900 combat-capable aircraft, 1,349 MBTs, 17 submarines, and 41 major surface combatants, plus a strong artillery, supported by a developed military industry and reserves.[53] In 2021, France had 203,250 active personnel, over 300 combat-capable aircraft, 222 MBTs, 8 submarines, and 22 major surface combatants. Artillery and reserves have also been significantly reduced.[54] Other European armies have also been reduced, in many cases substantially. The defence industry has also undergone a transformation, including significant cuts in production volume and capacity.[55] Despite limitations on arms spending, reductions in the size of the armed forces, etc., some European countries have significant defence capabilities. The European Union as a whole has a large share of the world's major arms exports. The two EU leaders (France and Germany) have achieved significant growth in their share of arms exports (Table 5).

Table 5. The 15 largest exporters of major arms, 2011–2015, 2016–2020

Exporter	**Share of arms exports (%)**		**Percentage change**
	2011–2015	**2016–2020**	
United States	32	37	+ 15
Russia	26	20	- 22
France	5.6	8.2	+ 44
Germany	4.5	5.5	+ 21
PRC	5.6	5.2	- 7.8
United Kingdom	4.6	3.3	- 27
Spain	3.5	3.2	- 8.4
Israel	1.9	3.0	+ 59
South Korea	0.9	2.7	+ 210
Italy	2.8	2.2	- 22
Netherlands	2.0	1.9	- 6.1
Ukraine	2.6	0.9	- 68
Turkey	0.6	0.7	30
Switzerland	1.1	0.7	- 35
Sweden	1.5	0.7	- 54
EU (total)	26	26	0

Source: Wezeman and Kiumowa and Wezeman 2021; SIPRI Arms Transfer Database, March 2021

French and German defence industries are technologically advanced, capable of developing and producing 4.5-generation jet fighters (e.g. Dassault *Rafale*), modern diesel-electric submarines (French *Scorpène*-class, German *Type 212* and *Type 214* SSK), tanks (*Leclerc*, *Leopard 2* MBTs), etc. Other countries – such as Italy, the Netherlands, Spain, Sweden – also have well-developed military industries capable of producing a range of military equipment, from small arms to electronics.[56] CEE countries, such as the Czech Republic, Slovakia, and Poland are also restructuring their defence industries with some success. The Polish *Krab* self-propelled howitzer, for example, has earned a good reputation on the Ukrainian battlefield, as has the *Piorun* MANPADS. The European defence industry also has experience in multinational projects such as the *Eurofighter* multirole combat aircraft, the *A400M* transport aircraft, the

NH90 helicopter, and the *Tiger* combat helicopter. In general, the narrative of a totally disarmed Europe does not stand up to criticism. The European military has considerable potential backed up by a well-developed military industry. As arms exporters, France and Germany are important global players. Technologically, only the US (and in some areas the PRC) are more advanced. However, there are areas where Europe lags behind the US or even the PRC. For example, Europe has not developed and built its own fifth generation fighter, and (as mentioned previously) some EU member states are buying the American *F-35*. Meanwhile, France, Germany, and Spain are collaborating on the Future Combat Air System (FCAS), which will consist of a New Generation Fighter (NGF) and swarming drones. According to Globalsecurity.org, the NGF is expected to replace platforms such as the Dassault *Rafale* and *Eurofighter Typhoon* around 2035–2040. Meanwhile, Italy is working with the UK and Japan to develop a next-generation fighter.[57] It clearly shows that Europe has a problem with coordinating development in key areas of defence and security, such as the new generation combat platforms. Airbus states on its website that 'the Future Combat Air System is a key instrument in ensuring future European autonomy and sovereignty in defence and security'. This sentence was placed there for marketing purposes, but there is some truth in it. An advanced weapon system (such as a sixth-generation fighter) developed in the EU with the participation of defence companies from EU member states would be a true example of strategic autonomy and a milestone on the road to EU self-reliance in security matters. Meanwhile, the fragmentation of the EU defence industry is one of its main weaknesses. There are simply too many companies, often offering similar products. This reduces economies of scale and synergies and also means that European suppliers compete not only with American, Russian, Chinese (or other) companies, but also with each other. However, reducing fragmentation is problematic for political reasons. The EU is divided into separate, national defence markets and governments protect their national defence industries.[58] As a result, equipment is not necessarily standardised, spending is duplicated, and public resources are misallocated. Moreover, EU member states are unable to maintain a full spectrum defence industrial base, due to lack of funding.[59] Military research and development programmes are increasingly expensive, as are the costs of the latest equipment.[60] Even European states with significant military budgets (such as Germany or France) may struggle to develop the latest weapon systems on their own. As a result, Europe falls behind the leading powers in terms of military technologies and its dependence on the US in this area may be growing. The EU is making some efforts to strengthen its defence industry through a common procurement law. The European Commission proposes a budget of €500 million for the period between 2022 and 2024.[61] However, compared to the current cost of military research and development and the latest equipment, the proposed amount is small and does not represent a breakthrough. Moreover, the list of problems and weaknesses is long and solving them will require more than an increase in funding.

Unlike the United States, or even China, Europe has limited global power projection capabilities (i.e. the ability to project military power to another theatre), in response to requirements of military operations.[62] Such a capability is a flexible tool for both military and political purposes.[63] Geoffrey Till emphasises the fact that '[…] maritime power projection can be used against a range of state or non-state adversaries, and with varying levels of intensity'.[64] The key element of effective power projection is the ability to prepare and execute a joint operation. It requires airlift, sealift, and amphibious operations capabilities (for troop deployment), as well as efficient systems of command and control, and logistics systems. In the maritime domain, from the perspective of great powers such as the US or the PRC, aircraft carrier strike groups, nuclear-powered submarines, and powerful amphibious assault forces are essential platforms of maritime power projection.[65]

Meanwhile, Europe lacks some critical power projection capabilities, such as air refuelling, transport aircraft, and high-end reconnaissance and surveillance drones.[66] According to The Military Balance (2022), in 2021 EU member states had 60 heavy transport aircraft (*A400M*) and over 160 medium transport aircraft (mostly many variants of *Hercules 130*).[67] Meanwhile, the United States Air Force alone have 182 heavy transport aircraft (36 *C5M Super Galaxy* and 146 *C-17A Globemaster*), and over 100 medium transport aircraft (*Hercules 130*).[68] The PRC has significantly expanded its airlift capabilities and possesses over 100 strategic (*Xian Y-20* and *Il-76*) and 130 tactical (*Shaanxi Y-8* and *Y-9*) airlifters.[69] Similarly, although the US aerial refuelling fleet has shrunk from 701 to 473 tankers, the US still has a significant advantage over the PRC (less than 20 tankers) and European armies (less than 30 tankers).[70] This is important, because air-to-air refuelling is essential for sustained combat operations and effective power projection. Meanwhile, NATO's air campaigns in Libya and Kosovo have demonstrated that air-to-air refuelling is a critical shortfall in European military capabilities.[71]

Europe's maritime power projection capabilities are also limited – the result of defence spending cuts in recent decades. Moreover, European navies have been reshaped to focus on low-end missions, such as counter-piracy. Collectively, EU member states had nearly 100 large surface combatants and over 50 submarines in 2021, which seems comparable (in numbers) to the US (over 120 large surface combatants and 68 submarines) and the PRC (80 large surface combatants and 59 submarines). However, China's People's Liberation Army Navy is expanding at an impressive rate, and the US has much more significant power projection capabilities than Europe. For example, the US Navy have 11 aircraft carriers compared to the mere 3 in Europe. Moreover, European navies are underinvested, ageing and overstretched, as they try to be present in the European theatre, as well as in distant regions such as the Indo-Pacific and the Libyan campaign in 2011, which demonstrated the limitations of European navies.[72] To improve the situation, the Coordinated Maritime Presences (CMP) tool was introduced and tested in the Gulf of Guinea.[73] In February 2022, the EU launched a CMP operation in the Northwest Indian Ocean, establishing a Maritime Area of Interest in the region.[74] Such an extension of the CMP to the Indo-Pacific shows the EU's ambition to have a permanent naval presence in a region of strategic importance and to enable Europe to protect its interests more effectively.[75] Indeed, the EU has experience in counter-piracy missions, such as the Operation *Atalanta* conducted at sea off the Horn of Africa (the EU's first naval operation). It also has the potential to protect sea lines of communication (SLOC's) and provide maritime security on the high seas against crime and robbery. This is vital for Europe's export-oriented economy, which could be adversely affected by any disruption to shipping lanes. Overall, Europe is capable of being a global maritime service provider but only in the fight against maritime piracy and organised crime. In a potential conflict between China and the US, the maritime domain will become a key battleground (e.g. fighting PLAN invasion forces sent to conquer Taiwan; US naval blockade of China). In such a scenario (disastrous for the European economy, which depends on trade with both great powers), Europe has almost no military assets, and in fact the EU can only show its flag in distant waters and call for a peaceful resolution of the conflict.

The EU has recognised the need to improve its power projection capabilities and in November 2022 it was announced that an EU Rapid Deployment Capacity (EU RDC) will be developed. It should consist of up to 5,000 troops and be rapidly deployable to respond to imminent threats and crisis situations. The EU RDC would have strategic enablers such as: strategic airlift, space-based communications, Intelligence, Surveillance and Reconnaissance (ISR), and cyber-defence capabilities. According to the plans, the EU RDC will reach full operational capability in 2025.[76] The European Defence Agency also expresses the need to improve its power projection capabilities, especially in the maritime domain. The EU should develop power projection based on long-range logistic support, naval aviation with strike capability and protection of naval forces. Strategic airlift capabilities should also be developed.[77]

The next area where Europe should strengthen its capabilities is space. As Bolder and Chavannes note: 'Space already is, and will only become more, crucial for military use' and this view is shared by military analysts.[78] In December 2019, NATO recognised space as the fifth operational domain for military operations.[79] Space is vital for satellite communications, intelligence, surveillance and reconnaissance, positioning, navigation and timing systems, Earth observation, early warning and meteorology. All of these are essential to the operational capabilities of armed forces.[80] The importance of space as an operational domain is prompting major powers to build and expand space forces. Both the PRC and the US have established independent space forces, while countries such as Russia, France, Spain, and Iran maintain combined air and space forces. Some other states have space commands, units and formations (e.g. Germany, UK) and are of course expanding their satellite networks. According to statista.com, at the beginning of 2022, there were over 4,800 satellites, of which over 2,900 belonged to the US, around 500 to the PRC and 169 to Russia (the rest of the world had 1,240 satellites).[81] Meanwhile, the Union of Concerned Scientists Satellite Database (2022) shows, that in April 2022 there were 5,465 satellites (US: 3,433, China 541, Russia 172, others 1,319). Of course, most of them are commercial or civilian, but the dominance of the United States and the strong position of China are evident. Military satellites are much less numerous. Here, too, the United States is the leader (231 satellites), followed by China and Russia (139 and 101, respectively). France, with 14 satellites, is the first EU power on this list. Italy has 8, Germany 7, and Spain 4 military satellites, fewer than Israel (11) and India (8), while the UK has 6. Some EU countries have a single military satellite, and some (such as Poland) are planning to introduce such capabilities. In general, there is a significant gap between the three leading powers and the rest of the world, although according to some sources, Russia relies on outdated technology, which hampered its military efforts in Ukraine.[82] In fact, the war in Ukraine proved the importance of satellites on today's battlefields, including those owned by private companies.[83] This confirms the experience of previous wars, such as the Gulf War (1990–1991), the Iraq War (2003–2011), Afghanistan (2001–2021), and many other armed conflicts.

As satellites play an important role in military operations, anti-satellite weapons (ASAT) are emerging. Several countries possess ASAT weapons, but only a few powers demonstrated such capabilities by shooting down their own satellites: India, People's Republic of China, Russia, and the United States.[84] Israel has tested an anti-ballistic missile that some experts believe could be adapted as an ASAT weapon.[85] What about EU member states? France will develop an anti-satellite laser weapon, although Defence Minister Florence Parly admitted that this is 'an area, in which France has fallen behind'.[86] Meanwhile, Germany has decided not to carry out direct ASAT missile tests.[87] In conclusion, as far as ASAT weapons are concerned, European capabilities in this area are severely limited, compared to the US, the PRC, or even Russia. Despite these limitations, Europe has many assets in the space domain. The space industry is developed, the European Space Agency (ESA) has achieved some successes, the *Galileo* global navigation satellite system became operational in 2016, and some EU member states have advanced military satellites. Europe therefore has the potential for development in space exploration, including in terms of security. However, it is hampered by two main factors. First, ESA's total budget for 2022 was only €7.15 billion,[88] compared to NASA's $24 billion. Secondly, the US and the PRC have significant military expenditures, which they use to fund research into the military uses of space. Some EU member states do the same, but – similar to the defence industry – fragmentation hinders efforts, and the European space industry does not operate as an integrated system. The ESA Council of Ministers has agreed to increase the agency's budget to €16.9 billion over the next five years, but it still has a long way to catch up with China and the US.[89] Second, the lack of coordination mentioned earlier makes it difficult for Europe to become an independent space power.

Conclusions

It is easy to find funny 'expectation versus reality' memes on the internet, depicting the disparity between (usually exorbitant) expectations and grim reality. The EU could also be portrayed in this way. Expectations – global leader, promoter of democracy, equal partner for both China and the US. Reality – highly developed and economically powerful entity, but dependent on US military power for defence. Moreover, the EU economy has benefited from globalisation, but the growing rivalry between China and the US threatens Europe's economic growth. As Zandee, Stoetnam, and Deen wrote: 'The EU faces a wider set of challenges and threats than ever before. In the global power rivalry between China, Russia and the United States, it is 'Europe' that runs the danger of becoming irrelevant and the object of great power actions rather being a global actor. The arc of instability around Europe is unlikely to turn into an arc of stability'.[90]

For the EU, maintaining the status quo (liberal world order) would be the most welcome scenario, but instead of cooperation, China and the US have chosen the path of rivalry, which is somewhat in line with the realist vision of international relations. There are many answers to the questions of what the future of Sino-American competition will look like, from hopes that both major powers – despite all tensions – will cooperate and have no choice but to find a way to manage their competition and continue to engage with each other,[91] to fears that conflict – even military conflict – is almost inevitable. Indeed, the new bipolarity (US-China) is a fact and in terms of balance of power, the rivalry between the two powers resembles the Cold War – hence the moniker Cold War 2.0.[92] The re-emergence of competing blocs is unfavourable for Europe, which will be pressured by Washington to support its policy against Beijing. For Europe, decoupling from the PRC is problematic because of the strong mutual economic ties. Either way, Europe has reason to be concerned, especially since it is not ready for another major crisis in international relations, even if Europe would not be directly involved. The side effect of a Sino-American conflict would be like an earthquake and a tsunami. Even if the epicentre of the earthquake is far away, the tsunami waves can cause great damage around the world. Especially as Europe has a lot of catching up to do in terms of security. As mentioned before, after the end of the Cold War, European states (with a few exceptions) reduced their defence capabilities below the level that would ensure their security.

Such a short-sighted policy could only work during a period of stabilisation in international relations, but when turbulence arose, it revealed Europe's weakness on security issues. As in the past, Europe must rely on America's military strength. However, the current escalation in US-China relations means greater US involvement in the Indo-Pacific region, making it necessary for Europe to improve its military capabilities. According to Jiří Šedivý (head of the EDA), the US is 'advising' Europe to invest in its strategic enablers, as there may come a time when the US will be fully engaged in Asia-Pacific and unable to support Europe.[93] However, America hopes that Europe can provide its own security seem dubious.[94] So the question is, does it always have to be this way – an emergency call to Uncle Sam?

As Kenneth Waltz has observed, the EU 'has all the tools – population, resources, technology, and military capabilities – but lacks the organisational ability and the collective will to use them'.[95] This is why the EU cannot become a great power. Current geopolitical crises are generating calls for a unified European response, with Berlin and Paris also calling for a more federal Europe. The European Union is perceived by some as moving towards a more federal system, but the ultimate effect of this direction is uncertain.[96] French President Emmanuel Macron calls for 'strategic autonomy' and a 'Made in Europe' strategy, while the German Chancellor Olaf Scholz supported a geopolitical European Union because Europe faces greater challenges than ever before.[97] In addition, Olaf Scholz wrote in *Foreign Policy* that: 'Germans are intent on becoming the guarantor of European security that our allies expect us to be, a bridge builder within the European Union and an advocate for multilateral solutions to global problems'.[98] Indeed, Germany has the economic, technological and political potential to lead Europe, but Berlin's policy following Russia's full-scale invasion of Ukraine has been criticised in some Central and Eastern European states. Germany is perceived as a reluctant supporter of Ukraine, which is damaging its reputation in these countries.[99] As the Polish analytical centre noted: 'The Russian invasion of Ukraine has undermined the principle of German policy, which is based on the idea that 'Europe's security can only be built with Russia, not against it'.'[100] Such an approach to Russia policy has consequences for the perception of Berlin, especially in Warsaw. Moreover, the Bundeswehr is currently weak and needs time to modernise and build up its combat capabilities. Germany's current military weakness, the lack of a nuclear deterrent, combined with the legacy of Berlin's policy towards Russia, means that Germany cannot currently be a security provider. Chancellor Olaf Scholtz announced a huge injection of funds into the German army (€100 billion), but it will take time to increase the Bundeswehr's combat capabilities, even if all goes according to plan. In this context, Berlin is not yet in a position to play a leading role in EU defence policy, so the US military presence remains essential for EU security. However, it has political implications: America can use its military presence as a tool to pressure Europe on the China issue.

Even if Europe were to improve its military security capabilities, building a coherent common security policy would be a challenge. Firstly, it is divided on issues such as threat perception and policy towards Washington, Beijing or Russia. For EU member states in the Mediterranean region, France or Germany, Russia is not an existential threat, while the Baltic states and Poland have a different perspective on this issue. Central and Eastern European societies (especially Poland and Romania) are also more pro-American than Western European ones. France may emphasise the need for the EU's 'strategic autonomy', while Germany speaks of a change of times (*Zeitenwende*) and a stronger Europe, but Poland is likely to be a supporter of the US and – if it realises its highly ambitious military modernisation plan – not 'America's donkey' but NATO's horse.

Even if Europe could overcome existing divisions and reach a compromise on security issues, many challenges remain. There are many differences in the armed forces of EU member states (equipment, training, etc.), so creating a coherent defence system would be a major challenge – like putting together a jigsaw puzzle with pieces that do not always fit together. Moreover, in such a scenario there would be many questions about the financing, command system, roles and responsibilities of such armed forces. Similarly, there are a number of potential complications, such as the issue of funding, in building up EU forces alongside or above the armies of the member states. Due to fragmentation and a lack of effective planning and coordination, the EU does not act as one in defence and its military strength is much weaker than the sum of its parts.[101] In general, the idea of strengthening the EU's defence capabilities still remains largely theoretical. Europe has a problem with implementing an effective defence and security policy. Without real military power, Europe can only talk about the EU as a 'global actor;' diplomacy without military does not work with regimes like Russia under

Vladimir Putin. Europe is currently reaping the bitter fruit of decades of defence neglect, but Russia's full-scale invasion of Ukraine has given a boost to the defence policies of some EU member states. France wants to transform its army to prepare for high-intensity conflicts, Germany announced a €100 billion package for its military modernisation, Poland plans to increase the size of its army and has signed some major arms deals with the US and South Korea, and other European states are also planning to increase military spending and the combat capabilities of their armed forces. EU leaders also stress the need to strengthen Europe's defence, especially since the conflict in Ukraine has shown that Europe is ill-prepared for a high-intensity war. It is becoming clear that there is a significant gap between the EU's 'expectations' and 'reality'. Europe would like to be able to secure its own backyard, but today it has to rely on America. In the near future, the EU may be able to build its own rapid deployment capacity to respond to imminent threats, but – even if everything goes according to plan – it will take some time to reach combat-ready status. So far, Europe is militarily unprepared for a great power clash and can only hope that the Sino-American rivalry does not escalate in the near future.

Notes

1 Leonard, Mark: 'Europe for itself'. *European Council on Foreign Relations*, July 24, 2018, retrieved 11.02.2023, from <https://ecfr.eu/article/commentary_europe_for_itself/>.

2 McCormick, John: *The European Superpower*. Palgrave Macmillan: London 2006; Leonard, Mark: *Why Europe Will Run the 21st Century?*. Fourth Estate: London 2011; Moravscik, Andrew: 'Europe Is Still a Superpower. And it's going to remain on for decades to come'. *Foreign Policy*, April 13, 2017, retrieved 18.09.2022, from <https://foreignpolicy.com/2017/04/13/europe-is-still-a-superpower/>; Reid, Thomas Roy: *The United States of Europe: The New Superpower and the End of American Supremacy*, Penguin Books: London 2005; Rifkin, Jeremy: *The European Dream: how European vision of the future is quietly eclipsing the American dream*. Penguin: New York 2004; Zielonka, Jan: *Europe as Empire: The Nature of the Enlarged European Union*. Oxford University Press: Oxford 2006.

3 Villup, Elina: 'The EU, Neither a Political Dwarf nor a Military Worm'. *International Catalan Institute for Peace*, 2015, retrieved 24.09.2022, from <https://www.icip.cat/perlapau/en/article/the-eu-neither-a-political-dwarf-nor-a-military-worm/>.

4 In 2006, Polish foreign minister, Radoslaw Sikorski, compared *Nord Stream 1* project to Molotov-Ribbentrop non-aggression pact between Nazi Germany and Soviet Union

5 Dempsey, Judy: 'Germany Continued illusions About China and Russia'. *Carnegie Europe*, October 20, 2022, retrieved 29.09.2022, from <https://carnegieeurope.eu/strategiceurope/88210>.

6 'National Defense Strategy of The United States of America. Including the 2022 Nuclear Posture Review and the 2022 Missile Defence Review'. *U.S. Department of Defense*, October 2022, retrieved 29.09.2022, from <https://www.defense.gov/News/News-Stories/Article/Article/3202438/dod-releases-national-defense-strategy-missile-defense-nuclear-posture-reviews/>.

7 'The China Threat'. *Federal Bureau of Investigation*, retrieved 15.11.2022, from <https://www.fbi.gov/investigate/counterintelligence/the-china-threat>.

8 'China-US Perceptions of Check: Falsehoods in Reality'. *Ministry of Foreign Affairs of the People's Republic of China*, June 19, 2022, retrieved 16.11.2022, from <https://www.mfa.gov.cn/eng/wjbxw/202206/t20220619_10706059.html>.

9 Donahoe, Patrick / Spencer, John: 'A Status Check On The Army's Preparation For the Next War'. *Modern War Institute at West Point*, June 07, 2021, retrieved 05.12.2022, from <https://mwi.usma.edu/a-status-check-on-the-armys-preparation-for-the-next-war/>.

10 Zhou, Laura: 'Risk of military conflict between US and China higher than ever, experts say'. *South China Morning Post*, January 24, 2020, retrieved 23.11.2022, from <https://www.scmp.com/news/china/diplomacy/article/3090314/risk-military-conflict-between-us-and-china-higher-ever>.

11 Ng Teddy: 'China's top military brass to be on high alert and ready for war amid mounting tensions with US'. *South China Morning Post*, October 19, 2022, retrieved 23.11.2022, from <https://www.scmp.com/news/china/military/article/3196462/chinas-top-military-brass-vow-be-high-alert-and-ready-war-amid-mounting-tension-us>.

12 Allison, Graham: 'The Thucydides Trap: Are the U.S. and China headed for War?'. *The Atlantic*, September 15, 2015, retrieved 18.09.2022, from <https://www.theatlantic.com/international/archive/2015/09/united-states-china-war-thucydides-trap/406756/>; Allison, Graham: *Destined for war. Can America and China escape Thucydidies Trap*? Houghton Mifflin Harcourt: Boston, New York, 2017.

13 Allison, Graham: 'The Thucydides Trap: Are the U.S. and China headed for War?'.

14 Perthes, Volker: 'Dimensions on rivalry: China, the United States, and Europe'. *China International Strategy Review* 3, 2021, p. 56.

15 Leonard, Mark: 'Europe's soft-power problem'. *The European Council of Foreign Relations*, May 05, 2022, retrieved 14.11.2022, from <https://ecfr.eu/article/europes-soft-power-problem/>.

16 Kagan, Robert: *Paradise and Power*. London: Atlantic Books: London 2004.

17 McCormick, John: *The European Superpower*, p. 6.

18 Pänke, Julian: 'Liberal Empire, Geopolitics and EU Strategy: Norms and Interests in European Foreign Policy Making'. *Geopolitics* 21(1), 2019, pp. 100–123; Streeck, Wolfgang: 'The European Union is a liberal empire, and is about to fall'. *LSE Brexit blog*, March 6, 2019, retrieved 18.10.2022, from <https://blogs.lse.ac.uk/brexit/2019/03/06/long-read-the-european-union-is-a-liberal-empire-and-it-is-about-to-fall/>.

[19] Behr, Hartmut / Stivachtis, Yannis A.: 'European Union: An Empire in New Clothes?'. In: edited by Behr, Hartmut / Stivactis, Yannis A. (eds.): *Revisiting the European Union as an Empire*, Routledge: London, 2015.

[20] 'China overtakes US as EU's biggest trading partner'. *BBC*, February 17, 2021, retrieved 19.10.2022, from <https://www.bbc.com/news/business-56093378>.

[21] McCormick, John: *The European Superpower*, p. 6.

[22] Riddervold, Marianne / Newsome, Akesemie: 'Transatlantic relations in times of uncertainty: crises and EU-US relations'. *Journal of European Integration* 40(5), 2018, p. 518.

[23] Dimitrova, Anna: 'The State of Transatlantic Relationship in the Trump Era'. *European Issues 545*, *Foundation Robert Schuman*, February 03, 2020, retrieved 16.12.2022, from <https://www.robert-schuman.eu/en/european-issues/0545-the-state-of-the-transatlantic-relationship-in-the-trump-era>.

[24] Aggestam, Elisabeth / Hyde-Price, Adrian: 'Double-Trouble: Trump, Transatlantic Relations and European Strategic Autonomy'. *Journal of Common Market Studies* 57 (S1), 2019, p. 126.

[25] 'Biden's presidency begins: a fresh start for the US but also for transatlantic relations'. *European External Action Service*, January 22, 2021, retrieved 21.12.2022, from <https://www.eeas.europa.eu/eeas/biden%E2%80%99s-presidency-begins-fresh-start-us-also-transatlantic-relations_en>.

[26] Brattberg, Erik: 'Transatlantic Relations After Biden's First 100 Days'. *Carnegie Endowment for International Peace*, May 06, 2021, retrieved 23.11.2022, from <https://carnegieendowment.org/2021/05/06/transatlantic-relations-after-biden-s-first-100-days-pub-84472>.

[27] 'Chapter Four: Europe'. *The Military Balance* 122 (1), 2022, p. 66, doi: 10.1080/04597222.2022.2022929.

[28] Hufbauer, Gary / Hogan, Mogan: 'Washington won't chip away at China's military with semiconductor sanctions'. *EastAsiaForum.org*, December 11, 2022, retrieved 21.12.2022, from <https://www.eastasiaforum.org/2022/12/11/washington-wont-chip-away-at-chinas-military-with-semiconductor-sanctions/>.

[29] Bermingham, Finman: '(The) EU will not follow US' China Policy, top diplomat says in fiery debate with lawmakers'. *South China Morning Posts*, November 23, 2022, retrieved 22.12.2022, from <https://www.scmp.com/news/china/article/3200632/eu-will-not-follow-us-china-policy-top-diplomat-says-fiery-debate-lawmakers>.

[30] Casarini, Nicola: 'A European strategic 'third-way?' The European Union between the traditional transatlantic alliance and the pull of Chinese market'. *China International Strategy Review* 4, 2022, p. 94.

[31] Bounds, Andy et al.: 'China calls EU to act independently of US foreign policy'. *Financial Times*, April 1, 2022, retrieved 18.11.2022, from <https://www.ft.com/content/5aff68f9-af65-4aa4-9c47-f4fbb35df48f>.

[32] Sofuoglu, Murat: 'Europe's recalibration of China's ties shows EU-US split'. *TRTWorld.com*, November 25, 2022, retrieved 27.12.2022, from <https://www.trtworld.com/magazine/europe-s-recalibration-of-china-ties-shows-eu-us-split-62860>.

[33] Casarini, Nicola: 'A European strategic 'third-way?', p. 92.

[34] Gramer, Robbie / Iyengar, Rishi: 'Europe's Great Catch-Up on China'. *Foreign Policy*, December 20, 2022, retrieved 23.12.2022, from <https://foreignpolicy.com/2022/12/20/europes-great-catch-up-on-china/>.

[35] Perthes, Volker: 'Dimensions on rivalry: China, the United States, and Europe'. *China International Strategy Review* 3, 2021, pp. 56.

[36] 'EU-China - A strategic outlook'. *European Commission*, March 12, 2019, retrieved 13.09.2022, from <https://ec.europa.eu/info/sites/default/files/communication-eu-china-a-strategic-outlook.pdf>.

[37] Buras, Piotr: 'The EU's unforgivable failure'. *European Council of Foreign Relations*, January 19, 2022, retrieved 21.11.2022, from <https://ecfr.eu/article/the-eus-unforgivable-failure/>; Forsberg, Thomas: 'The Power of the European Union. What explains the EU's (lack of) influence on Russia?' *Politiqueeuropéenne* 39(1), 2013, pp. 22–42; Verhofstdt, Guy: 'Europe's military weakness is indefensible!'. *EUObserver*, October 06, 2021, retrieved 21.11.2022, from <https://euobserver.com/opinion/153129>; Zandee, Dick / Stoetman, Adája / Deen, Bob: *The EU Strategic Compass for security and defence. Squaring ambition with reality*, Clingendale Report. Netherlands Institute of International Relations, Hague, 2021.

[38] Helwig, Niklas / Sinkkonen, Ville: 'Strategic Autonomy and the EU as a Global Actor: The Evolution, Debate and Theory of Contested Term'. *European Foreign Affairs Review* 27 (Special Issue), 2022, pp. 1–2.

[39] 'Shared Vision, Common Action: A Stronger Europe. A Global Strategy for the European Union's Foreign And Security Policy'. *European External Action Service*, December 15, 2019, retrieved 04.10.2022, from <https://www.eeas.europa.eu/eeas/global-strategy-european-unions-foreign-and-security-policy_en>.

[40] Helwig, Niklas / Sinkkonen, Ville: 'Strategic Autonomy and the EU … '. pp. 6–7.

[41] Howorth, Jolyon: 'Strategic autonomy and EU-NATO cooperation: threats or opportunity for transatlantic defence relations?'. *Journal of European Integration* 40(5), 2018, pp. 523–537; Aggestam, Elisabeth / Hyde-Price, Adrian: 'Double-Trouble: Trump, Transatlantic Relations and European Strategic Autonomy'. *Journal of Common Market Studies* 57, 2019, pp. 114–127.

[42] In 1998, the Saint-Malo declaration stated that the EU must have the capacity for autonomous action, backed up by credible military forces, the means to decide to use them, and a readiness to do so, in order to respond to military crises. In March 2022, two weeks after Russia started a full-scale invasion of Ukraine, in the Versailles Declaration, the EU Heads of State or Government announced that the EU, confronted with growing instability, strategic competition, and security threats, decided to take more responsibility for its security, including bolstering its defence capabilities. Twenty-four years elapsed between both abovementioned papers, during which the EU's real combat capability remained almost the same – that is, minimal. During this time, the majority of EU member states even reduced their military expenditures and defence capabilities.

[43] 'Europe must take greater responsibility of its own security - EU Heads of States and Government agree'. *European External Action Service*, June 26, 2018, retrieved 02.12.2022, from <https://www.eeas.europa.eu/node/47738_en>.

44 Kwiatkowska, Monika: 'Defence Forces of the European Union: prospects and ambitions'. *European Journal of Geopolitics* 10, 2022, p. 77.

45 Herszehorn, David: 'Europe's NATO problem'. *Politico.eu*, February 14, 2019, retrieved 21.02.2023, from <https://www.politico.eu/article/europe-nato-problem-defense-procurement-training-research/>.

46 Machi, Vivienne: 'How the F-35 swept Europe, and the competition it could soon face'. *DefenceNews.com*, September 04, 2022, retrieved 11.01.2022, from <https://www.defensenews.com/global/europe/2022/09/04/how-the-f-35-swept-europe-and-the-cometition-it-could-soon-face/>.

47 Kirk-Wade, Esme / Balakrishnan, Sanjana: 'Defence spending pledges by NATO members state since Russia invaded Ukraine'. *House of Common Library*, August 11, 2022, retrieved 12.01.2023, from <https://commonslibrary.parliament.uk/defence-spending-pledges-by-nato-members-since-russia-invaded-ukraine/>.

48 Bergmann, Max / Lamond, James /Cicarelli, Siena: 'The Case for EU Defense. A New Way Forward for Trans-Atlantic Security Relations'. *The Center for American Progress*, June 01, 2021, retrieved 17.11.2022, from <https://www.americanprogress.org/article/case-eu-defense/>.

49 Ruane, Kevin: *The Rise and Fall of the European Defence Community. Anglo-American Relations and the Crisis of European Defence*, Palgrave MacMillan: London, 2000.

50 'The Common Security and Defence Policy'. *European External Action Service*, August 12, 2021, retrieved 03.01.2022, from <https://www.eeas.europa.eu/eeas/common-security-and-defence-policy_en>.

51 Vanhoonacker, Sophie / Dijkstra, Hylke /Maurer, Heidi: 'Understanding the Role of Bureaucracy in the European Security and Defence Policy: The State of the Art'. *European Integration online Papers (EIoP)*: 14 (Special Issue 1), 2010, pp. 1–33, accessed 21.11.2022, from <http://eiop.or.at/eiop/texte/2010-004a.htm>.

52 Angelet, Bruno: 'The war against Ukraine and European defence: when will we square the circle?'. *Egmont. Royal Institute for International Relations*, November 10, 2022, retrieved 10.01.2023, from <https://www.egmontinstitute.be/the-war-against-ukraine-and-european-defence-when-will-we-square-the-circle/>.

53 'NATO'. *The Military Balance* 91 (1), 1991, pp. 55–58.

54 'Chapter Four: Europe'. *The Military Balance* 122 (1), 2022, pp. 104–108.

55 Sköns, Elisabeth: 'The European Defence Industry'. *Columbia International Affairs Online*, March 2022, retrieved 23.11.2022, from <https://ciaotest.cc.columbia.edu/casestudy/ske01/>.

56 Wiśniewski, Rafał: 'Defence industry in the European Union. Challenges and opportunities in times of economic crisis'. *Przegląd Strategiczny* (*Strategic Review*) 2, 2012, pp. 98–100.

57 Gallardo, Cristina: 'UK, Japan, Italy join forces to develop next-generation fighter jets'. *Politico.eu*, December 9, 2022, retrieved 30.10.2023, from <https://www.politico.eu/article/uk-japan-italy-join-forces-to-develop-next-generation-fighter-jets/>.

58 Wiśniewski, Rafał: 'Defence industry in the European Union. Challenges and opportunities in times of economic crisis', pp. 101–103.

59 Gressel, Gustav / Witney, Nick: 'Out of the dark: Reinventing European defence cooperation'. *European Council on Foreign Relations*, March 18, 2022, retrieved 21.01.2023, from <https://ecfr.eu/article/out-of-the-dark-reinventing-european-defence-cooperation/>.

60 Jones, Ben: 'Choices and dilemmas for European defence acquisition: alone: together or "off-the-shelf"'. In: *Solving the European defence market, Brussel: European Liberal Forum*, 2018, pp. 23–44.

61 'Defence Industry: EU to reinforce the European defence industry through common procurement with €500 million instrument'. *European Commission*, July 19, 2022, retrieved 23.10.2023, from <https://ec.europa.eu/commission/presscorner/detail/en/IP_22_4491>.

62 'DOD Dictionary of Military and Associated Terms'. *U.S. Department of Defense*, Washington DC: The Joint Staff, 2020, p. 85.

63 Stach, Łukasz: 'The Philippines maritime forces and its maritime power projection capabilities: unfulfilled ambitions?'. *Defense & Security Analysis* 37(4), 2021, pp. 416.

64 Till, Geoffrey: *Asia's Naval Expansion. An arms race in the making?*. Routledge: London, New York, 2012, p. 133.

65 Stach, Łukasz: 'The Philippines maritime forces…', pp. 415–416.

66 Bergmann, Max / Lamond, James /Cicarelli, Siena: 'The Case for EU Defense…'.

67 'Chapter Four: Europe'. *The Military Balance* 122 (1), 2022, pp. 65.

68 'Chapter Three: North America'. *The Military Balance* 122 (1), 2022, pp. 56–59.

69 'Chapter Six: Asia'. *The Military Balance* 122 (1), 2022, p. 261.

70 Wolton, Timothy/Clark, Bryan: 'Resilient Aerial Refuelling: Safeguarding the US Military's Global Reach'. *Centre for Defense Concepts and Technology, Hudson Institute,* November 2021, retrieved 18.01.2023, from <https://www.hudson.org/national-security-defense/resilient-aerial-refueling-safeguarding-the-us-military-s-global-reach>.

71 'Major boost to NATO's aerial refuelling capability'. *North Atlantic Treaty Organisation*, 2016, retrieved 11.01.2023, from <https://shape.nato.int/2016/major-boost-to-natos-aerial-refuelling-capability>.

72 Morcos, Pierre / Wall, Colin: 'Are European navies ready for high-intensity warfare?'. *War-on-rocks. Texan National Security Review*. January 31, 2022, retrieved 23.01.2023, from <https://warontherocks.com/2022/01/are-european-navies-ready-for-high-intensity-warfare/>.

73 'Coordinated Maritime Presence'. *European External Action Service,* December 03, 2021, retrieved 12.12.2022, from <https://www.eeas.europa.eu/eeas/coordinated-maritime-presences_en>.

74 'Coordinated Maritime Presences: Council extends implementation in the Gulf of Guinea for two years and establishes a new maritime Area of Interest in the North-Western Indian Ocean'. *European Council*, February 21, 2022, retrieved 18.01.2023, from <https://www.consilium.europa.eu/en/press/press-releases/2022/02/21/coordinated-maritime-presences-council-extends-implementation-in-the-gulf-of-guinea-for-2-years-and-establishes-a-new-concept-in-the-north-west-indian-ocean/?utm_source=dsms-auto&utm_medium=email&utm_campaign=Coordinated%20Maritime%20Presences%3A%20Council%20extends%20implementation%20in%20the%20Gulf%20of%20

Guinea%20for%20two%20years%20and%20establishes%20a%20new%20Maritime%20Area%20of%20Interest%20in%20the%20North-Western%20Indian%20Ocean>.

[75] Nováky, Niklas: 'The Coordinated Maritime Presences concept and the EU's naval ambitions in the Indo-Pacific'. *European View* 21 (1), 2022, pp. 60–61.

[76] 'EU Rapid Deployment Capacity'. *European External Action Service*, November 15, 2022, retrieved 21.11.2022, from <https://www.eeas.europa.eu/eeas/eu-rapid-deployment-capacity_en>.

[77] 'The EU Capability Development Priorities. 2018 CDP Revision'. *European Defence Agency*, December 12, 2018, retrieved 19.09.2022, from <https://eda.europa.eu/docs/default-source/eda-publications/eda-brochure-cdp>.

[78] Bolder, Patrick / Chavannes, Ester: 'Military Space Developments: Challenge and Opportunities for Defense and Industry'. *Hague Centre for Strategic Studies*, October 21, 2020, retrieved 19.11.2022, from <https://www.jstor.org/stable/resrep26763#metadata_info_tab_contents>.

[79] 'NATO's approach to space', *North Atlantic Treaty Organisation*, October 06, 2022, retrieved 18.11.2022, from <https://www.nato.int/cps/en/natohq/topics_175419.htm>.

[80] Carai, Gianluca: 'The 'Land Approach' to the Space Domain. Developing Space Expertise in Land Forces'. *Transforming Joint Air and Space Power. The Journal of the JAPCC* 32, Summer 2021, pp. 13–17.

[81] 'Number of satellites in orbit by major country as of January 1, 2022'. *Statista.com*, July 27, 2022, retrieved 19.11.2022, from <https://www.statista.com/statistics/264472/number-of-satellites-in-orbit-by-operating-country/>.

[82] Dobrynin, Sergiei / Krutov, Mark: 'In Russia's War On Ukraine, Effective Satellites Are Few And Far Between'. *Radio Free Europe*, April 11, 2022, retrieved 21.11.2022, from <https://www.rferl.org/a/russia-satellites-ukraine-war-gps/31797618.html>.

[83] Borowitz, Mariel: 'War in Ukraine highlights the growing strategic importance of private satellites companies'. *Phys.org*, August 16, 2022, retrieved 22.11.2022, from <https://phys.org/news/2022-08-war-ukrainehighlights-strategic-importance.html>.

[84] Smith, Mark: 'Anti-satellite weapons: History, types and purpose'. *Space.com*, August 10, 2021, retrieved 29.09.2022, from <https://www.space.com/anti-satellite-weapons-asats>.

[85] Oppal-Rome, Barbara: 'Israeli Experts: Arrow-3 Could Be Adapted for Anti-Satellite Role'. *Spacenews.com*, November 9, 2009, retrieved 09.09.2022, from <https://spacenews.com/israeli-experts-arrow-3-could-be-adapted-anti-satellite%E2%80%82role/>.

[86] 'France to develop anti-satellite laser weapon'. *France24.com*, July 25, 2019, retrieved 09.09.2022, from <https://www.france24.com/en/20190725-france-develop-anti-satellite-laser-weapons-defence-minister>.

[87] Si-soo, Park: 'Japan, Germany declare moratorium on anti-satellite missile tests'. *Spacenews.com*, September 14, 2022, retrieved 16.10.2022, from <https://spacenews.com/japan-germany-declare-moratorium-on-anti-satellite-missile-tests/>.

88 'ESA budget 2022'. *European Space Agency*, 18 January, 2022, retrieved 23.01.2023, from <https://www.esa.int/ESA_Multimedia/Images/2022/01/ESA_budget_2022>.

89 Tani, Caterina: 'European Space Agency €16B budget not enough to catch up with US and China, says industry'. *Sciencebusiness.net*, November 24, 2022, retrieved 03.03.2023, from <https://sciencebusiness.net/news/european-space-agency-eu169b-budget-not-enough-catch-us-and-china-says-industry>.

90 Zandee, Dick / Stoetman, Adája / Deen, Bob: *The EU Strategic Compass for security and defence. Squaring ambition with reality*, 2021, p. 1.

91 Zhao, Suisheng / Dan, Guo: 'A New Cold War? Causes and Future of the Emerging US-China Rivalry'. *Vestnik RUDN. International Relations* 19(1), 2019, p. 9.

92 Bekkevold, Inge Jo: '5 Ways the U.S.-China Cold War Will Be Different From the Last One'. *Foreign Policy*, December 29, 2022, retrieved 30.01.2023, from <https://foreignpolicy.com/2022/12/29/us-china-cold-war-bipolar-global-order-stability-biden-xi/>.

93 Gridneff, Ilya: 'Why Europe's defence industry can't keep up'. *Politico.eu*, October 11, 2022, retrieved 11.01.2023, from <https://www.politico.eu/article/europe-defense-military-industry-keep-up-demands/>.

94 Deni, John: 'What Tanks in Ukraine Tell Us About America in Pacific'. *Defence One*, February 7, 2023, retrieved 11.02.2023, from <https://www.defenseone.com/ideas/2023/02/what-tanks-ukraine-tell-us-about-america-pacific/382682/>.

95 Waltz, Kenneth: 'NATO expansion: A realist's view'. *Contemporary Security Policy* 21(2), 2000, p. 26.

96 Leigh, Michael: 'The European Union's federal dilemma'. *Geopolitical Intelligence Services*, January 2021, retrieved 21.01.2022, from <https://www.gisreportsonline.com/r/federal-eu/>.

97 'Europe is our future - and that future is in our hands'. *Bundesregierung*, August 29, 2022, retrieved 09.02.2023, from <https://www.bundesregierung.de/breg-en/news/scholz-speech-prague-charles-university-2079558>.

98 Scholz, Olaf: 'The Global Zeitenwende. How to Avoid a New Cold War in Multipolar Era'. *Foreign Policy*, December 5, 2022, retrieved 11.02.2023, from <https://www.foreignaffairs.com/germany/olaf-scholz-global-zeitenwende-how-avoid-new-cold-war>.

99 Dempsey, Judy: 'Judy Asks: Is Germany Damaging Europe's Position on Ukraine?'. *Carnegie Europe*, January 27, 2022, retrieved 21.01.2023, from <https://carnegieeurope.eu/strategiceurope/86288>; Fix, Liana: 'On the Ukraine War, Germany Has a Leadership Problem. Here's Why'. *Council on Foreign Relations*, October 14, 2022, retrieved 08.02.2023, from <https://www.cfr.org/in-brief/ukraine-war-germany-has-leadership-problem-heres-why>.

100 Gotkowska, Justyna: 'The war in Ukraine: consequences for the Bundeswehr and Germany's policy in NATO'. *Centre for Eastern Studies*, March 20, 2022, retrieved 11.02.2023, from <https://www.osw.waw.pl/en/publikacje/osw-commentary/2022-03-30/war-ukraine-consequences-bundeswehr-and-germanys-policy-nato>.

101 Kwiatkowska, Monika: 'Defence Forces of the European Union…'. p. 77.

Bibliography

'Biden's presidency begins: a fresh start for the US but also for transatlantic relations'. *European External Action Service*, January 22, 2021, retrieved 21.12.2022, from <https://www.eeas.europa.eu/eeas/biden%E2%80%99s-presidency-begins-fresh-start-us-also-transatlantic-relations_en>.

'Chapter Four: Europe'. *The Military Balance* 122 (1), 2022, pp. 64–163, doi: 10.1080/04597222.2022.2022929.

'Chapter Six: Asia'. *The Military Balance* 122 (1), 2022, pp. 218–317, doi: 10.1080/04597222.2022.2022931.

'Chapter Three: North America'. *The Military Balance* 122 (1), 2022, pp. 28–63, doi: 10.1080/04597222.2022.2022928.

'China overtakes US as EU's biggest trading partner'. *BBC*, February 17, 2021, retrieved 19.10.2022, from <https://www.bbc.com/news/business-56093378>.

'China-US Perceptions of Check: Falsehoods in Reality'. *Ministry of Foreign Affairs of the People's Republic of China*, June 19, 2022, retrieved 16.11.2022, from <https://www.mfa.gov.cn/eng/wjbxw/202206/t20220619_10706059.html>.

'Coordinated Maritime Presence'. *European External Action Service*, December 03, 2021, retrieved 12.12.2022, from <https://www.eeas.europa.eu/eeas/coordinated-maritime-presences_en>.

'Coordinated Maritime Presences: Council extends implementation in the Gulf of Guinea for two years and establishes a new maritime Area of Interest in the North-Western Indian Ocean'. *European Council*, February 21, 2022, retrieved 18.01.2023, from <https://www.consilium.europa.eu/en/press/press-releases/2022/02/21/coordinated-maritime-presences-council-extends-implementation-in-the-gulf-of-guinea-for-2-years-and-establishes-a-new-concept-in-the-north-west-indian-ocean/?utm_source=dsms-auto&utm_medium=email&utm_campaign=Coordinated%20Maritime%20Presences%3A%20Council%20extends%20implementation%20in%20the%20Gulf%20of%20Guinea%20for%20two%20years%20and%20establishes%20a%20new%20Maritime%20Area%20of%20Interest%20in%20the%20North-Western%20Indian%20Ocean>.

'Defence Industry: EU to reinforce the European defence industry through common procurement with €500 million instrument'. *European*

Commission, July 19, 2022, retrieved 23.10.2023, from <https://ec.europa.eu/commission/presscorner/detail/en/IP_22_4491>.

'DOD Dictionary of Military and Associated Terms'. *U.S. Department of Defense*, Washington DC: The Joint Staff, 2020.

'ESA budget 2022'. *European Space Agency*, 18 January, 2022, retrieved 23.01.2023, from <https://www.esa.int/ESA_Multimedia/Images/2022/01/ESA_budget_2022>.

'EU Rapid Deployment Capacity'. *European External Action Service*, November 15, 2022, retrieved 21.11.2022, from <https://www.eeas.europa.eu/eeas/eu-rapid-deployment-capacity_en>.

'EU-China - A strategic outlook'. *European Commission*, March 12, 2019, retrieved 13.09.2022, from <https://ec.europa.eu/info/sites/default/files/communication-eu-china-a-strategic-outlook.pdf>.

'Europe is our future - and that future is in our hands'. *Bundesregierung*, August 29, 2022, retrieved 09.02.2023, from <https://www.bundesregierung.de/breg-en/news/scholz-speech-prague-charles-university-2079558>.

'Europe must take greater responsibility of its own security - EU Heads of States and Government agree'. *European External Action Service*, June 26, 2018, retrieved 02.12.2022, from <https://www.eeas.europa.eu/node/47738_en>.

'France to develop anti-satellite laser weapon'. *France24.com*, July 25, 2019, retrieved 09.09.2022, from <www.france24.com/en/20190725-france-develop-anti-satellite-laser-weapons-defence-minister>.

'Major boost to NATO's aerial refuelling capability'. *North Atlantic Treaty Organisation*, 2016, retrieved 11.01.2023, from <https://shape.nato.int/2016/major-boost-to-natos-aerial-refuelling-capability>

'National Defense Strategy of The United States of America. Including the 2022 Nuclear Posture Review and the 2022 Missile Defence Review'. *U.S. Department of Defense*, October 2022, retrieved 29.09.2022, from <https://www.defense.gov/News/News-Stories/Article/Article/3202438/dod-releases-national-defense-strategy-missile-defense-nuclear-posture-reviews/>.

'NATO's approach to space', *North Atlantic Treaty Organisation*, October 06, 2022, retrieved 18.11.2022, from <https://www.nato.int/cps/en/natohq/topics_175419.htm>.

'NATO'. *The Military Balance* 91 (1), 1991, pp. 46–79, DOI: 10.1080/04597229108460029.

'Number of satellites in orbit by major country as of January 1, 2022'. *Statista.com*, July 27, 2022, retrieved 19.11.2022, from<www.statista.com/statistics/264472/number-of-satellites-in-orbit-by-operating-country/>.

'Shared Vision, Common Action: A Stronger Europe. A Global Strategy for the European Union's Foreign And Security Policy'. *European External Action Service,* December 15, 2019, retrieved 04.10.2022, from <https://www.eeas.europa.eu/eeas/global-strategy-european-unions-foreign-and-security-policy_en>.

'The China Threat'. *Federal Bureau of Investigation*, retrieved 15.11.2022, from <https://www.fbi.gov/investigate/counterintelligence/the-china-threat>.

'The Common Security and Defence Policy'. *European External Action Service*, August 12, 2021, retrieved 03.01.2022, from <https://www.eeas.europa.eu/eeas/common-security-and-defence-policy_en>.

'The EU Capability Development Priorities. 2018 CDP Revision'. *European Defence Agency*, December 12, 2018, retrieved 19.09.2022, from <https://eda.europa.eu/docs/default-source/eda-publications/eda-brochure-cdp>.

Aggestam, Elisabeth / Hyde-Price, Adrian: 'Double-Trouble: Trump, Transatlantic Relations and European Strategic Autonomy'. *Journal of Common Market Studies* 57 (S1), 2019, pp. 114–127.

Allison, Graham: 'The Thucydides Trap: Are the U.S. and China headed for War?'. *The Atlantic*, September 15, 2015, retrieved 18.09.2022, from <https://www.theatlantic.com/international/archive/2015/09/united-states-china-war-thucydides-trap/406756/>.

Allison, Graham: *Destined for war. Can America and China escape Thucydidies Trap*? Houghton Mifflin Harcourt: Boston, New York, 2017.

Angelet, Bruno: 'The war against Ukraine and European defence: when will we square the circle?'. *Egmont. Royal Institute for International Relations*, November 10, 2022, retrieved 10.01.2023, from <https://www.egmontinstitute.be/the-war-against-ukraine-and-european-defence-when-will-we-square-the-circle/>.

Behr, Hartmut / Stivachtis, Yannis A.: 'European Union: An Empire in New Clothes?'. In: edited by Behr, Hartmut / Stivactis, Yannis A. (eds.): *Revisiting the European Union as an Empire*, Routledge: London, 2015.

Bekkevold, Inge Jo: '5 Ways the U.S.-China Cold War Will Be Different From the Last One'. *Foreign Policy*, December 29, 2022, retrieved 30.01.2023, from <https://foreignpolicy.com/2022/12/29/us-china-cold-war-bipolar-global-order-stability-biden-xi/>.

Bergmann, Max / Lamond, James /Cicarelli, Siena: 'The Case for EU Defense. A New Way Forward for Trans-Atlantic Security Relations'. *The Center for American Progress*, June 01, 2021, retrieved 17.11.2022, from <https://www.americanprogress.org/article/case-eu-defense/>.

Bermingham, Finman: '(The) EU will not follow US' China Policy, top diplomat says in fiery debate with lawmakers'. *South China Morning Posts*, November 23, 2022, retrieved 22.12.2022, from <https://www.scmp.com/news/china/article/3200632/eu-will-not-follow-us-china-policy-top-diplomat-says-fiery-debate-lawmakers>.

Bolder, Patrick / Chavannes, Ester: 'Military Space Developments: Challenge and Opportunities for Defense and Industry'. *Hague Centre for Strategic Studies*, October 21, 2020, retrieved 19.11.2022, from <https://www.jstor.org/stable/resrep26763#metadata_info_tab_contents>.

Borowitz, Mariel: 'War in Ukraine highlights the growing strategic importance of private satellites companies'. *Phys.org*, August 16, 2022, retrieved 22.11.2022, from <phys.org/news/2022-08-war-ukrainehighlights-strategic-importance.html>.

Bounds, Andy et al.: 'China calls EU to act independently of US foreign policy'. *Financial Times*, April 1, 2022, retrieved 18.11.2022, from <https://www.ft.com/content/5aff68f9-af65-4aa4-9c47-f4fbb35df48f>.

Brattberg, Erik: 'Transatlantic Relations After Biden's First 100 Days'. *Carnegie Endowment for International Peace*, May 06, 2021, retrieved 23.11.2022, from <https://carnegieendowment.org/2021/05/06/transatlantic-relations-after-biden-s-first-100-days-pub-84472>.

Buras, Piotr: 'The EU's unforgivable failure'. *European Council of Foreign Relations*, January 19, 2022, retrieved 21.11.2022, from <https://ecfr.eu/article/the-eus-unforgivable-failure/>.

Carai, Gianluca: 'The 'Land Approach' to the Space Domain. Developing Space Expertise in Land Forces'. *Transforming Joint Air and Space Power. The Journal of the JAPCC* 32, Summer 2021, pp. 13–17.

Casarini, Nicola: 'A European strategic 'third-way?' The European Union between the traditional transatlantic alliance and the pull of Chinese market'. *China International Strategy Review* 4, 2022, pp. 91–107.

Dempsey, Judy: 'Germany Continued illusions About China and Russia'. *Carnegie Europe*, October 20, 2022, retrieved 29.09.2022, from <https://carnegieeurope.eu/strategiceurope/88210>.

Dempsey, Judy: 'Judy Asks: Is Germany Damaging Europe's Position on Ukraine?'. *Carnegie Europe*, January 27, 2022, retrieved 21.01.2023, from <https://carnegieeurope.eu/strategiceurope/86288>.

Deni, John: 'What Tanks in Ukraine Tell Us About America in Pacific'. *Defence One*, February 7, 2023, retrieved 11.02.2023, from <https://www.defenseone.com/ideas/2023/02/what-tanks-ukraine-tell-us-about-america-pacific/382682/>.

Dimitrova, Anna: 'The State of Transatlantic Relationship in the Trump Era'. *European Issues 545, Foundation Robert Schuman*, February 03, 2020, retrieved 16.12.2022, from <https://www.robert-schuman.eu/en/european-issues/0545-the-state-of-the-transatlantic-relationship-in-the-trump-era>.

Dobrynin, Sergiei / Krutov, Mark: 'In Russia's War On Ukraine, Effective Satellites Are Few And Far Between'. *Radio Free Europe*, April 11, 2022, retrieved 21.11.2022, from <https://www.rferl.org/a/russia-satellites-ukraine-war-gps/31797618.html>.

Donahoe, Patrick / Spencer, John: 'A Status Check On The Army's Preparation For the Next War'. *Modern War Institute at West Point*, June 07, 2021, retrieved 05.12.2022, from <https://mwi.usma.edu/a-status-check-on-the-armys-preparation-for-the-next-war/>.

Fix, Liana: 'On the Ukraine War, Germany Has a Leadership Problem. Here's Why'. *Council on Foreign Relations*, October 14, 2022, retrieved 08.02.2023, from <https://www.cfr.org/in-brief/ukraine-war-germany-has-leadership-problem-heres-why>.

Forsberg, Thomas: 'The Power of the European Union. What explains the EU's (lack of) influence on Russia?' *Politiqueeuropéenne* 39(1), 2013, pp. 22–42.

Gallardo, Cristina: 'UK, Japan, Italy join forces to develop next-generation fighter jets'. *Politico.eu*, December 9, 2022, retrieved 30.10.2023, from <https://www.politico.eu/article/uk-japan-italy-join-forces-to-develop-next-generation-fighter-jets/>.

Gotkowska, Justyna: 'The war in Ukraine: consequences for the Bundeswehr and Germany's policy in NATO'. *Centre for Eastern Studies*, March 20, 2022, retrieved 11.02.2023, from <https://www.osw.waw.pl/en/publikacje/osw-commentary/2022-03-30/war-ukraine-consequences-bundeswehr-and-germanys-policy-nato>.

Gramer, Robbie / Iyengar, Rishi: 'Europe's Great Catch-Up on China'. *Foreign Policy*, December 20, 2022, retrieved 23.12.2022, from <https://foreignpolicy.com/2022/12/20/europes-great-catch-up-on-china/>.

Gressel, Gustav / Witney, Nick: 'Out of the dark: Reinventing European defence cooperation'. *European Council on Foreign Relations*, March 18, 2022, retrieved 21.01.2023, from <https://ecfr.eu/article/out-of-the-dark-reinventing-european-defence-cooperation/>.

Gridneff, Ilya: 'Why Europe's defence industry can't keep up'. *Politico.eu*, October 11, 2022, retrieved 11.01.2023, from <https://www.politico.eu/article/europe-defense-military-industry-keep-up-demands/>.

Helwig, Niklas / Sinkkonen, Ville: 'Strategic Autonomy and the EU as a Global Actor: The Evolution, Debate and Theory of Contested Term'. *European Foreign Affairs Review* 27 (Special Issue), 2022, pp. 1–20.

Herszehorn, David: 'Europe's NATO problem'. *Politico.eu*, February 14, 2019, retrieved 21.02.2023, from <https://www.politico.eu/article/europe-nato-problem-defense-procurement-training-research/>.

Howorth, Jolyon: 'Strategic autonomy and EU-NATO cooperation: threats or opportunity for transatlantic defence relations?'. *Journal of European Integration* 40(5), 2018, pp. 523–537.

Hufbauer, Gary / Hogan, Mogan: 'Washington won't chip away at China's military with semiconductor sanctions'. *EastAsiaForum.org*, December 11, 2022, retrieved 21.12.2022, from <www.eastasiaforum.org/2022/12/11/washington-wont-chip-away-at-chinas-military-with-semiconductor-sanctions/>.

Jones, Ben: 'Choices and dilemmas for European defence acquisition: alone: together or "off-the-shelf"'. In: *Solving the European defence market, Brussel: European Liberal Forum*, 2018, pp. 23–44.

Kagan, Robert: *Paradise and Power.* London: Atlantic Books: London 2004.

Kirk-Wade, Esme / Balakrishnan, Sanjana: 'Defence spending pledges by NATO members state since Russia invaded Ukraine'. *House of Common Library*, August 11, 2022, retrieved 12.01.2023, from <https://commonslibrary.parliament.uk/defence-spending-pledges-by-nato-members-since-russia-invaded-ukraine/>.

Kwiatkowska, Monika: 'Defence Forces of the European Union: prospects and ambitions'. *European Journal of Geopolitics* 10, 2022, pp. 75–83.

Leigh, Michael: 'The European Union's federal dilemma'. *Geopolitical Intelligence Services*, January 2021, retrieved 21.01.2022, from <https://www.gisreportsonline.com/r/federal-eu/>.

Leonard, Mark: 'Europe for itself'. *European Council on Foreign Relations*, July 24, 2018, retrieved 11.02.2023, from <https://ecfr.eu/article/commentary_europe_for_itself/>.

Leonard, Mark: 'Europe's soft-power problem'. *The European Council of Foreign Relations*, May 05, 2022, retrieved 14.11.2022, from <https://ecfr.eu/article/europes-soft-power-problem/>.

Leonard, Mark: *Why Europe Will Run the 21st Century?*. Fourth Estate: London 2011.

Machi, Vivienne: 'How the F-35 swept Europe, and the competition it could soon face'. *DefenceNews.com*, September 04, 2022, retrieved 11.01.2022, from <www.defensenews.com/global/europe/2022/09/04/how-the-f-35-swept-europe-and-the-cometition-it-could-soon-face/>.

McCormick, John: *The European Superpower.* Palgrave Macmillan: London 2006.

Moravscik, Andrew: 'Europe Is Still a Superpower. And it's going to remain on for decades to come'. *Foreign Policy,* April 13, 2017, retrieved 18.09.2022, from <https://foreignpolicy.com/2017/04/13/europe-is-still-a-superpower/>.

Morcos, Pierre / Wall, Colin: 'Are European navies ready for high-intensity warfare?'. *War-on-rocks. Texan National Security Review.* January 31, 2022, retrieved 23.01.2023, from <https://warontherocks.com/2022/01/are-european-navies-ready-for-high-intensity-warfare/>.

Ng Teddy: 'China's top military brass to be on high alert and ready for war amid mounting tensions with US'. *South China Morning Post*, October

19, 2022, retrieved 23.11.2022, from <https://www.scmp.com/news/china/military/article/3196462/chinas-top-military-brass-vow-be-high-alert-and-ready-war-amid-mounting-tension-us>.

Nováky, Niklas: 'The Coordinated Maritime Presences concept and the EU's naval ambitions in the Indo-Pacific'. *European View* 21 (1), 2022, pp. 56–65.

Oppal-Rome, Barbara: 'Israeli Experts: Arrow-3 Could Be Adapted for Anti-Satellite Role'. *Spacenews.com*, November 9, 2009, retrieved 09.09.2022, from <spacenews.com/israeli-experts-arrow-3-could-be-adapted-anti-satellite%E2%80%82role/>.

Pänke, Julian: 'Liberal Empire, Geopolitics and EU Strategy: Norms and Interests in European Foreign Policy Making'. *Geopolitics* 21(1), 2019, pp. 100–123.

Perthes, Volker: 'Dimensions on rivalry: China, the United States, and Europe'. *China International Strategy Review* 3, 2021, pp. 56–65.

Reid, Thomas Roy: *The United States of Europe: The New Superpower and the End of American Supremacy*, Penguin Books: London 2005.

Riddervold, Marianne / Newsome, Akesemie: 'Transatlantic relations in times of uncertainty: crises and EU-US relations'. *Journal of European Integration* 40(5), 2018, pp. 505–521.

Rifkin, Jeremy: *The European Dream: how European vision of the future is quietly eclipsing the American dream*. Penguin: New York 2004.

Ruane, Kevin: *The Rise and Fall of the European Defence Community. Anglo-American Relations and the Crisis of European Defence*, Palgrave MacMillan: London, 2000.

Scholz, Olaf: 'The Global Zeitenwende. How to Avoid a New Cold War in Multipolar Era'. *Foreign Policy*, December 5, 2022, retrieved 11.02.2023, from <https://www.foreignaffairs.com/germany/olaf-scholz-global-zeitenwende-how-avoid-new-cold-war>.

Si-soo, Park: 'Japan, Germany declare moratorium on anti-satellite missile tests'. *Spacenews.com*, September 14, 2022, retrieved 16.10.2022, from <spacenews.com/japan-germany-declare-moratorium-on-anti-satellite-missile-tests/>.

Sköns, Elisabeth: 'The European Defence Industry'. *Columbia International Affairs Online*, March 2022, retrieved 23.11.2022, from <https://ciaotest.cc.columbia.edu/casestudy/ske01/>.

Smith, Mark: 'Anti-satellite weapons: History, types and purpose'. *Space.com*, August 10, 2021, retrieved 29.09.2022, from <><www.space.com/anti-satellite-weapons-asats>.

Sofuoglu, Murat: 'Europe's recalibration of China's ties shows EU-US split'. *TRTWorld.com*, November 25, 2022, retrieved 27.12.2022, from <www.trtworld.com/magazine/europe-s-recalibration-of-china-ties-shows-eu-us-split-62860>.

Stach, Łukasz: 'The Philippines maritime forces and its maritime power projection capabilities: unfulfilled ambitions?'. *Defense & Security Analysis* 37(4), 2021, pp. 414–434.

Streeck, Wolfgang: 'The European Union is a liberal empire, and is about to fall'. *LSE Brexit blog*, March 6, 2019, retrieved 18.10.2022, from <https://blogs.lse.ac.uk/brexit/2019/03/06/long-read-the-european-union-is-a-liberal-empire-and-it-is-about-to-fall/>.

Tani, Caterina: 'European Space Agency €16B budget not enough to catch up with US and China, says industry'. *Sciencebusiness.net*, November 24, 2022, retrieved 03.03.2023, from <sciencebusiness.net/news/european-space-agency-eu169b-budget-not-enough-catch-us-and-china-says-industry>.

Till, Geoffrey: *Asia's Naval Expansion. An arms race in the making?*. Routledge: London, New York, 2012.

U.S. Department of Defense. 2018. 'Summary of the 2018 National Defense Strategy of the United States of America. Sharpening the American's Military Competitive Edge'. Department of Defense. Accessed 6 December 2022. <https://dod.defense.gov/Portals/1/Documents/pubs/2018-National-Defense-Strategy-Summary.pdf>

Union of Concerned Scientists. 2022. 'UCS Satellite Database'. *Union of Concerned Scientists*, May 1. Accessed 18 November 2022. <https://www.ucsusa.org/resources/satellite-database>

Vanhoonacker, Sophie / Dijkstra, Hylke /Maurer, Heidi: 'Understanding the Role of Bureaucracy in the European Security and Defence Policy: The State of the Art'. *European Integration online Papers (EIoP)*: 14

(Special Issue 1), 2010, pp. 1–33, accessed 21.11.2022, from <http://eiop.or.at/eiop/texte/2010-004a.htm>.

Verhofstdt, Guy: 'Europe's military weakness is indefensible!'. *EUObserver*, October 06, 2021, retrieved 21.11.2022, from <https://euobserver.com/opinion/153129>.

Villup, Elina: 'The EU, Neither a Political Dwarf nor a Military Worm'. *International Catalan Institute for Peace*, 2015, retrieved 24.09.2022, from <https://www.icip.cat/perlapau/en/article/the-eu-neither-a-political-dwarf-nor-a-military-worm/>.

Waltz, Kenneth: 'NATO expansion: A realist's view'. *Contemporary Security Policy* 21(2), 2000, pp. 23–38.

Wezeman, Pieter D., Alexandra Kuimova and Siemont T. Wezeman. 2021. 'Trends in International Arms Transfers'. *SIPRI Fact Sheet, Stockholm International Peace Research Institute*, March. <https://doi.org/10.55163/CBZJ9986>

Wiśniewski, Rafał: 'Defence industry in the European Union. Challenges and opportunities in times of economic crisis'. *Przegląd Strategiczny (Strategic Review)* 2, 2012, pp. 95–113.

Wolton, Timothy / Clark, Bryan: 'Resilient Aerial Refuelling: Safeguarding the US Military's Global Reach'. *Centre for Defense Concepts and Technology, Hudson Institute,* November 2021, retrieved 18.01.2023, from <https://www.hudson.org/national-security-defense/resilient-aerial-refueling-safeguarding-the-us-military-s-global-reach>.

Zandee, Dick / Stoetman, Adája / Deen, Bob: *The EU Strategic Compass for security and defence. Squaring ambition with reality*, Clingendale Report. Netherlands Institute of International Relations, Hague, 2021.

Zhao, Suisheng / Dan, Guo: 'A New Cold War? Causes and Future of the Emerging US-China Rivalry'. *Vestnik RUDN. International Relations* 19(1), 2019, pp. 9–21.

Zhou, Laura. 2020. 'Risk of military conflict between US and China higher than ever, experts say'. *South China Morning Post*, January 24. Accessed 23 November 2022. <https://www.scmp.com/news/china/diplomacy/article/3090314/risk-military-conflict-between-us-and-china-higher-ever>.

Zielonka, Jan: *Europe as Empire: The Nature of the Enlarged European Union*. Oxford University Press: Oxford 2006.

Public Diplomacy and Popular Culture: American and Chinese Soft Power in Europe

Przemysław Łukasik

> Understanding is based on a share basis, and those were and still are the values personified by Western civilisation, which, like a bridge over the Atlantic Ocean, connects two cousins with some precious blood ties. [...] Understanding, ultimately, should rely on common sense, which avoids extremes and the squabbling between opposites. Some tensions in transatlantic relations do, and will, remain.[1]

> The Chinese nation does not carry aggressive or hegemonic traits in its genes. The Party cares about the future of humanity and wishes to move forward in tandem with all progressive forces around the world. China has always worked to safeguard world peace, contribute to global development and preserve international order.[2]

Soft power

The concept of power is a crucial category in international relations.[3] It has multiple meanings, such as strength, energy, authority, might or ability. As a basic concept in relation to other terms, it cannot be explained by reference to them, so it is relatively difficult to define it.[4] In the sociological literature it is associated with might, power status or empire. In international relations theory, power is usually associated with the enforcement of one's will and has been defined as the control of one political entity by another, even against its will.[5] It has also been defined as the ability to persuade others to do things they would not otherwise do. We can distinguish the following three types of approaches to the concept of power: the traditional approach, that is, state power that depends on state assets; the neorealist approach, that is, the ability to determine the rules of operation and the final outcome of negotiations;

and the structural approach, that is, the ability to influence the structures of the global economy and to impose dominant values and rules of operation, that must be observed by other countries, their political institutions and elites.[6]

The notion of power as a neutral concept that does not require domination was popularised in the early 2000s by the American political scientist Joseph Nye who introduced the concept of soft power.[7] Nye worked in the Carter and Clinton administrations, and together with Robert Keohane, he developed the theory of complex interdependence. In analysing international relations, Nye concluded that states should focus on cooperation rather than rivalry in their struggle for survival and power. As a neoliberal, Nye believed in democracy, human freedom, and equal opportunity, and he also saw significant interdependence in international relations. The origin of the term 'soft power' is related to the search for intangible power assets. In his book entitled *The Rise and Fall of the Great Powers: Economic Change and Military Conflict from 1500 to 2000* of 1987, the British historian Paul Kennedy proclaimed the end of the US imperial power[8] as a result of 'imperial overstretch, as in the case of other powers in human history'. In 1990, Nye wrote *Bound to Lead. The Changing Nature of American Power*, in which he challenged Kennedy and suggested that American power would have to be modified and adapted to skilful use of 'hard power' and 'soft power', in order to prevail.[9] Before Nye used the term 'soft power', other scholars had also tried to address these issues. Pierre Bourdieu wrote about symbolic power, Max Weber on 'legitimate authority', Michel Foucault about 'governmentality', and Jürgen Habermas about 'communicative action'.

According to the theory of international relations, states pursue their goals and clash with other states that are also trying to increase their power. A state has power when it is able to impose its will on others or at least protect itself from the imposition of that will. According to Nye, state hard power is determined by the following clearly defined assets: population, territory, raw materials, economy, and army. Hard power is the so-called first face of power, which makes it possible to achieve goals by force or bribery. According to Nye, Americans learned about the limits of hard power, when the United States lost the Vietnam War. The U.S., lacking long-term strategy and wise leadership, was doomed to failure. Nye argued that after the collapse of the USSR, Americans should develop power based on cooperation, that is, soft power, expressed in agenda setting, persuasion, and attractiveness. He quoted the eighteenth-century philosopher David Hume who argued that no man is powerful enough to achieve his goals alone.[10] Kenneth Boulding called the ability to create trust-based networks that enable groups to work together in order to achieve common goals 'the integrative power'.[11] The war the United States launched against Iraq in 2003 was supposed to prove that *hard power* sometimes destroys the efforts of *soft power.* As a result, another book was published in 2004, that introduced the concept of 'smart power', understood as the ability to combine the assets of hard and soft power into effective strategies.[12] Nye also conducted a thorough analysis of the concept of smart power itself. He emphasised that successful soft power depends on the attitude of another party and the level of credibility of a given country. Sources of soft power should be embedded in the culture, political values, and foreign policy of the country using them. However, he also pointed out that soft power is determined by civil society and not by the government. The positive attractiveness of a society is created by a shared attitude to values, such as charity, competence, or beauty. In the face of constant information overload, the rivalry for attention and recognition is crucial. In this context, Nye wrote about the need for daily communication, strategic communication, and the role of public diplomacy. The ultimate victory in this rivalry will be achieved by the most reliable countries. In the information age, 'it may be about a matter of whose narrative wins'. Thus, the narrative becomes the currency of soft power.[13]

Similarly to many historical concepts, Nye's theory plays the double explanatory and performative role. Soft power explained the important role of non-material assets of power in the post-Cold War reality. Also, it encouraged countries to analyse their own image and soft assets needed to adjust them correctly for the implementation of their own goals of foreign policy.

Joseph Nye once said that soft power is like giving birth to a child, but it is primarily a matter of experience and environment that determines who that child will be. In doing so, he correctly anticipated that his concept could be interpreted and used in many different ways. For 30 years, the theory of soft power has been criticised and analysed by political scientists and academics interested in international relations. The very idea of efficiently transforming soft power assets into global power of a given country has been questioned. Niall Ferguson, a Scottish professor of history, said that buying a pair of American shoes or watching Hollywood movies does not necessarily lead to increased admiration for the United States.[14] Nye was criticised for the lack of a solid theoretical background that would explain, systematise and detail his concepts.[15] For Nye, soft power is the potential of a country's attractiveness, related to foreign policy and popularisation of culture and democratic values, but he does not explain the theoretical background of this process. Moreover, there are different methods of measuring soft power, but – as critics point out – they are based on opinion polls and assess a declarative image of a given country, as perceived by the respondents. Nye's analysis focuses on the influence of governmental institutions and public diplomacy, and, to a lesser extent, it recognises the role of non-governmental organizations, business entities, or social media.[16] Soft power is particularly criticised by Chinese scholars, albeit from an interesting perspective. Chinese analyses point to an unnatural division between hard and soft power since a country's attractiveness depends on hard power, which is expressed in political and military capabilities. According to Far East researchers, soft power is the most effective, when it is combined with hard power.[17] The Chinese also accuse Nye of Americanising and mis-universalising the term. In their view, democratic values and culture do not have to be attractive and so 'enticing' in all countries. The example of China shows that a country's attractiveness in terms of investment and economic cooperation can be much more critical.[18]

The measurable tools that countries use to build soft power are national branding and public diplomacy. Both of these instruments are based on the analysis of objective and subjective data, which allows countries to be ranked according to such indices as national brands, or soft power 30.[19] National branding is promoted as a country's most important asset in the global economic market. A high ranking should encourage investment, increase the number of tourists and attract educated workers from other countries. Branding power is determined by the following factors: foreign investment (government regulations, employees), society (image, security, quality of life, corruption), and produced goods and services (market, tourism).

The history of public diplomacy began at the end of the First World War. At the Paris Peace Conference, secret negotiations between world powers were criticised, and transparency of decisions announced by 'ambassadors of opinion' and journalists was demanded. Nowadays, public diplomacy is an effort to build good relations with the population of given countries with the purpose of arousing curiosity, but also to be able to present certain values. Countries try to use the activities of celebrities (sportspeople, artists, etc., who act as unofficial ambassadors of the country), world events (Olympic Games), international activities of countries (within the UN), and activities of national cultural institutions and media. As a result, all activities aimed at arousing interest, involvement, and influencing foreign public opinion, conducted by another country or international organization, can be defined as public diplomacy. A good example is so-called niche diplomacy, that is, the creation of a country's image by popularising its values in the international forum, such as the Canadian government's involvement in international environmental protection projects and in combating the problem of anti-personnel mines.[20] On the other hand, Norway, one of the richest countries in the world, is called a 'humanitarian superpower' for its participation in peacekeeping and peacebuilding processes.[21]

The U.S. and China are among the 30 leading soft power countries (the U.S. is at the top of the list, while China is at the bottom).[22] According to analysts, China has earned a place in this group thanks to its rich culture (most cultural monuments on the list of World Heritage Sites). China also stands out for having won the most Olympic medals in the most recent editions of the Summer and Winter Olympic Games (first and second place, respectively), for having one of the largest art markets, and for the number of foreign tourists visiting the homeland of Confucius). Education and entrepreneurship are also strong advantages of this country. The U.S. has earned its place at the top of the list because of its superiority in education, culture, and digital technologies. Americanisation has permanently popularised the American mass culture around the world, and American universities are among the best in the world and host the most foreign students. The U.S. is also home to technologically innovative companies (Google, Meta, Microsoft) located in Silicon Valley. Both countries' rankings are lowered by opinions about their governments and foreign policies. Beijing is criticised for violating human rights and freedoms (small number of Internet users and blocking access to websites or violating the rights of several dozen of minorities, e.g. Uyghurs). The administration of President Donald Trump was not trusted and discouraged other actors due to its unpredictability and unilateral approach.

Soft power in America and China

> Through the 20th century until now, the United States (US) has had a unique and lasting influence on European political, economic, social, and cultural affairs. US cultural phenomena, ranging from consumer styles and mass entertainment to education practices and forms of social communication, have represented a profoundly influential range of soft power resources through which the US has shaped, enticed, and aggravated European identities, desires, and futures.[23]

So wrote Giles Scott-Smith. During the Cold War, American cultural soft power in Europe was a part of the anti-communist campaign leading to progressive Americanisation.[24] Defence-oriented cooperation between the United States and Western Europe, based on shared political values and cultural exchange, has become the foundation of the transatlantic community. Defined by social and political scientist Karl Deutsch in 1957 as a 'pluralistic security community', the Euro-Atlantic area after 1945 followed the course of integration of the transatlantic political actors. By integration, we mean the acquisition, within a territorial unit, of a 'sense of community' – the belief, held by the actors, that the resolution of the problems should be carried out preferably without recourse to force and through the institutionalisation of political processes – which leads to the creation of institutions and strong and widespread practices that ensure the peaceful resolution of problems within this community.[25] After the fall of the USSR, the American government stopped funding public diplomacy in Europe, which led to the dissolution of the United States Information Agency in 1999. This decision was made because the ideological adversary, the Soviet Union, had dissolved, but also because of the post-Cold War belief that the values of democratic freedoms and free-market economics were widely shared. In addition, the State Department's Bureau of Educational and Cultural Affairs (ECA) was established, taking over the staff and functions of the defunct USIA. After the September 11 attacks, de-radicalisation became one of the tasks of cultural diplomacy, that is, an attempt to combat political and religious extremism that could lead to terrorism.[26] In this sense, attempts were made to influence the Muslim community in Europe, the Middle East, and around the world. Traditional means of cultural diplomacy were also used in order to strengthen transatlantic ties and the sense of cultural community. This was particularly important, as the interventions in Iraq and Afghanistan drew strong criticism, especially from Western Europe, against the George W. Bush administration and the American hegemony itself. The 'strategic directions' of American cultural diplomacy, defined by the National Security Strategy developed by the US presidential administration, are implemented by the Department of State and its partners, such as the US Agency for International Development (USAID). The purpose of educational projects or cultural exchanges is to promote American leadership and advance U.S. foreign policy objectives, to preserve the U.S. economic interests, and in a broader context, to build 'trust and mutual understanding among nations' and to promote democracy and 'civic participation'.[27]

The famous America Houses and American Libraries organised in Europe after the Second World War in Europe have been continued in various forms in the so-called American Spaces. In cooperation with local partners (schools and libraries), this programme provides access to 650 sites around the world where various activities are carried out.[28] Among the partners, non-governmental organizations or certain cities have become increasingly important. The success of American cultural diplomacy is linked to the positive reaction of Europeans to American cinema, music, and sports.

The reception of American soft power is also influenced by the attitude of the American political leaders residing in the White House. In the twenty-first century, transatlantic relations have been challenged by the division between old and new Europe as a result of the Iraq conflict (George W. Bush), the U.S. pivot to Southeast Asia (Obama), and the prioritisation of unilateralism and economic interests over international alliances and principles (Donald Trump). During the presidency of Donald Trump, European politicians expressed their mistrust of the American partner, repeatedly raising the idea of European defence autonomy and the creation of a European army.[29] The full-scale Russian attack on Ukraine in February 2022 has consolidated the importance of the American military potential for European security. The Americans are concerned about China's growing economic influence in Europe. In response to China's Belt and Road Initiative, the United States and some other rich countries established the Build Back Better World Partnership.[30] It envisages support for infrastructure development in low- and medium-income countries. By 2035 more than USD 40 trillion will be invested in the construction of roads, bridges, airports, ports, and power plants. The project is supported by the OECD and the Three Seas Initiative and is intended to create a positive image of developing countries to implement their aid package, the Chinese have established the China International Development Cooperation Agency, and the country has become one of the ten most active countries in this field of operations.[31] According to research, China's influence is noticeable, although it is not perceived as unambiguously positive.

In 2021, China solemnly commemorated the 100th anniversary of the Chinese Communist Party. The paramount leader of China, Xi Jinping, chose the solution to the problem of overwhelming poverty and the creation of a relatively prosperous society as the greatest 'internal' achievement of the last century. He also indicated that the goal for the next 100 years would be the creation of 'a great modern socialist country'. Regarding foreign policy, he said: 'We must continue working to promote the building of a human community with a shared future. Peace, concord, and harmony are ideas the Chinese nation has pursued and carried forward for more than 5,000 years'.[32]

The image of a peaceful and friendly power focused on economic development and cooperation based on mutual benefits is at the very centre of what we could call Chinese soft power. The foundations of this approach lie in traditional Confucian values, but they also express the flexibility and adaptability of the Chinese people. From the perspective of the Chinese government, harmonious international relations are necessary for the country's further economic development, while the image of a peaceful power is meant to protect against fears arising from China's growing strength. Economic cooperation with developed and developing countries, based on a mutual benefit, is intended to provide access to markets and cheap raw materials.[33] The ambassadors of Chinese public diplomacy are both figures from the past and current members of the public. Confucius is a symbol of the national renaissance and traditional values. This thinker, eradicated by the Chinese communists under Mao Zedong, is currently being rehabilitated. In 2011, a monument to him was erected at Tiananmen Square, and the anniversary of his birthday (September 28) is celebrated with great solemnity. Confucianism has become a source of Chinese soft power around the world. With its focus on the rebirth of personal virtues (the same level of life for oneself and others) as the foundation of humanity, it fits perfectly with the concept of China's peaceful growth in harmony with the rest of the world. In 2004, the

Confucian Institutes project was launched to popularise the Chinese language and culture abroad. By 2021 there were 525 of them in several dozen countries on six continents, with more than 9 million students.[34] The ambassador of China's image seen as a global power focused on trade exchange and peaceful relations is the Chinese admiral and sailor Zheng He. From 1405 to 1433, he travelled to Java, India, and the African coast, establishing friendly relations with the tribes he encountered, presenting them with gifts, and providing them with information about the Chinese empire. He did not establish any colonies, nor did he occupy any discovered territories, thus creating favourable conditions for future trade exchanges.[35] Other important ambassadors of China are sportsmen, such as Li Ning, a gymnast, Yao Ming, a basketball player, and Ma Lin, a table tennis player,[36] followed by the director Zhang Yimou and Jackie Chan, the star of spectacular action films.[37]

The Chinese use global events to build a positive image of their country. The 2008 Olympic Games in Beijing showed China's success in many contexts. China was presented as a power to be reckoned with. The image of rich Chinese tradition, presented in the media, went hand in hand with the country's economic success, technological advancement, and increasing concern for the environment.[38]

In the international forum, China's soft power activities are mostly economic cooperation that provides access to raw materials, technologies, and communication nodes. The New Silk Road Initiative, launched in 2013, is an instrument of Chinese policy in both global and regional contexts. Connecting the Middle Kingdom with Asian and European countries through roads, railways, and maritime routes has been presented in the media and at various events as a new Marshall Plan in which all parties win (the project's goals are coordination of policies, free trade, financial integration and establishment of interpersonal ties). Certain projects within this initiative should be characterised by high-quality and environmentally friendly approaches. One hundred and forty-seven countries have signed the declaration of cooperation within the project. In the geopolitical context, its significance is also noted as ending the domination of maritime powers and providing China with more opportunities for economic expansion.[39]

China is a major investor in Europe. In 2016, the Chinese became the owners of the Greek port of Piraeus and, in 2017, of the Belgian port of Zeebrugge. In 2015 they bought KUKA AG, called the 'pearl of German industry' in the field of industrial robotics and automation of manufacturing processes in the automotive, medical, and energy industries.[40] China uses global trade in ancient and contemporary Chinese art to promote the image of a cultural empire. The Chinese art market is the second largest in the world and a major source of revenue for the country (in 2018, China accounted for over 20 % of the global art market worth $63 billion) and creates an image of China as a modern and liberal country.[41] Chinese art is bought by both increasingly wealthy domestic buyers and foreigners (old oil paintings and contemporary art).

Chinese soft power is characterised by these three themes. In Beijing, the understanding of soft power is more complex. From the Chinese perspective, all types of activities, except for military and security issues, can be described as 'soft use of power'. As a result, financial investments, activities in international relations, economic power, and diplomatic actions can be used as a means of imposing policies. The basis of the Chinese *modus operandi* is, as specified by Sun Tzu, the author of *The Art of War*, the consideration of all factors (weather, natural topography, intelligence reports, surprise effect, enemy morale) in the development of a strategy, destabilise the enemy's plans, destroy his alliances and finally defeat his army.[42]

If the currency of soft power is narrative, in China's case, it takes the form of information warfare. China and Russia are described as authoritarian states that use information as so-called 'hard power'. By manipulating broadcast content, China tries to destabilise democratic countries, especially by using state officials in 'wolf warrior diplomacy'. Diplomats use speeches and social media posts that attack other countries.[43] An exception to the rule of 'peaceful growth' is the 'One China' policy, which aims to consolidate all territories considered Chinese under the control of the Beijing government. In this way, the Chinese want to end the period of 'national humiliation' caused by European colonialism, Japanese occupation during World War II, and the Chinese civil war and destabilisation of the country. The Chinese historical policy is focused on the identification of the complete unification of the Chinese lands, including Taiwan, with the project of growth of the economic, political, and military position of the country.[44]

In the early twenty-first century, polls showed positive or neutral opinions of the Chinese state.[45] More recently, despite the noticeable growth of Chinese influence, respondents have more positive opinions of the U.S. than of China. China's image has been weakened by several factors, such as a lack of trust regarding the concealment of information about COVID-19 in the early stages of the pandemic or negative media opinions about the Belt and Road Initiative projects, resulting from higher-than-expected costs and debts incurred by various countries. China is viewed negatively for its authoritarian rule, which restricts freedom in Hong Kong and the Xinjiang province. The most negative opinion of China is typical for the developed countries, where politicians are trying to force the closure of one of China's important soft power institutions, the Confucius Institutes.[46]

Henry Kissinger argued that the 'continental symptoms of cultural identity' of the United States and China, followed by economic and political successes, could convince people that their policies are in the general interest of humanity and lead to tensions between the two countries.[47] He also hoped that they would avoid the 'Thucydides trap', that is, a direct confrontation between a threatened empire and a would-be power.

The reference to soft power assets by Americans and Chinese may help avoid the aforementioned confrontation, but it should be primarily in the name of building peaceful international relations. China's 'peaceful growth', seen in Europe in the form of investments in companies and ports, the Belt and Road Initiative, as well as the network of the Confucius Institutes, has improved the image of the Middle Kingdom.[48] It has also galvanised Americans, who responded with their own projects, such as Build Buck Better World. The transatlantic community, based on shared values and interests, is more popular, research shows. American smart power in Europe, based on cultural diplomacy, trade exchange, and military protection through NATO, seems impregnable.

Notes

1 Arnold, Maik / Łukasik, Przemyslaw: *Europe and America in the mirror. Culture, Economy and History*. Nomos: Kraków 2012, p. 54.

2 Speech by Xi Jinping at a Celebration of the 100th Anniversary of the Communist Party of China Xi Jinping, General Secretary of the Central Committee of the Communist Party of China (CPC), President of China, and Chairman of the Central Military Commission, delivered a speech at a ceremony marking the CPC's 100th anniversary on July 1, 2021, at Tiananmen Square in Beijing. Retrieved January 20, 2022 from: <https://www.fmprc.gov.cn/ce/celv/eng/xwdt/t1889004.htm>.

[3] Dahl, Robert A.: 'The concept of Power', *Behavioral Science*, No. 2, Vol. 3,1957, pp. 203.

[4] Lukas, Steven: 'Power and the Battle for Hearst and Minds', *Millennium: Journal of International Studies'*, No. 33, Issue 3, 2005, pp. 447.

[5] Barnett, Michael / Duvall, Raymond: 'Power in International Politics', *International Organization*, Issue 1, vol. 59, 2005, pp. 39.

[6] Smouts, Marie-Cloude: 'International Organizations and Inequality among States', *International Social Science Journal*, No. 144, 1995, pp. 234.

[7] The term of soft power is related to a very old idea, quoted by the Chinese philosopher Mencius, who lived during the Warring States period: 'Win the people, if you will to win the empire'. See: Joseph S. Nye, *'Notes for a Soft Power Research Agenda'*. In: Berenskoetter, Felix / Williams, Michael (eds.): *Power in world politics*. Routledge: Abingdon2008, pp. 162. See also: Joseph S. Nye, 'The *Benefits* of *Soft Power*', *Harvard Business School Working Knowledge for Business Leaders*, February 8, 2004.

[8] Kennedy, Paul: *The Rise, and Fall of the Great Powers: Economic Change and Military Conflict from 1500 to 2000*. Vintage Books: New York, 1989.

[9] Nye, Joseph S.: *Bound to Lead: The Changing Nature of American Power*. Basic Books New York: 1990.

[10] Nye, Joseph S.: *The Future of Power*. Public Affairs: New York 2011, pp. 66.

[11] Boulding, Kenneth E.: *Three Faces of Power*. Sage Publications: Newbury Park, California 1989.

[12] Nye, Joseph S.: *Soft Power: The Means to Success in World Politics*. Public Affairs: New York 2004.

[13] Nye, Joseph S.: *The Future of Power*. Public Affairs: New York 2011, pp. 66.

[14] Ferguson, Niall: 'Think Again: Power', *Foreign Policy*, January-February 2003. Retrieved November 12, 2021 from: <https://foreignpolicy.com/2009/11/03/think-again-power/>.

[15] Layne, Christopher: ' The Unbearable Lightness of Soft Power',. In: Parmar, Inderjeet / Cox, Michael (eds.): *Soft Power and US Foreign Policy. Theoretical, Historical and Contemporary Perspectives*. Routledge: London-New York 2010, pp. 51–82.

[16] Byong-kuen, Jhee / Nae-young, Lee: 'Measuring Soft Power in East Asia. An Overview of Soft Power in East Asia on Affective and Normative Dimensions'. In: Sook, Jang Lee, Melissen, Jan (eds.): *Public Diplomacy and Soft Power in East Asia*. Palgrave Macmillan: New York 2011.

[17] Mingijang, Li: ' Introduction. Soft Power: Nurture Not Nature'. In: Mingijang, Li (ed.): *Soft Power: China's Emerging Strategy in International Politics*. Lexington Books: Lanham 2009.

[18] Yongnian, Zheng / Chi, Zhang: '"Soft Power" and Chinese Soft Power'. In: Lai, Hong / Lu, Yiyi (eds.): *China's Soft Power and International Relations*. Routledge: London-New York 2012, pp. 21–39. See also: Jura, Jarosław / Kałużyńska, Kaja: 'Not Confucius, nor Kung Fu: Economy and Business as Chinese Soft Power in Africa'. *African East Asian Affairs. The China Monitor*, 2013, Issue 1, pp. 42–69.

[19] Melissen, Jan: 'The New Public Diplomacy: Between Theory and Practice'. In: Melissen, Jan (ed.): *The New Public Diplomacy. Soft Power in International Relations*. Palgrave Macmillan: London 2005, pp. 3–28.

20 O'Shea, Kevin D.: 'Revitalizing Canadian Public Diplomacy', *Canadian Global Affairs Institute*, September 2016. Retrieved November 12, 2021 from: <https://www.cgai.ca/revitalizing_ canadian_ public_ diplomacy>).

21 Roy, Chiraag / Ware, Anthony / Laoutides, Costas: 'The political economy of Norwegian peacemaking in Myanmar's peace process', *Third World Quarterly*, Volume 42, Issue 9, 2021, pp. 2172–2188.

22 National Brands 2021. Retrieved November 12, 2021 from: <https://brandirectory.com/rankings/ nation-brands/>. See also: The Soft Power Overall Ranking 2019, Retrieved August 12, 2021 from: <https://softpower30.com/>.

23 Scott-Smith, Giles: 'Transatlantic Cultural Relations, Soft Power, and the Role of US Cultural Diplomacy in Europe', *European Foreign Affairs Review*, Volume 24, Special Issue, 2019, pp. 21–41.

24 See: Pells, Richard: *Not Like Us: How Europeans have Loved, Hated, and Transformed American Culture since World War II.* Basic Books: New York 1998. See also: Grazia de, Victoria: *Irresistible Empire: America's Advance through Twentieth Century Europe.* University Press: Harvard 2006.

25 Deutsch, Karl: *Political Community in the North Atlantic Area.* Princeton University Press: Princeton 1957.

26 Zaharna, Rhonda: *Battles to Bridges: US Strategic Communication and Public Diplomacy after 9/11.* Palgrave Macmillan: London 2014, pp. 31.

27 Scott-Smith, Giles: 'Transatlantic Cultural Relations, Soft Power, and the Role of US Cultural Diplomacy in Europe', *European Foreign Affairs Review, Review*, Volume 24, Special Issue, 2019, pp. 21 – 41.

28 American Spaces, *Annual Report* (2019). Retrieved November 12, 2021 from: <https://americanspaces.state.gov/wp-content/uploads/sites/292/LORES_AmSpaces 2019 Report.pdf>.

29 Łukasik, Przemyslaw: 'NATO Without the USA: How Long Will the Alliance Survive Without American Leadership? '. In: Christensen, Carsten Sander / Maisaia, Vakhtang: *NATO and the Future of European and Asian Security.* IGI Global: Hershey 2021.

30 The White House: *FACT SHEET: President Biden and G7 Leaders Launch Build Back Better World (B3W) Partnership.* Retrieved June 12, 2021 from: <https://www.whitehouse.gov/briefing-room/ statements-releases/2021/06/12/fact-sheet-president-biden-and-g7-leaders-launch-build-back-better-world-b3w-partnership/>.

31 Bureau of Educational and Cultural Affairs: *Functional Bureau Strategy* 2018. Retrieved November 12, 2021 from: <https://www.state.gov/documents/organization/284589.pdf>.

32 Speech by Xi Jinping at a Celebration of the 100th Anniversary of the Communist Party of China Xi Jinping, General Secretary of the Central Committee of the Communist Party of China (CPC), President of China, and Chairman of the Central Military Commission, delivered a speech at a ceremony marking the CPC's 100th anniversary on July 1, 2021, at Tiananmen Square in Beijing. Retrieved January 20, 2022 from: <https://www.fmprc.gov.cn/ce/celv/eng/xwdt/t1889004.htm>.

33 Kurlantzick, Joshua: *Charm Offensive. How China's Soft Power Is Transforming the World.* Yale University Press: New Haven London 2007.

34 The Institutes are called an instrument of cultural diplomacy or the 'Chinese Trojan Horse'. According to critics, their goal is to show a selective propagandistic image of

China, in which Mao Zedong is seen as a positive figure, while the issues of human rights violations or the 1989 Tiananmen Square Massacre are avoided. The US National Security Agency's 2017 report suggested that the institutes should be shut down, as they act as undercover units of Chinese intelligence. Most of the over 100 institutes that closed down in the US due to criticism are said to be continuing their activities, albeit under different brands. See: Peterson, Rachelle: 'American Universities Are Welcoming China's Trojan Horse', *Foreign Policy*, May 9, 2017. Retrieved November 19, 2022, from: <https://foreignpolicy.com/2017/05/09/american-universities-are-welcoming-chinas-trojan-horse-confucius-institutes/>. See also: Edwards, Lee: 'Confucius Institutes: China's Trojan Horse', *The Heritage Foundation*, May 27, 2021. Retrieved November 19, 2022 from: <https://www.heritage.org/homeland-security/commentary/confucius-institutes-chinas-trojan-horse>. See also: Peterson, Rachelle / Oxnevad, Ian / Yan, Flora (eds:) 'After Confucius Institutes. China's Enduring Influence on American Higher Education', *National Association of Scholars*. Retrieved June 15, 2022 from: <https://www.nas.org/reports/after-confucius-institutes/full-report>.

35 Mote, Frederick W.: *Imperial China: 900-1800*. Harvard University Press: Cambridge 1999, pp. 614–615.

36 Basketball player Yao Ming was the first Chinese player in the NBA and a world-renowned athlete. Ma Lin is a three-time Olympic champion and a nine-time world champion in what is traditionally considered a Chinese specialty, table tennis. Li Ning is an Olympic Champion who has been called the 'Prince of Gymnastics'. After his professional career ended, he founded the sportswear company that ranks third in the Chinese market, only behind Nike and Adidas.

37 Zhang Yimou was the author of the scenario for the opening and closing ceremonies of the 2008 Beijing Olympic Games. He refuses to divide Chinese films into anti-government and pro-government but is sometimes called a propagandist. His critics accuse him of making nationalistic films designed to promote pride and arouse xenophobic feeling against the United States. Particularly criticised was the film 'Hero', in which he portrayed the tyrannical emperor Qin Shi Huang and his fight for the unification of China under his rule in a very positive context. The film was seen as an example of subservience to the government and the Communist Party. See: Zhang, Le Evans: 'Yimou's Hero and the Temptations of Fascism', *Film International*, Volume 2, Number 2, 1 March 2004, pp. 14–23. See also: Larson, Wendy: 'North American reception of Zhang Yimou's Hero'. In: Rawnsley, Gary D. / Ming-Yeh T.: *Global Chinese Cinema. The Culture and Politics of 'Hero'*. Routledge: New York-London 2010. Hong Kong-born Jackie Chan participated in the 100th anniversary of the Communist Party and declared the will to join it. See: Davies, Rebecca: 'Jackie Chan Declares: "I Want to Be a Chinese Communist Party Member"', *Variety*, July 14, 2021. Retrieved November 12, 2021 from: <https://variety.com/2021/film/news/jackie-chan-join-communist-party-1235019781/>.

38 International Audiences & Visitors agree: Beijing Passed with Flying Colours, *News Release*, 5 September 2008. Retrieved November 12, 2021 from: <https://www.nielsen.com/wp-content/uploads/sites/3/2019/04/press_release4-2.pdf>; Wardęga, Joanna: 'The Image of the Beijing Olympic Games as Constructed in Chinese Media'. In: Zemanek,

Adina (ed.): *Media in China. China in the media. Processes, Strategies, Images, Identities.* Jagiellonian University Press: Kraków 2014, pp. 57–72.

39 President Xi Jinping Delivers Important Speech and Proposes to Build a Silk Road Economic Belt with Central Asian Countries, 2013/09/07, Embassy of the People's Republic of China in the Republic of Guyana. Retrieved November 12, 2021 from: <https://www.mfa.gov.cn/ce/cegy/eng/zgyw/t 1076334.htm>. See also: Vision and Actions on Jointly Building Silk Road Economic Belt and 21st Century Maritime Silk Road, March 2015. Retrieved November 12, 2021 from: <https://www.fmprc.gov.cn/eng/topics_ 665678/2015zt/xjpcxbayzlt 2015nnh /201503/t20150328_705553.html>. See: Bai, Gao: 'The High-Speed Railway and China's Grand Strategy in the 21st Century'. In: Zhengyu, Wu (ed.): *Toward 'Land' or Toward 'See'?, Naval War College Review*, vol. 66, no. 3, 2013. See: Belt and Road Initiative. Retrieved November 12, 2021 from: <https://www.beltroad-initiative.com/belt-and-road/>.

40 Johnson, Keith: 'In Odyssey for Chinese, Greece Sells Its Fabled Port of Piraeus', *Foreign Policy*, April 8, 2016. Retrieved November 19, 2022 from: <https://foreign-policy.com/2016/04/08/in-odyssey-for-chinese-greece -sells-its-fabled-port-of-piraeus/>. See also: 'China increases its influence on Belgian seaports', *The Brussels Times*, Thursday, 26 December 2019. Retrieved November 19, 2022 from: <https://www.brusselstimes.com/86085/chinas-influence-on-europes-ports-keeps-growing>. See: 'Germany's Weber: Chinese purchase of Kuka shows we must protect European firms', *Reuters*, January 28, 2019. Retrieved November 19, 2022 from: <https://www.reuters.com/article/us-europe-companies-idUSKCN1PM1DJ>.

41 Witek, Michał: 'Chinese Contemporary Art: Between Market and Freedom'. In: Gacek, Łukasz and Trojnar, Ewa (eds.): *China at the beginning of the 21st century*, Jagiellonian University Press, Cracow 2014. 'China is the second-largest art market', *Seo Agency China*. Retrieved August 24, 2019 from: <https://seoagencychina.com/china-is-the-second-largest-art-market/>.

42 Smith, Kidder: 'The Military Texts: The Sunzi'. In: De Bary, Theodore / Bloom, Irene. (eds.): *Sources* of *Chinese tradition*. Vol. 1, *From earliest times* to *1600*. Columbia University Press: New York 1999.

43 Walker, Christopher: 'What is sharp power?' *Journal of Democracy*, Volume 29, Issue 3, July 2018, pp. 9–23. Retrieved January 20, 2022 from: <https://www.journalofdemocracy.org/articles/what-is-sharp-power>; see: Martin, Peter: *China's Civilian Army: The Making of Wolf Warrior Diplomacy.* Oxford University Press, 2021. See: Birtles, Bill: 'Xi Jinping hints at a shift in China's "Wolf Warrior" diplomacy. But does this mean we'll see a change in relations with Australia?' *www.abc.net*, 4 June 2021. Retrieved January 20, 2022 from: <https://www.abc.net.au/news/2021-06-04/china-signals-shift-in-wolf-warrior-diplomacy /100186166>.

44 Wang, Zheng: *Never Forget National Humiliation: Historical Memory in Chinese Politics and Foreign Relations*. Columbia University Press: New York 2014.

45 'Nation Poll Shows China Viewed Positively by Most Countries', March 5, 2005, Retrieved November 19, 2022 from: <https://drum.lib.umd.edu/bitstream/handle /1903/10666/China_ Mar05_art.pdf;jsessionid=F3ED75B01A8CDC69A41CAD70BCEA3BCC?sequence=2>.

46 Kurlantzick, Joshua: 'Why China's Global Image Is Getting Worse, Council on Foreign Affairs', *Council on Foreign Relations*, January 24, 2022. Retrieved November 19, 2022 from: <https://www.cfr.org/in-brief/why-chinas-global-image-getting-worse>. See: Silver, Laura/ Huang, Christine / Clancy, Laura: 'Across 19 countries, more people see the U.S. than China favourably – but more see China's influence growing', *Pew Research*, June 29, 2022. Retrieved November 19, 2022 from: <https://www.pewresearch.org/fact-tank/2022/06/29/across-19-countries-more-people-see-the-u-s-than-china-favorably-but-more-see-chinas-influence-growing/>.

47 Kissinger, Henry: *On China*, Penguin Press: London, 2011, pp.51.

48 China's rise 'will not come at the cost of any other country, will not stand in the way of any other country, nor pose a threat to any other country' – convinced the Chinese Prime Minister Wen Jiabao in 2004. See: Pan, Esther: 'The Promise and Pitfalls of China's "Peaceful Rise"', *Council on Foreign Affairs*, April 14, 2006. Retrieved November 12, 2021 from: </promise-and-pitfalls-chinas-peaceful-rise>. See also: Shambaugh, David (ed.) *Power Shift. China and Asia's New Dynamics.* University of California Press, Berkeley, 2006. See:. Sutter, Robert G.: *China's Rise in Asia: Promises and Perils.* Rowman & Littlefield Publishers: Lanham, 2005, pp. 12–16.

Bibliography

American Spaces, *Annual Report* (2019). Retrieved November 12, 2021 from: <https://americanspaces.state.gov/wp-content/uploads/sites/292/LORES_> AmSpaces 2019 Report.pdf.

Arnold, Maik / Łukasik, Przemyslaw: *Europe and America in the Mirror. Culture, Economy and History.* Nomos: Kraków 2012.

Bai, Gao: 'The High-Speed Railway and China's Grand Strategy in the 21st Century'. In: Zhengyu, Wu (eds.): *Toward 'Land' or Toward 'See'?, Naval War College Review,* vol. 66, no. 3, 2013. See: Belt and Road Initiative. Retrieved November 12, 2021 from: <https://www.beltroad-initiative.com/belt-and-road/>.

Barnett, Michael / Duvall, Raymond: 'Power in International Politics', *International Organization,* Issue 1, vol. 59, 2005, pp. 39.

Birtles, Bill: 'Xi Jinping hints at a shift in China's "Wolf Warrior" diplomacy. But does this mean we'll see a change in relations with Australia?' *<www.abc.net>*, 4 June 2021. Retrieved January 20, 2022 from: <https://www.abc.net.au/news/2021-06-04/china-signals-shift-in-wolf-warrior-diplomacy> /100186166.

Boulding, Kenneth E.: *Three Faces of Power.* Sage Publications: Newbury Park, California 1989.

Bureau of Educational and Cultural Affairs: *Functional Bureau Strategy* 2018. Retrieved November 12, 2021 from: <https://www.state.gov/documents/organization/284589.pdf>.

Byong-kuen, Jhee / Nae-young, Lee: 'Measuring Soft Power in East Asia. An Overview of Soft Power in East Asia on Affective and Normative Dimensions'. In: Sook, Jang Lee, Melissen, Jan (eds.): *Public Diplomacy and Soft Power in East Asia.* Palgrave Macmillan: New York 2011.

'China is the second-largest art market', *Seo Agency China.* Retrieved August 24, 2019 from: <https://seoagencychina.com/china-is-the-second-largest-art-market/>.

'China increases its influence on Belgian seaports', *The Brussels Times*, Thursday, 26 December 2019. Retrieved November 19, 2022 from: <https://www.brusselstimes.com/86085/chinas-influence-on-europes-ports-keeps-growing>.

Dahl, Robert A.: 'The concept of Power', *Behavioral Science*, No. 2, Vol. 3, 1957, pp. 203.

Davies, Rebecca: 'Jackie Chan Declares: "I Want to Be a Chinese Communist Party Member"', *Variety*, July 14, 2021. Retrieved November 12, 2021 from: <https://variety.com/2021/film/news/jackie-chan-join-communist-party-1235019781/>

Deutsch, Karl: *Political Community in the North Atlantic Area.* Princeton University Press: Princeton 1957.

Edwards, Lee: 'Confucius Institutes: China's Trojan Horse', *The Heritage Foundation*, May 27, 2021. Retrieved November 19, 2022 from: <https://www.heritage.org/homeland-security/commentary/confucius-institutes-chinas-trojan-horse>.

Ferguson, Niall: 'Think Again: Power', *Foreign Policy*, January-February 2003. Retrieved November 12, 2021 from: <https://foreignpolicy.com/2009/11/03/think-again-power/>.

'Germany's Weber: Chinese purchase of Kuka shows we must protect European firms', *Reuters*, January 28, 2019. Retrieved November 19, 2022 from: <https://www.reuters.com/article/us-europe-companies-idUSKCN1PM1DJ>.

Grazia de, Victoria: *Irresistible Empire: America's Advance through Twentieth Century Europe.* University Press: Harvard 2006.

International Audiences & Visitors agree: Beijing Passed with Flying Colours, *News Release*, 5 September 2008. Retrieved November 12, 2021 from: <https://www.nielsen.com/wp-content/uploads/sites/3/2019/04/press_release4-2.pdf;>

Johnson, Keith: 'In Odyssey for Chinese, Greece Sells Its Fabled Port of Piraeus', *Foreign Policy*, April 8, 2016. Retrieved November 19, 2022 from: <https://foreignpolicy.com/2016/04/08/in-odyssey-for-chinese-greece> -sells-its-fabled-port-of-piraeus/.

Jura, Jarosław / Kałużyńska, Kaja: 'Not Confucius, nor Kung Fu: Economy and Business as Chinese Soft Power in Africa'. *African East Asian Affairs. The China Monitor*, 2013, Issue 1, pp. 42–69.

Kennedy, Paul: *The Rise, and Fall of the Great Powers: Economic Change and Military Conflict from 1500 to 2000.* Vintage Books: New York, 1989.

Kissinger, Henry: *On China*, Penguin Press: London, 2011, pp. 51.

Kurlantzick, Joshua: *Charm Offensive. How China's Soft Power Is Transforming the World.* Yale University Press: New Haven London 2007.

Kurlantzick, Joshua: 'Why China's Global Image Is Getting Worse, Council on Foreign Affairs', *Council on Foreign Relations*, January 24, 2022. Retrieved November 19, 2022 from: <https://www.cfr.org/in-brief/why-chinas-global-image-getting-worse>.

Speech by Xi Jinping at a Celebration of the 100th Anniversary of the Communist Party of China Xi Jinping, General Secretary of the Central Committee of the Communist Party of China (CPC), President of China, and Chairman of the Central Military Commission, delivered a speech at a ceremony marking the CPC's 100th anniversary on July 1, 2021, at Tiananmen Square in Beijing. Retrieved January 20, 2022 from: <https://www.fmprc.gov.cn/ce/celv/eng/xwdt/t1889004.htm>.

Larson, Wendy: 'North American reception of Zhang Yimou's Hero'. In: Rawnsley, Gary D. / Ming-Yeh T.: *Global Chinese Cinema. The Culture and Politics of 'Hero'.* Routledge: New York-London 2010.

Layne, Christopher: 'The Unbearable Lightness of Soft Power'. In: Parmar, Inderjeet / Cox, Michael (eds.): *Soft Power and US Foreign Policy. Theoretical, Historical and Contemporary Perspectives.* Routledge: London-New York 2010, pp. 51–82.

Lukas, Steven: 'Power and the Battle for Hearst and Minds', *Millennium: Journal of International Studies*', No. 33, Issue 3, 2005, pp. 447.

Łukasik, Przemyslaw: 'NATO Without the USA: How Long Will the Alliance Survive Without American Leadership?'. In: Christensen, Carsten Sander / Maisaia, Vakhtang: *NATO and the Future of European and Asian Security*. IGI Global: Hershey 2021.

Martin, Peter: *China's Civilian Army: The Making of Wolf Warrior Diplomacy.* Oxford University Press, 2021.

Melissen, Jan: 'The New Public Diplomacy: Between Theory and Practice'. In: Melissen, Jan (ed.): *The New Public Diplomacy. Soft Power in International Relations.* Palgrave Macmillan: London 2005, pp. 3–28.

Mingijang, Li: ' Introduction. Soft Power: Nurture Not Nature'. In: Mingijang, Li (ed.): *Soft Power: China's Emerging Strategy in International Politics*. Lexington Books: Lanham 2009.

Mote, Frederick W.: *Imperial China: 900-1800.* Harvard University Press: Cambridge 1999, pp. 614–615.

National Brands 2021. Retrieved November 12, 2021 from: <https://brandirectory.com/rankings/nation-brands/>.

'Nation Poll Shows China Viewed Positively by Most Countries', March 5, 2005, Retrieved November 19, 2022 from: <https://drum.lib.umd.edu/bitstream/handle> /1903/10666/China_ Mar05_art.pdf;jsessionid=F3ED75B01A8CDC69A41CAD70BCEA3BCC?sequence=2.

Nye, Joseph S.: *Bound to Lead: The Changing Nature of American Power.* Basic Books New York: 1990.

Nye, Joseph S.: *'Notes for a Soft Power Research Agenda'*,. In: Berenskoetter, Felix / Williams, Michael (eds.): *Power in world politics.* Routledge: Abingdon 2008, pp. 162.

Nye, Joseph S.: *Soft Power: The Means to Success in World Politics.* Public Affairs: New York 2004.

Nye, Joseph S.: 'The *Benefits* of *Soft Power*', *Harvard Business School Working Knowledge for Business Leaders*, February 8, 2004.

Nye, Joseph S.: *The Future of Power.* Public Affairs: New York 2011, pp. 66.

O'Shea, Kevin D.: 'Revitalizing Canadian Public Diplomacy', *Canadian Global Affairs Institute*, September 2016. Retrieved November 12,

2021 from: <https://www.cgai.ca/revitalizing_> canadian_ public_ diplomacy.

Pan, Esther: 'The Promise and Pitfalls of China's "Peaceful Rise"', *Council on Foreign Affairs*, April 14, 2006. Retrieved November 12, 2021 from: / promise-and-pitfalls-chinas-peaceful-rise.

Pells, Richard: *Not Like Us: How Europeans have Loved, Hated, and Transformed American Culture since World War II.* Basic Books: New York 1998.

Peterson, Rachelle: 'American Universities Are Welcoming China's Trojan Horse', *Foreign Policy*, May 9, 2017. Retrieved November 19, 2022, from: <https://foreignpolicy.com/2017/05/09/american-universities-are-welcoming-chinas-trojan-horse-confucius-institutes/>.

Peterson, Rachelle / Oxnevad, Ian / Yan, Flora (eds:) 'After Confucius Institutes. China's Enduring Influence on American Higher Education', *National Association of Scholars.* Retrieved June 15, 2022 from: <https://www.nas.org/reports/after-confucius-institutes/full-report>.

President Xi Jinping Delivers Important Speech and Proposes to Build a Silk Road Economic Belt with Central Asian Countries,2013/09/07, EMBASSY OF THE PEOPLE'S REPUBLIC OF CHINA IN THE REPUBLIC OF GUYANA. Retrieved November 12, 2021 from: <https://www.mfa.gov.cn/ce/cegy/eng/zgyw/t> 1076334.htm.

Roy, Chiraag / Ware, Anthony / Laoutides, Costas: 'The political economy of Norwegian peacemaking in Myanmar's peace process', *Third World Quarterly*, Volume 42, Issue 9, 2021, pp. 2172–2188.

Shambaugh, David (ed.) *Power Shift. China and Asia's New Dynamics.* University of California Press, Berkeley, 2006.

Silver, Laura / Huang, Christine / Clancy,Laura: 'Across 19 countries, more people see the U.S. than China favourably – but more see China's influence growing', *Pew Research*, June 29, 2022. Retrieved November 19, 2022 from: <https://www.pewresearch.org/fact-tank/2022/06/29/across-19-countries-more-people-see-the-u-s-than-china-favorably-but-more-see-chinas-influence-growing/>.

Smith, Kidder: 'The Military Texts: The Sunzi'. In: De Bary, Theodore / Bloom, Irene. (eds.): *Sources* of *Chinese tradition*. Vol. 1, *From earliest times* to *1600.* Columbia University Press: New York 1999.

Smouts, Marie-Cloude: 'International Organizations and Inequality among States', *International Social Science Journal*, No. 144, 1995, pp. 234.

Speech by Xi Jinping at a Celebration of the 100th Anniversary of the Communist Party of China Xi Jinping, General Secretary of the Central Committee of the Communist Party of China (CPC), President of China, and Chairman of the Central Military Commission, delivered a speech at a ceremony marking the CPC's 100th anniversary on July 1, 2021, at Tiananmen Square in Beijing. Retrieved January 20, 2022 from: <https://www.fmprc.gov.cn> /ce/celv/ eng/xwdt/t1889004.htm

Sutter, Robert G.: *China's Rise in Asia: Promises and Perils*. Rowman & Littlefield Publishers: Lanham, 2005, pp. 12–16.

Scott-Smith, Giles: 'Transatlantic Cultural Relations, Soft Power, and the Role of US Cultural Diplomacy in Europe', *European Foreign Affairs Review*, Volume 24, Special Issue, 2019, pp. 21 – 41.

The Soft Power Overall Ranking 2019, Retrieved August 12, 2021 from: <https://softpower30.com/>.

The White House: *FACT SHEET: President Biden and G7 Leaders Launch Build Back Better World (B3W) Partnership.* Retrieved June 12, 2021 from: <https://www.whitehouse.gov/briefing-room/> statements-releases/2021/06/12/fact-sheet-president-biden-and-g7-leaders-launch-build-back-better-world-b3w-partnership/.

Wardęga, Joanna: 'The Image of the Beijing Olympic Games as Constructed in Chinese Media'. In: Zemanek, Adina (ed.): *Media in China. China in the media. Processes, Strategies, Images, Identities.* Jagiellonian University Press: Kraków 2014, pp. 57–72.

Walker, Christopher: 'What is sharp power?' *Journal of Democracy*, Volume 29, Issue 3, July 2018, pp. 9–23. Retrieved January 20, 2022 from: <https://www.journalofdemocracy.org/articles/what-is-sharp-power>.

Wang, Zheng: *Never Forget National Humiliation: Historical Memory in Chinese Politics and Foreign Relations*. Columbia University Press: New York 2014.

Witek, Michał: 'Chinese Contemporary Art: Between Market and Freedom'. In: Gacek, Łukasz and Trojnar, Ewa (eds.): *China at the beginning of the 21st century*, Jagiellonian University Press, Cracow 2014.

Vision and Actions on Jointly Building Silk Road Economic Belt and 21st Century Maritime Silk Road, March 2015. Retrieved November 12, 2021 from: <https://www.fmprc.gov.cn/eng/topics_> 665678/2015zt/ xjpcxbayzlt 2015nnh /201503/t20150328_705553.html.

Yongnian, Zheng / Chi, Zhang: '"Soft Power" and Chinese Soft Power'. In: Lai, Hong / Lu,Yiyi (eds.): *China's Soft Power and International Relations*. Routledge: London-New York 2012, pp. 21–39.

Zaharna, Rhonda: *Battles to Bridges: US Strategic Communication and Public Diplomacy after 9/11.* Palgrave Macmillan: London 2014, pp. 31.

Zhang, Le Evans: 'Yimou's Hero and the Temptations of Fascism', *Film International*, Volume 2, Number 2, 1 March 2004, pp. 14–23.

Central and Eastern Europe vis-à-vis China and the US

Przemysław Łukasik

> This is why we built the Three Seas Initiative, which is completely in harmony with the European Union, with the objectives of transatlantic security conference, and at the same time it's strengthening our identity and strengthening our economic power vis-à-vis China. China is trying to enter exactly the same zone through other initiatives. One of them is 17+1. China is buying the harbors like Piraeus next to Athens in Greece and in other places all over Europe, because they are using the enormous power of state to enter into this part of Europe, which is less developed. This is exactly why the investments from the United States at this juncture is so much needed, also to stop not only the Russian aggression, but also more silent but equally challenging Chinese policy vis-à-vis – this part of the world.[1]

A community of shared values and different incomes: One Europe or two Europes

Central and Eastern Europe is comprised of the Baltic States, Central Europe, Eastern Europe, and Southern and Eastern Europe (mainly the Balkans), that is, the former communist countries from the Eastern Bloc and the Warsaw Pact. Central and Eastern European countries joined the European Union (EU) in the following three stages: eight countries joined in May 2004 (Estonia, Latvia, Lithuania, Czech Republic, Slovakia, Poland, Hungary and Slovenia), followed by Romania and Bulgaria in 2007 and Croatia in July 2013. These countries are sometimes referred to as 'new Europe'. The notion of 'old' and 'new' Europe was introduced into the political science discourse by Donald Rumsfeld in 2003. He distinguished between the Western European countries that had joined NATO before and opposed the American intervention in Iraq and the new NATO members from Central and Eastern Europe that supported the intervention. In Western Europe the term of 'old and new Europe' was seen as derogatory and divisive among the US allies. The pro-American stance of the Central and Eastern European countries was and is still a way of showing appreciation for the security guarantees of the strongest NATO army.[2]

According to the World Bank analysis, all 10 countries that joined the EU in 2004 and 2007 have completed their transition to advanced market economies.[3] However, Bank's final report ten years later described the region as underperforming, similar to the countries of Southern Europe.[4] Low income and GDP per capita below 50% of the EU average level were attributed to the 2008 financial crisis and other factors, such as a lack of skilled labour and access to markets.[5] The region's population is shrinking (from 108 million in 2000 to 101 million in 2021), while its inhabitants are emigrating (over 640 thousand in 2017).[6] The significant income gap between Western and Scandinavian countries and Central and Eastern Europe and the Balkans is gradually widening, calling into question the strength of EU convergence.

The European Union is supposed to create a European space by transforming the territories of the member states into a single economic and normative system. The cohesion policy, which is supposed to eliminate the differences in the development of certain regions, is supposed to guarantee stable and peaceful relations in Europe by creating a European welfare community. The funds of the Cohesion Fund are slowly closing the gap between the most developed and the least developed regions (it is expected that the GDP per capita of the less developed regions will increase by up to 5% by 2023).[7] As an example of the success of Central Europe, Poland has overtaken the two countries with the longest EU membership, Greece and Portugal, in terms of GDP per capita (while in terms of purchasing power, Poland ranks 22nd out of 27 EU countries).[8] As the Cohesion Reports point out, internal regional disparities are also growing in the rapidly developing member states. As a result of the lack of investment in research and development in the less developed regions, the innovation-related gap in Europe is also widening. The ageing and shrinking of Europe's population, followed by the migration of mostly young and educated people to more developed EU countries with better living conditions, is also exacerbating development disparities.[9]

The disparities in income and development are prompting the countries of Central and Eastern Europe to take steps to boost their economies. The five countries of the region – Lithuania, Latvia, Estonia, Slovakia and Slovenia – joined the Eurozone, expecting to benefit from faster economic growth, higher incomes, lower borrowing and payment costs, and the elimination of currency exchange costs. Although in opinion polls show people are satisfied with joining the Eurozone, it has not led to a significant improvement in living conditions.[10] In search of better wages, medical care, and social benefits, people from the Baltic states are migrating to Western Europe. These factors, followed by low birthrates, could to depopulation in the three countries (according to the UN, the populations of Latvia, Lithuania, and Estonia will shrink by 22%, 17%, and 13%, respectively).[11]

Although few doubt the geopolitical significance of the decision to join the EU and the democratisation of the region, the economic benefits of membership are sometimes denied because of the persistent wealth gap between old and new Europe.[12] One of the reactions to this development gap is scepticism about the European Union. Semi-periphery development, the middle-income trap, or the 'golden cage of Europeanisation within the EU' are terms used to express doubts about the economic benefits of EU membership for Central and Eastern European countries.[13] In countering these accusations, the EU institutions have often pointed out that the benefits accruing to member states do not only result from the positive net balance between national expenditure and transfers received from the EU budget, as there are also indirect benefits resulting, for example, from policies coordinated and financed by the EU. Member states also benefit from direct intra-EU investment, intra-EU trade, and EU network effects.[14] Moreover, for certain national politicians, blaming the EU institutions for failures may be a convenient way to escape from the promises they have made. The perception of development differences between the western and eastern parts of the EU is also an element of the more complex debate on the evolution of the European Union. The lack of an effective solution to EU crises, such as the Eurozone crisis or the migrant crisis, and the shift in power at its core raise questions about the future. The promotion of 'diversification of integration' in the EU is seen by supporters of the federalist European state as an important step towards integration.[15] For others, however, it is a resignation from the idea of full integration. From the wider perspective, it may lead to an intensification of differences, not only in terms of development but also with regard to the EU itself. Following the UK's exit from the EU, the role of the Franco-German duo has increased significantly. This could lead to a so-called asymmetric confederation, in which a small group of stronger countries takes decisions.[16]

Three Seas Initiative vs. USA

Central and Eastern Europe has never developed stable foundations as a unified political entity (although some attempts were made, e.g. in the inter-war period). The reasons for this were different interests and different cultural or economic conditions. Contemporary regional integration projects were developed on the basis of eliminating the differences between the East and West of the continent after the Cold War. The cooperation projects in Central and Eastern Europe emerged from the process of the USSR's loss of influence in the region and the search by the former communist countries for a platform for cooperation that would link them with the Western countries. The first of these projects was the Central European Initiative, which was initiated by Austria in 1992 and involved mainly post-communist countries from Central, Eastern, and Southern Europe.[17] It is a platform for political, economic, cultural, and scientific cooperation between the regions of the Baltic Sea, Danube River, Adriatic Sea, and Black Sea regions. The platform currently has 17 members: Albania, Belarus, Bosnia and Herzegovina, Bulgaria, Croatia, Czechia, Hungary, Italy, Moldova, Montenegro, North Macedonia, Poland, Romania, Serbia, Slovakia, Slovenia, and Ukraine.

Another initiative with an impact on geopolitical relations in Central Europe is the mechanism of cross-border and inter-regional European cooperation called the Visegrád Group. It has been active since 1991 (under this name since 1993), and its aim is to address regional challenges that require the cooperation of the following four member states: Czechia, Hungary, Poland, and Slovakia. The semi-formal nature of the cooperation and the weak coordination mechanism have made it impossible to create an expressive identity for the project.[18] As a result, it tends to express the foreign policy interests of certain member countries. The lack of a long-term vision of the project's development and role, the weakness of formal consultations, and the lack of integrity lead to its international marginalisation.[19] The member states were unable to find a common approach to the Russian-German Nord Stream 2 project or the outbreak of the war in Ukraine (Hungary tries not to condemn Russia). In addition, Poland, Czechia and Slovakia are perceived as more pro-EU, while Hungary are more sceptical in this context.[20] Negative experiences with the activities of the Visegrád Group have raised doubts about the real capacity to effectively finance such forms of cooperation in the region.

The Three Seas Initiative was launched by the presidents of Poland and Croatia, Andrzej Duda and Kolinda Grabar-Kitarović, as a response to the economic weakness of the regions, which account for about 28%of the EU's territory and 22% of its population, while producing only 10% of its GDP (as of 2018).[21] The initiative is intended to help Central and Eastern Europe leave behind its peripheral status within the EU and the label of 'New Europe'.[22] By harnessing growth dynamics, the region is supposed to overcome the role of a subordinate and auxiliary economy serving larger markets. The purpose of the Three Seas Initiative is also to create regional political subjectivity and a more effective expression of the interests of certain countries.

The preceding and following events were key determinants of the circumstances surrounding the origins of the Three Seas. The project was launched shortly after the Chinese government had announced the plan for the New Silk Road, that is, connecting the Middle Kingdom with Asian and European countries by road, rail, and sea routes (2013). Soon after, the American think tank Atlantic Council presented the analysis *Completing Europe – From the North-South Corridor to Energy, Transportation, and Telecommunications Union*, in which it emphasised the need to expand the transport infrastructure, that is, the North-South route from the Baltic Sea to the Adriatic Sea, which would connect Central Europe with the rest of the EU and complete the process of building the European single market (2014).[23] The aforementioned American analysis was inspiring enough to be favourably assessed by the decision-makers in the region. The Russian aggression against Crimea and Eastern Ukraine in 2014 was also significant, as it provided the unconvinced countries with the final proof of the invasive and neo-imperial goals of the Russian government. The negotiations on the status of Donbas and Crimea between Ukraine, Russia, Germany, and France, held in the Normandy format, failed. They also convinced the Central and Eastern European countries that Russia is not a threat to Germany or France, but, above all, a business partner. The project was launched during the persistent Russian and German efforts to launch the second line of the Nord Stream 2 gas pipeline, which would have bypassed the countries of the region, and exposed them to energy blackmail by the Russian government. The concept of Nord Stream not only deprived the countries of the region of the option of serving as a hub, but it would also preserve Europe's energy dependence on Russia.

First, the Three Seas Initiative aims to integrate the member states along the North-South routes by strengthening regional infrastructure in the areas of transport, energy, and telecommunications. Increasing the reliability and accessibility of such transport routes should encourage regional investment and contribute to the development of the Three Seas framework. Most of the projects (49%) are related to transport, including the construction and modernisation of international road and rail routes (e.g. Via Carpathia or Rail Baltica), and energy sources (37%), such as the Slovenian-Hungarian gas interconnector and the Croatian LNG terminal on the island of Krk. One of the energy projects implemented within the Three Seas Initiative is the Slovak project called Eastring. It envisages the development of gas transport infrastructure between Slovakia, Hungary, Romania, and Bulgaria. Poland could also become a new regional gas hub, as it has had the LNG terminal in Świnoujście since 2015, which allows receiving liquefied natural gas via sea routes, for example, from the Middle East and the US. By the end of 2022, the Baltic Pipe project, which will connect Poland with the Norwegian gas seabed in the North Sea, will be fully operational. Also, in 2022, the gas interconnectors will be launched, which will allow the transport of gas from Poland via Lithuania to the Baltic States and via Slovakia to Romania, Austria, and Hungary. The projects are largely co-finance by EU funds. The construction of the interconnector between Poland and Lithuania was co-financed from the EU budget in the amount of €266.3 million under the EU's Trans-European Networks for Energy (TEN-E) policy.[24] Projects related to cybersecurity are very few (e.g. the joint project of cross-border cyber-resilient digital infrastructure called The Three Seas Digital Highway, which should enable better and safer data transfer from the northern parts of the region to its southern parts).

As a result of the Three Seas Initiative, the reorientation of trade networks and energy transportation along North-South routes will have significant geopolitical consequences not only for the member states but also for Europe as a whole. However, the Three Seas Initiative should not become an alternative for the EU or its competitor. Its purpose is to consolidate economic cooperation between countries that are and will remain members of the European Union, while the interconnection of economic systems and infrastructure in Central and Eastern Europe along the North-South routes would be a final step towards the completion of the European Single Market.[25]

The project is also aimed at reducing the level of dependence on imports of Russian hydrocarbons, increasing the energy security of the members through energy diversification on the regional market, and facilitating new gas-related initiatives. The intensification of the war in Ukraine in 2022 and the disruption of gas supplies from Europe proved that the fears of the countries of the region about Russia's cynical use of energy sources were justified.

There are the following twelve full members of the Three Seas Initiatives: Austria, Bulgaria, Croatia, Czechia, Estonia, Hungary, Latvia, Lithuania, Poland, Romania, Slovakia, and Slovenia. In 2019, the Three Seas Investment Fund (€800 million) has been established. The partners of the Initiative are the United States, Germany, the European Commission, the European Investment Bank, and the World Bank. The support of the United States is of particular importance, as it declared financial assistance in the amount of USD 300 million. American involvement is seen as a way to limit Chinese influence in the region. Central and Eastern Europe sees an opportunity to revive trade with the US. Equally important is support for the implementation of projects financed by the EU funds (€155 billion from the European Regional Development Fund and the Cohesion Fund until 2020).[26] The success of the Three Seas projects could lead to greater internal cohesion and strengthen the entire EU economy. Finding new sources of investment for projects is one of the main challenges for the Three Seas countries. In view of the aforementioned aspects, there are some tendencies towards institutionalising cooperation and establishing a permanent office needed for coordination purposes. It also seems necessary to activate the Three Seas Initiative in the field of digitalisation, but it is the projects that invest in human resources, which may turn out to be crucial for the region (high level of education, healthcare, etc.), allowing to reduce the brain drain effect.[27]

Similar to the projects described previously, the Three Seas Initiative faces various challenges. Among the leading countries are Croatia, Poland, Romania, and Lithuania, accompanied by observing countries (e.g. Austria) or countries with an ambivalent approach (e.g. Hungary).[28] Czechia was suspicious from the very beginning. Its government saw the Initiative as an example of unnecessary multiplication of regional cooperation projects in the context of the existence of the Visegrád Group and other forms of activity. The Czech government saw the support of the US for the project and the lack of full membership for Germany as a source of unnecessary divisions.[29] A positive signal for the project is the ambition of the EU's strongest economy (Germany) to join the group on the basis of full membership in the future. The importance of the Three Seas Initiative, beyond the economic sphere, was demonstrated by the fact that Ukraine, after being attacked by Russia, was granted the status of a country participating in the project.

The image of the Three Seas Initiative is still poorly recognised, and the motives for its creation are presented in different ways. Among the negative comments, we can find those related to scepticism about the European Union, as well as the populism that allegedly led to the project. Attempts to eliminate development differences between eastern and western EU countries are presented as activities that lead to divisions within the European Union. Finally, there is dissatisfaction with the possibility of the USA or China gaining more influence in regional affairs. The project is also defined as an attempt by Poland to establish hegemony over its neighbours, as the country is the largest regional actor.[30]

USA and China in Central and Eastern Europe

The region of Central and Eastern Europe, like the entire European continent, is a theatre of Sino-American rivalry. Recognised as a 'strategic competitor' by its American adversary, China is a combination of the ancient Confucian civilisation and innovative smart power. Chinese achievements in the fields of artificial intelligence, manufacturing, and global Internet infrastructure management threaten the hitherto technologically omnipotent Americans, but they also encourage other countries to establish economic cooperation with the Middle Kingdom. While American power is based on democracy and capitalism, the Chinese rules of capitalism grew on the basis of a communist and authoritarian state. Both the U.S. and China are trying to influence the world and the countries in the region through their sticky power. In the case of the U.S., it is the popularisation of the liberal world order through the expansion of the global economic zone and personal freedoms, while China emphasises the importance of stable and predictable relations, though not necessarily liberal and transparent.[31] Europe sees the US as an ally and a security guarantor, while China is perceived as a powerful and friendly business partner. The value of trade exchange between the EU and China in 2019 reached €560 billion in 2019 (exports: €362 billion, imports: €198 billion), while the EU deficit was €164 billion. The Chinese approach to relations with various regions of the world, including Europe, is called minilateralism, that is, intensive cooperation with a few countries with the most significant influence in the region. The Beijing government gives a priority to the relations with the Western European countries that are more attractive in terms of investment and more advanced in terms of technology (France, Germany or the United Kingdom). The value of German goods (e.g. cars or machines) exported to China in 2019 was equal to the total exports of other EU countries.[32]

The Three Seas countries welcomed the concept of implementing China's Belt and Road Initiative with high hopes. The 17 plus 1 format for cooperation between Central and Eastern Europe and China, announced in 2012, was expected to promote economic cooperation. The simultaneous implementation of these two projects by various countries was seen as a great development opportunity. An example of this is Poland's plans to build the Solidarity Transport Hub in the form of a hub airport located between Warsaw and Łódź, focused on passenger and cargo traffic and supported by the international railway network. The projects are intended to make Central and Eastern Europe 'the economic heart of Europe', as Polish Prime Minister Mateusz Morawiecki has said.[33]

Meanwhile, except for a few countries, such as Hungary, Serbia, and Greece, the trade deficit between the region and China has been growing. In 2021, the Polish export to China reached €3 billion (about 1% of the total Polish export), while the import reached almost €40 billion.[34] The Belt and Road Initiative improved the image of China in Central and Eastern Europe and on the whole continent, but the growing project costs and the lack of significant growth of Chinese investments resulted in a noticeable decrease in enthusiasm for China and its projects in the Central European media in 2017.[35] The positive and neutral image of China declined as a result of the COVID-19 pandemics (except in Georgia and Hungary).[36] The 2020 polls confirmed that Europe had a mostly negative opinion of China, while in Central

Europe, opinions were mixed. Notably, the pandemics and the escalation of the Russo-Ukrainian war placed trade exchanges between Europe and China in the context of economic security and dependence on goods from the Far East. The European Commission identified 137 categories of products from various economic sectors (e.g. defence, health, digital technologies, electronics) in which the EU is strategically dependent on supplies from China.[37]

Cybersecurity concerns are leading European countries to consider excluding Chinese companies from the implementation of the 5G technology. It is believed that the involvement of the Chinese company Huawei in the development of 5G has brought significant consequences for security, that is, the risk of persecution of critics, collection of intelligence data, and theft of intellectual property by the Chinese government.[38] However, the idea of excluding Huawei from the implementation of the 5G network may result in increased costs for states (in the U.S., the increase in costs for several operators is estimated to reach several billion USD). Slovenia, which initially declared its intention to exclude Chinese companies from the process, did not adopt certain regulations in the end. In turn, work on these regulations in Poland did not go beyond the level of preparatory work in the Ministry of Digital Affairs. The moderation of certain countries can also be explained by the fear of possible retaliation by the Chinese government. China may close the market for Polish food products or hinder the delivery of important ingredients necessary for the production of medicines. The deterioration of Sino-Lithuanian relations is a serious warning in this context. In November 2021, the Lithuanian government agreed to the opening of the Taiwanese representative office in Vilnius, in which led to a diplomatic and economic response from China, recalling its ambassador from Vilnius and downgrading the diplomatic relations to the level of chargé d'affaires.[39] In addition, the Middle Kingdom has stopped exporting goods to this Baltic country, banned the import of goods with components manufactured in Lithuania, and suspended the transit of its goods transported through Lithuania. The situation of Lithuania, which fell victim to the asymmetrical trap of co-dependency, underscored the problem for all of Europe. Lithuanian companies exposed to the negative effects of the Chinese decisions were financially supported by the US and the EU, while Taiwan announced to invest in Lithuania. Shockingly, China called on Russia to help punish Lithuania.[40] As a result of the conflict, in 2021, the country withdrew from the China-Central and Eastern European

Countries Cooperation Framework (also known as 16/17+1). In August 2002, Latvia and Estonia also left the 16+1 format.[41] China's failure to clearly criticise Russia after its invasion of Ukraine or even to attempt to explain the Russian government, may be perceived as a threat by the countries in the region.[42]

Principles vs. reality

Opinion polls commissioned by the European Parliament and the European Commission and conducted in October 2021 showed that 68% of respondents saw the EU as a stable place in the unstable world, while the European Union offered good prospects for the future of Europe's youth (67%).[43] As shown by the polls conducted by the Eurobarometer for the European Parliament in spring 2022, the Russian invasion of Ukraine in February 2022increased support for the EU. Nearly two-thirds of EU residents (66%) described membership in the EU as a good thing, while 52% had a favourable opinion of the EU's image. For the majority, the war in Ukraine has shaken their belief in a safe and predictable future (61%). Respondents also said it was important to defend values such as freedom and democracy, even if meant higher living costs.

The Russo-Ukrainian war could lead to the unification of 'old' and 'new Europe' in terms of security and economy.[44] The transformation of the conflict in Ukraine from a perpetually smouldering conflict (since 2014) into an all-out war brought the security-related perspectives of the Western and Eastern EU countries closer together. Central and Eastern Europe, especially Poland, the Baltic states, and Romania, became increasingly concerned as they saw the disintegration of the international order and stabilisation due to Russian activities after 2014. NATO responded by increasing its military presence in the Eastern flank countries in order to deter military threats. The invasion of February 2022 showed the West not only Russia's aggressive and neo-imperial plans, but also the threats posed by economic dependence on Russian energy sources. As a result, the aforementioned concepts of building strategic European autonomy in the field of security, announced by the German and French leaders, have become seriously justified. Currently, the EU countries are planning to establish the EU Rapid Deployment Capability consisting of 5,000 troops to be deployed in various crises and with the aim of intensifying cooperation with NATO. Both structures are expected to develop a rapid decision-making process and expand command structures and a system of regular military manoeuvres.[45]

Central and Eastern Europe, like the whole of the EU, is looking for a conciliatory path in its relations with its ally and security guarantor (the United States) and its economically growing partner (China). However, the region is aware that for the Chinese government, the most important economic partners are the Western EU countries, while Central and Eastern Europe is mainly a trade hub between Western Europe and China, trying to profit from this transit (4,226 freight trains from China had crossed the Polish border between January and June 2022).[46] The Three Seas Initiative is intended to reorient cooperation in the region along the North-South axis, allowing it to evolve from its role as a transitional hub between East and West. Strengthening the transport infrastructure is intended to revitalise the region's economy and reduce the development gap with the Western EU countries. This reorientation is politically supported by the US, while EU funds are also intended to make Europe independent of Russian energy sources. There are fears in the U.S. that it will lose influence in Europe, while the European Union will become closely involved in China, but opinion polls show that these fears are unfounded. The EU-China Comprehensive Agreement on Investment (CAI), which was supposed to increase the access of European companies to the Chinese market, has still not been ratified, and one of the factors is the lack of American approval. The escalation of the Russian-Ukrainian war has underlined the importance of NATO and the US as an ally, especially for Central and Eastern Europe. China has become an important economic partner of Russia, but the image of the Middle Kingdom has definitely been worsened in the eyes of Europeans, as it did not condemn the Russian aggression against Ukraine, but the example of Lithuania proves that attempts to put pressure on China can cause a serious reaction of its government, which those Europeans who dream of good profitable business would like to avoid.[47]

Notes

1 'Polish Prime Minister Morawiecki on the COVID comeback, the Three Seas Initiative, and where the US is falling short'. *Atlantic Council*, 6.05.2021, retrieved July 22, 2022, from: <https://www.atlanticcouncil.org/news/transcripts/polish-prime-minister-morawiecki-on-the-covid-comeback-the-three-seas-initiative-and-where-the-us-is-falling-short/>.

2 'Outrage at "old Europe" remarks', *BBC News*, 23 January, 2003, retrieved July 22, 2022, from: <http://news.bbc.co.uk/2/hi/ europe/2687403.stm>. See also: Merkl, Peter H.: *The Distracted Eagle: The Rift between America and Old Europe.* Routledge: London & New York, 2005.

3 Alam, Asad et alii (eds.): *Unleashing Prosperity. Productivity Growth in Eastern Europe and the Former Soviet Union.* The World Bank: Washington, 2008.

4 Cano, Cristobal Ridao /Bodewig, Christan: *Growing United. Upgrading Europe's Convergence Machine. The World Bank Report on European Union.* World Bank: Washington, 2018.

5 'Central Europe and the Baltics', *The World Bank.* Retrieved July 22, 2022, from: <https://data. worldbank.org/region/central-europe-and-the-baltics>.

6 'Living conditions in Europe - income distribution and income inequality', *Eurostat*, June 2022, Retrieved July 30, 2022, from: <https://ec.europa.eu/eurostat/statistics-explained/index. php? Title = Living_conditions_in_Europe_-_income_distribution _and_income _inequality& oldid=528159 #Key _findings>.

7 'New Cohesion Report shows that differences between EU regions are narrowing thanks to EU support', *European Commission*, 9.02.2022. Retrieved July 22, 2022, from: <https://ec.europa. eu/ regional _ policy/en/ newsroom/ news/ 2022/02/02-09-2022-new-cohesion-report-shows-that-differences-between-eu-regions-are-narrowing-thanks-to-eu-support>.

8 Harper, Jo: 'Could Poland catch up with Germany's economy?', *Deutsche Welle*, 19.02.2020. Retrieved July 22, 2022, from: <https://www.dw.com/en/could-poland-catch-up-with-germanys-economy/a-52425523>.

9 Lutz, Wolfgang et alii. (eds.): *Demographic Scenarios for the EU - Migration Population and Education.* Publications Office of the European Union: Luxembourg, 2019. Retrieved July 22, 2022, from: <https://ec.europa.eu/jrc /en/publication /eur-scientific-and-technical-research-reports/ demographic-scenarios-eu>.

10 'The euro area', *Eurobarometer*, October 2021 - November 2021. Retrieved July 22, 2022, from: <https://europa.eu/eurobarometer /surveys/detail/2289>. See also: 'Politics and the European Union. Future of Europe', *European Parliament & European Commission*, September 2021 - October 2021. Retrieved July 22, 2022, from: <https://europa.eu/eurobarometer/surveys/detail/2554>.

11 Birka, Ieva: *Can Return Migration Revitalize the Baltics? Estonia, Latvia, and Lithuania Engage Their Diasporas, with Mixed* Asya: 'From selective integration into selective implementation: The link between differentiated integration and conformity with EU laws', *European Journal of Political Research*, Volume 53, Issue 4, November 2014. See: Schimmelfennig, Frank: 'Good governance and differentiated integration: Graded membership in the European Union'. *European Journal of Political Research*, Volume 55, Issue 4, November 2016. See also: Khoo, Jerald: 'Towards a Two-Speed Europe: National Sovereignty and the Absence of Political Integration in the Eurozone', *Columbia Journal of European Law*, Volume 22, Issue 1, 2015–2016, pp. 165–192.

The White Paper on the future of Europe. Reflections and scenarios for the EU27 by 2025, European Commission, Brussels, 1 March 2017, COM (2017)2025. Retrieved June 1, 2022, from: <https://ec.europa.eu/info/sites/default/files/ white _paper _on_the_future_of_europe_en.pdf>. See also:

Council Decision Establishing Permanent Structured Cooperation (PESCO) and determining the list of participating Member States, 14866/17, Brussels, 8 December 2017. Retrieved June 1, 2022, from: <https://eur-lex.europa.eu/legal-content/EN/TXT/PDF/?uri=CELEX:32017D2315&from=EN>. See: Council Regulation (EU) 2017/1939 of 12 October 2017 implementing enhanced cooperation on the establishment of the European Public Prosecutor's Office ('the EPPO') Brussels, 15 October 2017. Retrieved June 1, 2022, from: <https://eur-lex.europa.eu/legal-content/EN/TXT/?uri =CELEX %3A32017R1939&qid=1659704641124>.

Results. Migration Policy Institute: Washington, May 8, 2019, retrieved July 22, 2022, from: <https://www.migrationpolicy.org/article/can-return-migration-revitalize-baltics-estonia-latvia-and-lithuania-engage-their-diasporas>.

12 Bershidsky, Leonid: 'Piketty Thinks the EU Is Bad for Eastern Europe. He's Half Right', *Bloomberg*, 9.02.2018. Retrieved July 22, 2022, from: <https://www.bloomberg.com/opinion/articles/2018-02-09/piketty-thinks-the-eu-is-bad-for-eastern-europe-he-s-half-right#xj4y7vzkg>.

13 Stehrer, Robert / et alii. (eds.): *How EU funds tackle economic divide in the European Union*. Policy Department for Budgetary Affairs Directorate-General for Internal Policies, European Parliament, Brussels, PE 654.525, July 2020.Retrieved January 4, 2024, from: <https://www.europarl.europa.eu/RegData/etudes/STUD/2020/654525/IPOL_STU(2020)654525_EN.pdf>.

14 Vitte de, Bruno / Ott, Andrea / Vos, Ellen: *Between Flexibility and Disintegration. The Trajectory of Differentiation in EU Law.* Edward Elgar: Cheltenham-Northampton, 2017. See also: Zhelyazkova, Asya: 'From selective integration into selective implementation: The link between differentiated integration and conformity with EU laws', *European Journal of Political Research*, Volume 53, Issue 4, November 2014. See: Schimmelfennig, Frank: 'Good governance and differentiated integration: Graded membership in the European Union'. *European Journal of Political Research*, Volume 55, Issue 4, November 2016. See also: Khoo, Jerald: 'Towards a Two-Speed Europe: National Sovereignty and the Absence of Political Integration in the Eurozone", *Columbia Journal of European Law*, Volume 22, Issue 1, 2015–2016, pp. 165–192.

15 *The White Paper on the future of Europe. Reflections and scenarios for the EU27 by 2025*, European Commission, Brussels, 1 March 2017, COM (2017)2025. Retrieved June 1, 2022, from: <https://ec.europa.eu/info/sites/default/files/ white _paper _on_the_future_of_europe_en.pdf>. See also:

Council Decision Establishing Permanent Structured Cooperation (PESCO) and determining the list of participating Member States, 14866/17, Brussels, 8 December 2017.Retrieved June 1, 2022, from: <https://eur-lex.europa.eu/legal-content/EN/TXT/PDF/?uri=CELEX:32017D2315&from=EN>. See: Council Regulation (EU) 2017/1939 of 12 October 2017 implementing enhanced cooperation on the establishment of the European Public Prosecutor's Office ('the EPPO') Brussels, 15 October 2017.Retrieved June 1, 2022, from: <https://eur-lex.europa.eu/legal-content/EN/TXT/?uri =CELEX %3A32017R1939&qid=1659704641124>.

16 Grosse, Tomasz Grzegorz (eds.): *European Union Policies at a time of the Crisis.* Scholar Publishing House: Warsaw, 2017, pp. 281–306.

17 Orzelska-Stączek, Agnieszka: 'Inicjatywa Środkowoeuropejska a Trójmorze – odmienne koncepcje współpracy w Europie Środkowo-Wschodniej', *Studia Polityczne*, no. 1 (46)/2018, pp. 149–169.

18 Olejarz, Tomasz / Stępniewski, Tomasz: 'Grupa Wyszehradzka: status polityczny i specyfika działań międzynarodowych na przykładzie inicjatywy Partnerstwa Wschodniego Unii Europejskiej', *Rocznik Instytutu Europy Środkowo-Wschodniej*, no. 11(1)/2013, pp. 107–125.

19 Eberhardt, Piotr: 'Ekonomiczne i kulturowe podstawy Trójmorza', *Arcana. Kultura, Historia, Polityka*, no. 5(137)/2017, pp. 20–21.

20 Bayer, Lili / Cienski, Jan: 'The not-so-fantastic 4: Central Europe's divided Visegrad Alliance', *Politico*, January 7, 2022. Retrieved June 1, 2023, from: <https://www.politico.eu/article/central-europe-divided-visegrad-v4-alliance/>.

21 'The Three Seas Initiative Summit: European Commission Investments in Connectivity Projects Bucharest, Romania, 17-18 September 2018', *European Commission*. Retrieved June 1, 2023, from: <https://ec.europa.eu/info/sites/default/files/ the_three_seas_initiative_summit_en.pdf>.

22 Bajda, Piotr: *Inicjatywa Trójmorza 2016-2020 in statunascendi*, Collegium Interethnicum: Warszawa, 2020.

23 Jones, Jr., James L. /Olechnowicz, Pawel: *Completing Europe – From the North-South Corridor to Energy, Transportation, and Telecommunications Union*. Atlantic Council: Washington, 2014. Retrieved June 1, 2023, from: <https://www.ceep.be/www/wp-content/uploads/2014/11/Completing-Europe_Report.pdf>.

24 Gniazdowski, Mateusz: 'Trójmorze – nowy instrument w polskiej polityce zagranicznej', *Polski Przegląd Dyplomatyczny*, nr 4 (71)/2017, pp. 79.

25 Sprūds, Andris / Vargulis, Mārtiņš: *Three Seas Initiative Mapping National Perspectives*. Latvian Institute of International Affairs Riga, 2022.

26 See: Thomann, Pierre-Emmanuel: 'The Three Seas Initiative, a New Project at the Heart of European and Global Geopolitical Rivalries', *Rocznik Instytutu Europy* Środkowo-Wschodniej, 2019, vol. 17, subvol. 3, pp. 31–63. See also: Wike, Richard / Poushter, Jacob / Fetterolf, Janell / Schumacher, Schannon: *Ratings Remain Low Around Globe, While Views of U. S. Stay Mostly Favorable Trump foreign policies receive little support.* Pew Research Center: Washington 2020, pp. 41. See also: Szczerski, Krzysztof: *Utopia Europejska. Kryzys integracji i polska inicjatywa naprawy*. Biały Kruk: Kraków, 2017, pp. 251.

27 See: *Three Seas, Priority Projects*, retrieved June 1, 2023, from: <https://www.3seas.eu/about/progressreport>. 'Inauguration of gas interconnection between Poland and Lithuania, '*European Commission*, 5 May 2022,Retrieved June 1, 2023, from: <https://ec.europa.eu/info /news/inauguration-gas-interconnection-between-poland-and-lithuania-2022-may-05_en>. 'Poland is becoming Europe's gas hub': EU commissioner', *Polskie Radio*, 29.04.2022, retrieved June 1, 2023, from: <https://www.polskieradio.pl/395/7786/ Artykul/2948144,%e2%80%98Poland-is-becoming-Europe%e2%80%99s-gas-hub%e2%80%99-EU-commissioner>.

28 Bajda, Piotr: *Inicjatywa Trójmorza 2016-2020 in statu nascendi*. Collegium Interethnicum: Warszawa: 2020.

29 See: Dostál, Vít / Strážay, Tomáš / Végh, Zsuzsanna: 'The perspective of the Czech Republic, Hungary, and Slovakia on the Three Seas Initiative', *Association for International Affairs*, 24.06.2021, retrieved June 1, 2023, from: <https://www.amo.cz/en/the-perspective-of-the-czech-republic-hungary-and-slovakia-on-the-three-seas-initiative/>. See also: Ehl, Martin: 'The Three Seas Initiative through Czech Eyes: Unconvinced by Their Neighbour's Plans, '*The Polish Quarterly of International Affairs*, No. 2, Warsaw, 2017.

30 *The Three Seas Initiative Summit: European Commission Investments in Connectivity Projects*, Bucharest, Romania, 17-18 September 2018, European Commission. Retrieved June 1, 2023, from: <https://ec.europa.eu/info/sites/default/files/the_three_seas_initiative_summit_en.pdf>.

31 Sprūds, Andris / Vargulis, Mārtiņš: *Three Seas Initiative Mapping National Perspectives.* Latvian Institute of International Affairs: Riga, 2022.

32 Zbińkowski, Grzegorz: 'The Three Seas Initiative and its Economic and Geopolitical Effect on the European Union and Central and Eastern Europe', *Comparative Economic Research. Central and Eastern Europe*, 2019, vol. 22, no. 2, pp. 108–109. See also: Lewkowicz, Łukasz: 'The Three Seas Initiative in the Context of International Challenges', *Rocznik Instytutu Europy* Środkowo-Wschodniej, 17(2019), vol. 3, pp. 7–12. See: Kowal, Paweł/ Orzelska-Stączek, Agnieszka: *Inicjatywa Trójmorza: geneza, celeifunkcjonowanie.*WydawnictwoStudiówPolitycznychPolskiejAkademiiNauk: Warszawa, 2019, pp. 51–90. See: Soroka, George / Stępniewski, Tomasz: 'The Three Seas Initiative: Geopolitical Determinants and Polish Interests', *Rocznik Instytutu Europy* Środkowo-*Wschodniej*, 17, 2019, pp. 18–19. See: Ari, Ani / et alii.: *Infrastructure in Central, Eastern and Southeastern Europe. Benchmarking, Macroeconomic Impact, and Policy Issues*. International Monetary Fund: Washington: 2020, pp.1–110.

33 Lewicki, Grzegorz: *China's Belt and Road meets the Three Seas Initiative Chinese and US sticky power in the context of the COVID-19 pandemic and Poland's strategic interests.* Polish Economic Institute: Warsaw, 2020.

34 Bergsen, Pepijn: *The EU's unsustainable China strategy*, Chatham House: London, July 2021.

35 'GPW Launches Three Seas Exchanges Index', *The Warsaw Stock Exchange Group*, 2019-09-04. Retrieved June 1, 2023, from: <https://www.gpw.pl/news?cmn_id=108800&title=GPW+Launches+ Three+ Seas+Exchanges+Index>. See: Paszak, Paweł: *Xi Jinping's diplomacy: 2013-2020.* Institute of New Europe: Warsaw, 2020.

36 Brattberg, Erik / Le Corre, Philippe / Stronski, Paul / Waal de, Thomas: *China's Influence in Southeastern Central, and Eastern Europe. Vulnerabilities and Resilience in Four Countries.* Carnegie Endowment for International Peace: Washington, OCTOBER 2021.

37 Rutkowska, Elżbieta: 'Sieć 5G utknęła w rządowych gabinetach. Operatorzy nie wiedzą, czy będzie wolno współpracować z Huaweiem', *Gazeta Prawna*, 10 lutego 2022. Retrieved June 1, 2023, from: <https://serwisy.gazetaprawna.pl/telekomunikacja /artykuly/8353782,siec-5g-cyberbezpieczenstwo-wspolpraca-z-huaweiem.html>.

38 Turcsanyi, Richard / Kachlikova, Eva: 'The BRI and China's Soft Power in Europe: Why Chinese Narratives (Initially) Won',*Journal of Current Chinese Affairs*, 2020, Vol. 49(1), pp. 58–81.

[39] Brattberg, Erik / Le Corre, Philippe / Stronski, Paul / Waal de, Thomas: *China's Influence in Southeastern Central, and Eastern Europe. Vulnerabilities and Resilience in Four Countries.* Carnegie Endowment for International Peace: Washington, October 2021.

[40] Andrijauskas, Konstantinas: 'An Analysis of China's Economic Coercion Against Lithuania', *The Council on Foreign Relations*, May 12, 2022. Retrieved June 1, 2023, from: <https://www.cfr.org/blog/ analysis-chinas-economic-coercion-against-lithuania>.

[41] 'China, Russia Can Cooperate to Punish Lithuania: Global Times Editorial', *Global Times*, August 11, 2021, retrieved June 1, 2023, from: www.globaltimes.cn/. 'In the defense of a rules-based world order, every country has a role to play!' said Frank Jüris, China relations expert and research fellow at the ICDS' Estonian Foreign Policy Institute. See: Estonia, Latvia withdrawing from China's 16+1 cooperation format, 11.08.2022. Retrieved June 1, 2023, from: <https://news.err.ee/ 1608682231 /estonia-latvia-withdrawing-from-china-s-16-1-cooperation-format>.

[42] Karásková, Ivana: 'How China lost Central and Eastern Europe', *Mercator Institute for China Studies*, April 22, 2022. Retrieved June 1, 2023, from: short-analysis/ how-china-lost-central-and-eastern-europe>.

[43] 'EP Spring 2022 Survey: Rallying around the European flag - Democracy as anchor point in times of crisis', *European Parliament*. Retrieved June 1, 2023, from: <https:// europa.eu/eurobarometer/ surveys /detail/2792>.

[44] 'The 2022 Ukraine war saw the belated birth of a geopolitical EU' - Joseph Borell Fontelles. See: Borrell Fontelles, Josep: 'Europe in the Interregnum: our geopolitical awakening after Ukraine', *Grouped 'études géopolitiques*, 24.03.2022, retrieved June 1, 2023, from: July 30, 2022: <https:// geopolitique.eu/en/2022/03/24/ europe-in-the-interregnum-our-geopolitical-awakening-after-ukraine/>.

[45] A Strategic Compass for the EU, The Diplomatic Service of the European Union, October 28, 2021. Retrieved June 1, 2023, from: <https://www.eeas.europa.eu/eeas/ strategic-compass-security-and-defence-1_en/>.

[46] Stefaniak, Piotr: 'Nowy Jedwabny Szlak. Ruch tranzytowy zaczyna omijać Polskę?', *WNP.pl*, 1.08.2022. Retrieved June 1, 2023, from: <https://www.wnp.pl/logistyka/ nowy-jedwabny-szlak-ruch-tranzytowy-zaczyna-omijac-polske,607984.html>.

[47] Casarini, Nicola: 'A European strategic "third way?" The European Union between the traditional transatlantic alliance and the pull of the Chinese market', *China International Strategy Review.* The Institute of International and Strategic Studies: Peking University, 2022.

Bibliography

Alam, Asad et alii (eds.): *Unleashing Prosperity. Productivity Growth in Eastern Europe and the Former Soviet Union.* The World Bank: Washington, 2008.

Andrijauskas, Konstantinas: 'An Analysis of China's Economic Coercion Against Lithuania', *The Council on Foreign Relations*, May 12,

2022. Retrieved June 1, 2023, from: <https://www.cfr.org/blog/> analysis-chinas-economic-coercion-against-lithuania.

Ari, Ani / et alii.: *Infrastructure in Central, Eastern and Southeastern Europe. Benchmarking, Macroeconomic Impact, and Policy Issues*. International Monetary Fund: Washington: 2020, pp.1–110.

A Strategic Compass for the EU, The Diplomatic Service of the European Union, October 28, 2021. Retrieved June 1, 2023, from: <https://www.eeas.europa.eu/eeas/strategic-compass-security-and-defence-1_en>.

Bajda, Piotr: *Inicjatywa Trójmorza 2016-2020 in statunascendi*, Collegium Interethnicum: Warszawa, 2020.

Bayer, Lili / Cienski, Jan: 'The not-so-fantastic 4: Central Europe's divided Visegrad Alliance', *Politico*, January 7, 2022. Retrieved June 1, 2023, from: <https://www.politico.eu/article/central-europe-divided-visegrad-v4-alliance/>.

Bergsen, Pepijn: *The EU's unsustainable China strategy*, Chatham House: London, July 2021.

Bershidsky, Leonid: 'Piketty Thinks the EU Is Bad for Eastern Europe. He's Half Right', *Bloomberg*, 9.02.2018. Retrieved July 22, 2022, from: <https://www.bloomberg.com/opinion/articles/2018-02-09/piketty-thinks-the-eu-is-bad-for-eastern-europe-he-s-half-right#xj4y7vzkg>.

Birka, Ieva: *Can Return Migration Revitalize the Baltics? Estonia, Latvia, and Lithuania Engage Their Diasporas, with Mixed* Asya: 'From selective integration into selective implementation: The link between differentiated integration and conformity with EU laws', *European Journal of Political Research*, Volume 53, Issue 4, November 2014.

Borrell Fontelles, Josep: 'Europe in the Interregnum: our geopolitical awakening after Ukraine', *Grouped'études géopolitiques*, 24.03.2022, retrieved June 1, 2023, from: July 30, 2022: https:// geopolitique.eu/en/2022/03/24/europe-in-the-interregnum-our-geopolitical-awakening-after-ukraine/.

Brattberg, Erik / Le Corre, Philippe / Stronski, Paul / Waal de, Thomas: *China's Influence in Southeastern Central, and Eastern Europe. Vulnerabilities and Resilience in Four Countries.* Carnegie Endowment for International Peace: Washington, October 2021.

Cano, Cristobal Ridao /Bodewig, Christan: *Growing United. Upgrading Europe's Convergence Machine. The World Bank Report on European Union.* World Bank: Washington, 2018.

Casarini, Nicola: 'A European strategic 'third way?' The European Union between the traditional transatlantic alliance and the pull of the Chinese market', *China International Strategy Review.* The Institute of International and Strategic Studies: Peking University, 2022.

'Central Europe and the Baltics', *The World Bank*. Retrieved July 22, 2022, from: https://data. <worldbank.org/region/central-europe-and-the-baltics>.

'China, Russia Can Cooperate to Punish Lithuania: Global Times Editorial', *Global Times*, August 11, 2021, retrieved June 1, 2023, from: <www.globaltimes.cn>./.

Council Decision Establishing Permanent Structured Cooperation (PESCO) and determining the list of participating Member States, 14866/17, Brussels, 8 December 2017.Retrieved June 1, 2022, from: <https://eur-lex.europa.eu/legal-content/EN/TXT/PDF/?uri=CELEX>:32017D2315&from=EN.

Council Regulation (EU) 2017/1939 of 12 October 2017 implementing enhanced cooperation on the establishment of the European Public Prosecutor's Office ('the EPPO') Brussels, 15 October 2017.Retrieved June 1, 2022, from: <https://eur-lex.europa.eu/legal-content/EN/TXT/?uri=CELEX%3A32017R1939&qid=1659704641124>.

Dostál, Vít / Strážay, Tomáš / Végh, Zsuzsanna: 'The perspective of the Czech Republic, Hungary, and Slovakia on the Three Seas Initiative', *Association for International Affairs*, 24.06.2021, retrieved June 1, 2023, from: <https://www.amo.cz/en/the-perspective-of-the-czech-republic-hungary-and-slovakia-on-the-three-seas-initiative/>. Eberhardt, Piotr: 'Ekonomiczne i kulturowe podstawy Trójmorza', *Arcana. Kultura, Historia, Polityka*, no. 5(137)/2017, pp. 20–21.

Ehl, Martin: 'The Three Seas Initiative through Czech Eyes: Unconvinced by Their Neighbour's Plans', *The Polish Quarterly of International Affairs*, No. 2, Warsaw, 2017.

'EP Spring 2022 Survey: Rallying around the European flag - Democracy as anchor point in times of crisis', *European Parliament*. Retrieved

June 1, 2023, from: <https://europa.eu/eurobarometer/> surveys / detail/2792.

Estonia, Latvia withdrawing from China's 16+1 cooperation format, 11.08.2022. Retrieved June 1, 2023, from: <https://news.err.ee/> 1608682231 / estonia-latvia-withdrawing-from-china-s-16-1-cooperation-format.

Gniazdowski, Mateusz: 'Trójmorze – nowy instrument w polskiej polityce zagranicznej', *Polski Przegląd Dyplomatyczny*, nr 4 (71)/2017, pp. 79.

'GPW Launches Three Seas Exchanges Index', *The Warsaw Stock Exchange Group*, 2019-09-04. Retrieved June 1, 2023, from: <https://www.gpw.pl/news?cmn_id=108800&title=GPW+Launches+> Three+Seas+Exchanges+Index.

Grosse, Tomasz Grzegorz (eds.): *European Union Policies at a time of the Crisis.* Scholar Publishing House: Warsaw, 2017, pp. 281–306.

Harper, Jo: 'Could Poland catch up with Germany's economy?', *Deutsche Welle*, 19.02.2020. Retrieved July 22, 2022, from: <https://www.dw.com/en/could-poland-catch-up-with-germanys-economy/a-52425523>.

Jones, Jr., James L. /Olechnowicz, Pawel: *Completing Europe – From the North-South Corridor to Energy, Transportation, and Telecommunications Union.* Atlantic Council: Washington, 2014. Retrieved June 1, 2023, from: <https://www.ceep.be/www/wp-content/uploads/2014/11/Completing-Europe_Report.pdf>.

Karásková, Ivana: 'How China lost Central and Eastern Europe', *Mercator Institute for China Studies*, April 22, 2022. Retrieved June 1, 2023, from: short-analysis/how-china-lost-central-and-eastern-europe.

Khoo, Jerald: 'Towards a Two-Speed Europe: National Sovereignty and the Absence of Political Integration in the Eurozone', *Columbia Journal of European Law*, Volume 22, Issue 1, 2015–2016, pp. 165–192.

Kowal, Paweł / Orzelska-Stączek, Agnieszka: *Inicjatywa Trójmorza: geneza, celeifunkcjonowanie.*Wydawnictwo Studiów Politycznych Polskiej Akademii Nauk: Warszawa, 2019, pp. 51–90.

Lewicki, Grzegorz: *China's Belt and Road meets the Three Seas Initiative Chinese and US sticky power in the context of the COVID-19 pandemic and Poland's strategic interests.* Polish Economic Institute: Warsaw, 2020.

Lewkowicz, Łukasz: 'The Three Seas Initiative in the Context of International Challenges', *Rocznik Instytutu Europy* Środkowo-Wschodniej, 17(2019), vol. 3, pp. 7–12.

'Living conditions in Europe - income distribution and income inequality', *Eurostat*, June 2022, Retrieved July 30, 2022, from: <https://ec.europa.eu/eurostat/statistics-explained/index>. php? Title = Living_conditions_in_Europe_-_income_distribution _and_income _inequality&oldid=528159 #Key _findings.

Lutz, Wolfgang et alii. (eds.): *Demographic Scenarios for the EU - Migration Population and Education.* Publications Office of the European Union: Luxembourg, 2019. Retrieved July 22, 2022, from: <https://ec.europa. eu/jrc> /en/publication /eur-scientific-and-technical-research-reports/ demographic-scenarios-eu.

Merkl, Peter H.: *The Distracted Eagle: The Rift between America and Old Europe.* Routledge: London & New York, 2005.

'New Cohesion Report shows that differences between EU regions are narrowing thanks to EU support', *European Commission*, 9.02.2022. Retrieved July 22, 2022, from: <https://ec.europa>. eu/ regional _ policy/ en/ newsroom/ news/2022/02/02-09-2022-new-cohesion-report-shows-that-differences-between-eu-regions-are-narrowing-thanks-to-eu-support.

Olejarz, Tomasz / Stępniewski, Tomasz: 'Grupa Wyszehradzka: status polityczny i specyfika działań międzynarodowych na przykładzie inicjatywy Partnerstwa Wschodniego Unii Europejskiej', *Rocznik Instytutu Europy Środkowo-Wschodniej*, no. 11(1)/2013, pp. 107–125.

Orzelska-Stączek, Agnieszka: 'Inicjatywa Środkowoeuropejska a Trójmorze – odmienne koncepcje współpracy w Europie Środkowo-Wschodniej', *Studia Polityczne*, no. 1 (46)/2018, pp. 149–169.

'Outrage at "old Europe" remarks', *BBC News*, 23 January, 2003, retrieved July 22, 2022, from: <http://news.bbc.co.uk/2/hi/europe/2687403.stm>.

Paweł Paszak, *Xi Jinping's diplomacy: 2013-2020.* Institute of New Europe: Warsaw, 2020.

'Poland is becoming Europe's gas hub: EU commissioner', *Polskie Radio*, 29.04.2022, retrieved June 1, 2023, from: <https://www.polskieradio. pl/> 395/7786/ Artykul/2948144,%e2%80%98Poland-is-becoming-Europe%e2%80%99s-gas-hub%e2%80%99-EU-commissioner.

'Polish Prime Minister Morawiecki on the COVID comeback, the Three Seas Initiative, and where the US is falling short'. *Atlantic Council*,

6.05.2021, retrieved July 22, 2022, from: <https://www.atlanticcouncil.org/news/transcripts/polish-prime-minister-morawiecki-on-the-covid-comeback-the-three-seas-initiative-and-where-the-us-is-falling-short/>.

'Politics and the European Union. Future of Europe' *European Parliament & European Commission*, September 2021 - October 2021. Retrieved July 22, 2022, from: <https://europa.eu/eurobarometer> /surveys/detail/2554.

Results. Migration Policy Institute: Washington, May 8, 2019, retrieved July 22, 2022, from: <https://www.migrationpolicy.org/article/can-return-migration-revitalize-baltics-estonia-latvia-and-lithuania-engage-their-diasporas>.

Rutkowska, Elżbieta: 'Sieć 5G utknęła w rządowych gabinetach. Operatorzy nie wiedzą, czy będzie wolno współpracować z Huaweiem', *Gazeta Prawna*, 10 lutego 2022. Retrieved June 1, 2023, from: <https://serwisy.gazetaprawna.pl/telekomunikacja> / artykuly/8353782,siec-5g-cyberbezpieczenstwo-wspolpraca-z-huaweiem.html.

Schimmelfennig, Frank: 'Good governance and differentiated integration: Graded membership in the European Union'. *European Journal of Political Research*, Volume 55, Issue 4, November 2016.

Soroka, George / Stępniewski, Tomasz: 'The Three Seas Initiative: Geopolitical Determinants and Polish Interests', *Rocznik Instytutu Europy* Środkowo-*Wschodniej*, 17, 2019, pp. 18–19.

Sprūds, Andris / Vargulis, Mārtiņš: *Three Seas Initiative Mapping National Perspectives.* Latvian Institute of International Affairs: Riga, 2022.

Stefaniak, Piotr: 'Nowy Jedwabny Szlak. Ruch tranzytowy zaczyna omijać Polskę?', *WNP.pl*, 1.08.2022. Retrieved June 1, 2023, from: <https://www.wnp.pl/logistyka/nowy-jedwabny-szlak-ruch-tranzytowy-zaczyna-omijac-polske,607984.html>.

Stehrer, Robert / et alii. (eds.): *How EU funds tackle economic divide in the European Union*. Policy Department for Budgetary Affairs Directorate-General for Internal Policies, European Parliament, Brussels, PE 654.525, July 2020.Retrieved January 4, 2024, from: <https://www.europarl.europa.eu/RegData/etudes/STUD/2020/654525/IPOL_STU>(2020)654525_EN.pdf.

Szczerski, Krzysztof: *Utopia Europejska. Kryzys integracji i polska inicjatywa naprawy*. Biały Kruk: Kraków, 2017, pp. 251.

'The euro area', *Eurobarometer*, October 2021 - November 2021. Retrieved July 22, 2022, from: <https://europa.eu/eurobarometer> /surveys/detail/2289.

The White Paper on the future of Europe. Reflections and scenarios for the EU27 by 2025, European Commission, Brussels, 1 March 2017, COM (2017)2025. Retrieved June 1, 2022, from: <https://ec.europa.eu/info/sites/default/files/> white _paper _on_the_future_of_europe_en.pdf.

The White Paper on the future of Europe. Reflections and scenarios for the EU27 by 2025, European Commission, Brussels, 1 March 2017, COM (2017)2025. Retrieved June 1, 2022, from: <https://ec.europa.eu/info/sites/default/files/> white _paper _on_the_future_of_europe_en.pdf.

'The Three Seas Initiative Summit: European Commission Investments in Connectivity Projects Bucharest, Romania, 17-18 September 2018', *European Commission*. Retrieved June 1, 2023, from: <https://ec.europa.eu/info/sites/default/files/> the_three_seas_initiative_summit_en.pdf.

Thomann, Pierre-Emmanuel: 'The Three Seas Initiative, a New Project at the Heart of European and Global Geopolitical Rivalries', *Rocznik Instytutu Europy* Środkowo-Wschodniej, 2019, vol. 17, subvol. 3, pp. 31–63.

Three Seas, Priority Projects, retrieved June 1, 2023, from: <https://www.3seas.eu/about/progressreport>. 'Inauguration of gas interconnection between Poland and Lithuania, '*European Commission*, 5 May 2022, Retrieved June 1, 2023, from: <https://ec.europa.eu/info> /news/inauguration-gas-interconnection-between-poland-and-lithuania-2022-may-05_en.

The Three Seas Initiative Summit: European Commission Investments in Connectivity Projects, Bucharest, Romania, 17–18 September 2018, European Commission. Retrieved June 1, 2023, from: <https://ec.europa.eu/info/sites/default/files/> the_three_seas_initiative_summit_en.pdf.

Turcsanyi, Richard / Kachlikova, Eva: 'The BRI and China's Soft Power in Europe: Why Chinese Narratives (Initially) Won', *Journal of Current Chinese Affairs*, 2020, Vol. 49(1), pp. 58–81.

Wike, Richard / Poushter, Jacob / Fetterolf, Janell / Schumacher, Schannon: *Ratings Remain Low Around Globe, While Views of U. S. Stay Mostly Favorable Trump foreign policies receive little support.* Pew Research Center: Washington 2020, pp. 41.

Vitte de, Bruno / Ott, Andrea / Vos, Ellen: *Between Flexibility and Disintegration. The Trajectory of Differentiation in EU Law.* Edward Elgar: Cheltenham-Northampton, 2017.

Zbińkowski, Grzegorz: 'The Three Seas Initiative and its Economic and Geopolitical Effect on the European Union and Central and Eastern Europe', *Comparative Economic Research. Central and Eastern Europe*, 2019, vol. 22, no. 2, pp. 108–109.

Zhelyazkova, Asya: 'From selective integration into selective implementation: The link between differentiated integration and conformity with EU laws', *European Journal of Political Research*, Volume 53, Issue 4, November 2014.

Peace and Development: The European Union as a World Leader?

Przemysław Łukasik

> With all its pros and cons, the contemporary world has its origins in Europe. In this westernmost fortress protecting Eurasia, the Age of Enlightenment and the Industrial Revolution occurred, with their effects seen everywhere around us. These effects, good and bad, are impacted by the geographical location of Europe.[1]

Tim Marshall, a British journalist, expert on foreign policy and diplomacy, and the author of this quote, saw Europe's success in its favourable climate, good soil, and rivers along which goods could be rafted to the seas. These geographical factors have always given Europe an advantage over other parts of the world. However, for Marshall, another factor was far more critical. European integration had brought peace to a warring Europe. As he jokingly said, the European Union was founded on the assumption that France and Germany would embrace each other so tightly that neither of them would be able to strike the other, bound as they were in this loving embrace.[2] Today, the European Union, united in a 'peaceful embrace' and associated with development and economic welfare, is well on its way to becoming a global leader. However, the possible questions of the EU's power status raise even more questions. Can a non-state entity, such as the EU, be a power at all?[3] What are the premises of the EU's power status or what does this status entail?[4] Will the outbreak of the Russo-Ukrainian War and the demographic crisis undermine the foundations of the EU's power status?[5]

Evolution of the international order and its conditions

> The first threat, an external one, is related to the new geopolitical situation in the world and around Europe. An increasingly, let us call it, assertive e China, especially on the seas, Russia's aggressive policy towards Ukraine and its neighbours, wars, terror and anarchy in the Middle East and in Africa, with radical Islam playing a major role, as well as worrying declarations by the new American administration all make our future highly unpredictable neighbors first time in, our history, in an increasingly multipolar external world, so many are becoming openly anti-European, or Eurosceptic at best.[6]

In his book, *The Jungle Grows Back*: *America* and *Our Imperilled World*, Robert Kagan, a leading American political analyst warned that the international liberal global order symbolised by the 'garden', where cooperation rather than competition is encouraged, geopolitics is replaced by geoeconomics, cosmopolitanism prevails over tribalism, is threatened by the 'ever-growing jungle' (authoritarianism, geopolitical ambitions, aggressive attitudes and great power spheres of interest). The weakening power of the United States or its retreat from the role of the guarantor of this liberal order could, as he predicted, drive the world into instability and chaos.[7] Indeed, contemporary international relations are characterised by increasing dynamism. Growing multipolarity and interdependence are persistent global trends, although globalisation, especially in the economic context, is like a coin with two sides. It assigns the roles of winners and losers to different countries in the global economic game. On the one hand, it reduces the level of asymmetry between the major powers, such as the US and China, and gives a boost to the development of emerging powers. On the other hand, it widens the gap between the richest and the poorest which can lead to instability, create tensions and weaken the often-fragile foundations of some countries. Growing instability or state fragility has been demonstrated in the evolution of the concept of a *failed state* and its extension by the category of entities called *fragile states*. The current indicators of state instability show versatility and multipolarity in certain aspects.[8] The fragility of North African or Middle East states is an indirect threat to Europe (evidenced by migrations to Europe due to the Arab Spring, etc.). The development of the Russian-Ukrainian conflict from the hybrid 'new war' (2014–22) to an all-out war (since 2022) proves the vulnerability of the EU and NATO countries to destabilisation. Recent NATO operations in Libya or Afghanistan have shown that humanitarian interventions only temporarily stabilise the situation.

Contemporary international relations are described as shifting from the American hegemony to a multipolar system. The 'growth of the East', namely of China, Japan, or India, is a challenge to American hegemony.[9] The multipolar world also includes new regional powers such as Brazil and South Africa.[10] The US, which is experiencing an economic crisis and a growing deficit caused, among other things, by its military involvement in Iraq and Afghanistan, is trying to maintain development by seeking allies who share the same values. The Americans define international change as a return to great power rivalry. The 2018 US security strategy links the slow decline of the international order to the activities of China and Russia. The strategy describes these two states as 'revisionist powers' that 'seek to shape the world according to their authoritarian model'. However, the rising importance of China and Russia is not generally seen as a factor leading inevitably to confrontation.[11] Nevertheless, there is a palpable rivalry between China and the US for zones of influence, for example, in Europe.[12] As a result, the American response is more measured, rejecting unilateralism or the creation of new alliances. The US administration's response is close cooperation between allies and gradual evolution within the existing US security architecture. The Americans want an increased presence and strengthening of the existing alliances in Southeast Asia and the North Atlantic Treaty Organization. The Atlantic and Pacific Partnership is designed to enable cooperation within the regional network coordinated by NATO.[13] Due to this integration, the international consultation network is to be established to include countries such as Australia, Japan, South Korea, and New Zealand (in addition to NATO countries), that is, more than 30 countries.

At present, Europe (NATO and EU member states) identifies various threats to security, such as terrorism, violation of the rules of the international order by states and non-state actors, cyber-terrorism, and migrations that threaten borders. Europeans also see Russia's aggressive operations as the most challenging factor for Euro-Atlantic security, while China's growing power and international position are seen as both a challenge and a source of change in the international order. These changes could either raise Europe's status to a third pillar alongside the global powers of the US and China or accelerate its marginalisation and dependency.

Serious demographic changes in Europe could be a symptom of the decline of the West as a whole. Long-term factors determining Europe's future are the ageing of Europeans and a declining population compared to the rest of the world (in 1900, Europeans represented 25% of the global population, while in 2060, they will represent only 5% of all people). A smaller population will also lead to lower productivity (in 2017, Europe produced 22% of the world's GDP; by 2030, it will be only 20%).[14] However, Europeans see threats to international security as the most serious. The Russo-Ukrainian conflict, which turned into an all-out war in February 2022, made EU countries aware of the need to develop hard power and a defence-oriented community. The Russo-Ukrainian war also exposed the negative aspects of international economic dependencies. Russia's energy policy is a good example of this trend.[15]

Evolution of the importance of power status premises

> Our troubled past has given to a peace spanning seven decades and to an enlarged Union of 500 million citizens living in freedom in one of the world's most prosperous economies. The images of battles and fields in Verdun, or of a continent separated by the Iron Curtain and the Berlin Wall, have been replaced by a Union standing out as a beacon of peace and stability [...] The EU is now the place where Europeans can enjoy a unique diversity of culture, ideas and traditions in a Union covering four million square kilometers.[16]

The concepts of power and the status of power have changed constantly. They are also defined differently by adherents to realist and neoliberal approaches to international relations. Realists refer to the two key concepts of security and power. In the international anarchist reality, the ability of the state to survive (protect its borders) and increase its power (conduct independent policies) are the most important values. Realists describe international relations as a constant struggle for limited resources in which one party gains profits while another one suffers losses.

According to realists, the assets necessary to achieve the status of power are as follows: geographical conditions, territory, type of borders, natural resources, economy, the character of the nation, quality of diplomacy, national fighting spirit, population, and military power. Neoliberals can see shortcomings in relations between countries (focusing on the selfish interests of states), but they believe they should be based on values such as democracy and human rights to enable the creation of peaceful international relations. A liberal international order focuses on development, exchange, and international cooperation, which should be mutually beneficial.[17] The interdependence of countries and the institutionalisation of cooperation based on trust, law, and procedures are supposed to regulate relations between political actors and interfere with rivalry. Constructivists have a similar approach to international relations, believing that norms and ideas can change relations between countries and expose the performative role of the international relations discourse (conflict-based relations or cooperation-based relations).[18]

In sociological literature, power is defined as authority or influence, and in international relations, it is associated with power, power status, or empire. In the theory of international relations, power is usually associated with getting your way, defined as the control of one political entity by another, even against its will.[19] It has also been defined as the ability to persuade others to do something they would not otherwise do.[20] We can distinguish three ways of defining the concept of power: the traditional approach, that is, state power that depends on state assets; the neorealist approach, that is, the ability to determine the rules of operation and the final outcome of negotiations; and the structural approach, that is, the ability to shape the structures of the global economy, imposing dominant values and rules of operation that other countries, their political institutions, and elites, must respect.[21] In this context, the German sociologist Max Weber presented an interesting theory when he tried to convince us that power is a method of gaining an advantage without using physical force.[22] Power, defined as a neutral term that does not require domination, was popularised in the early twenty-first century by the American political scientist Joseph Nye. According to him, soft power is an attractive power to convince and persuade based on such assets as culture, values, and foreign policy.[23]

As a result, the concept of power is a central category in international relations, although it is also multidimensional and differently defined. Power is an asset to reach the global leader of power status level, the latter being assigned to a state or non-state entity with sufficient power used to surpass other countries, resulting in an important global role.[24] Thus, from the EU perspective, it becomes crucial to consider the EU's position in terms of power status and its dynamics.

Contemporary political analysis alternates between a more realist and a more neoliberal view of international relations. The choice of one of these two approaches is usually determined by the scale of challenges faced by an entity seeking power status. With regard to the discussion on the possible power status of the EU, the pro- or anti-approach is a symptom of support for one of the paradigms, although not always. The rejection of the EU's role as a global leader may also stem from the belief that power status is only ascribable to states.[25] Moreover, the EU has long had no ambitions for global influence (the Common Foreign and Security Policy, with the exception of relations with the US and the PRC, has mainly focused on stabilisation and cooperation with neighbouring countries and regions). However, the main realist arguments against the European Union's power status are economic downturn, demographic crisis, and military weakness. The EU's power status is perceived mainly in the context of neoliberal bridging and merging of worlds. The history of the EU is a practical confirmation of the statement that economic interdependence leads to permanent cooperation and, thus, confirms peace. As a result, the EU is the world's largest coalition or a political union, the largest market, and the largest aid donor in the world. According to the neoliberal theory, the EU is the only superpower besides the United States, and its relative strength has been steadily increasing.[26] The permanent foundations of the EU's continuous growth are supposed to be as follows: high PCI, long-term institutional advantages, and convergence of fundamental national interests between the EU countries and other great powers.

In the 2010s, the EU's power status became the subject of greater analysis in 2010s thanks to the following two factors.[27] The first was the enlargement of the EU to include 12 Central and Eastern European and Balkan countries. The voluntary cooperation of countries with developed market economies was supplemented by former communist countries. The result was a community of 27 countries (followed by Croatia in 2013 and with the United Kingdom leaving the EU in 2020), covering an area of over 4 million square kilometres and a population of 445 million people. The second factor was the erosion of the popularity of the United States, which, under the leadership of George W. Bush, launched military interventions in Afghanistan and Iraq as a part of the global war on terrorism. Criticism of American unilateralism and militarism in Europe and the United States itself turned into anti-Americanism. It was the moment when hard power began to be distinguished from soft power in the discourse on the premises of militarism. This distinction, introduced by Joseph Nye, has become very popular with the EU as a good example. The EU community was supposed to perceive neighbouring entities as potential friends, in contrast to the United States, which saw every independent entity as a potential enemy. The increased power of the EU takes the form of peaceful and voluntary expansion of the community and permanent transformation of its members. Undoubtedly, the EU was and is a transformative force, delivering dynamic liberalism followed by the stability and prosperity of social democracy. Europe, based on a communitarian model of society, economy, and citizenship, more focused on cooperation rather than rivalry, may be better prepared for the challenges of the twenty-first century than the United States. As a subject of international relations, the EU is an excellent example of giving a new meaning to the notion of power status by playing the role of 'soft, gentle power'.[28] The EU's popularity and success are based not on domination but on the imposition of discipline. The premises of Europeanisation, such as the EU funds and unrestricted mobility across its borders, are too attractive to refuse.

Evolution of subjects of power status

> We must be realistic and recognize that the current phase in history and global politics requires us to think and act in terms of power (hence, the phrase 'the language of power'). The war against Ukraine is the latest and most dramatic illustration of this.[29]

The EU exerts influence on surrounding entities primarily through peaceful means (civilian power), the popularisation of democratic values (normative power), support for transformation (transformative power), development, and humanitarian assistance or multilateral cooperation (cooperative power).The EU prefers soft methods, not only in terms of hard-headed arguments but also due to political practice and within the EU's system of political norms known as 'European values'. The most relevant values in the context of international relations include promoting democratic values, such as respect for human rights, the peaceful settlement of disputes, and respect for international law.[30] The role of the EU as a model of friendly international relations is emphasised. The causal effect of the EU's soft power is its attractiveness in international relations through its foreign policy, political system, social attitudes, and the power of its values. Thanks to its attraction capacity, the EU is an influential political actor in implementing democratic and economic reforms in neighbouring countries, leading to EU enlargement. As a civil and normative power, the EU promotes the culture of non-militarism and reconciliation through cooperation and support for EU values, human rights, and democracy. EU soft power aims to combine diplomacy with multilateralism.

The development of the EU as a subject of power status is the primary goal of the discourse between the member states and the EU's institutions. In 2017 the European Commission presented *The White Paper on the Future of Europe. Reflections and Scenarios for the EU27 by 2025*, in which it was stated that despite the undeniable success of the European integration project, the EU is still subject to criticism that it is an institution that does too little or, on the contrary, interferes too much in the affairs of Europeans.[31] In his open letter to the heads of state and government of the member states the then President of the European Council, Donald Tusk, saw the reason for the criticism of the European integration project in the 'decline of the spirit of the elites supporting the European Union', and 'the end of the belief in liberal democracy', as well as in the emergence of the 'anti-EU and nationalist movement [...] led by national egoism in the Community itself'.[32] He also warned that the possible disintegration of the EU would make the EU dependent on the three powers: the United States, Russia, and China. Recurrent criticism has focused on the EU's internal problems and limited ability to respond to challenges outside the EU. The global financial and banking crisis, which was most severe in 2008–09, the Eurozone problems, the migrant crisis, Brexit, and the escalation of the Russian-Ukrainian war, are all significant crises facing the EU. The main problem, however, is the identity problem linked to various aspects of the EU's power status. The EU project is based on the idea of gradual integration. Today's Union, which is in part an international organization, a confederation, and a federation, has come a long way in terms of development, from the Coal and Steel Community to the Economic and Legal community, with a joint parliament, human rights, and the European Neighbourhood Policy. However, there remains dispute between federalists who support the idea of Europe of nations, that is, the idea of the EU as an organization that is an instrument of cooperation between states. Supporters of federalisation see the United States of Europe not only as an opportunity to deepen integration but as an opportunity for the EU to acquire all the attributes of power. In the face of resistance from some member states, the

European Commission adopted the idea of 'diversified integration'.[33] Among five scenarios for the future development of the EU, the idea was to form alliances of willing countries that would like to intensify cooperation in certain areas, or for the EU to strengthen cooperation in a smaller number of areas.[34] Examples of such intensified cooperation of willing countries are establishing the European Public Prosecutor's Office and structural collaboration security field.[35] Diversified integration offers the possibility of a flexible conciliatory intensification of integration and different development variants. It also undermines the rule of uniform application of the EU law and the protection of national interests. Europe's 'Variable geometry' and lack of uniformity can hamper the EU's effective functioning outside its borders.

The currently emerging new model of integration is sometimes called an 'asymmetric confederation' because of the growing imbalance between the strength and influence of large countries (Germany and France) and smaller nations in EU decision-making'.[36] The critical decisions on tackling the Eurozone, migration, and Russo-Ukrainian wars were taken in Berlin and Paris. The emergence of the EU leadership of France and Germany is evidenced by the fact that it was not the EU members but the heads of government of the two countries who participated in the Normandy format negotiations in Minsk. Both countries are trying to achieve their own goals within the EU (e.g. improving the competitiveness of the German economy through the energy transition (Energiewende) policy or implementing France's postcolonial policy towards Africa) instead of executing the shared visions of the member states. The weakening of integration is reflected in the cohesion policy, as its benefits have been transferred from less developed to more developed countries. Farmers in the original 12 founding members of the EU still receive more funding than those who have joined since 2004.The need for the EU's development as a subject of power status is justified by the search for 'strategic autonomy'. The standard defence policy would end the EU's development dichotomy of being an economic power and a political dwarf. As not only soft power but also a hard power, Europe will be able to effectively protect the global liberal order without seeking the help of great powers ('soft power is a delicate glove on an iron hand').[37] Finally, it will not be forced to choose between the two great rivals, the US and China.[38] Current EU strategic policy focuses on responding to external conflicts and crises, building the capabilities of EU partners (NATO is still the most important), and protecting the EU and its citizens. The EU's credibility is to be enhanced through increased spending on the army (including 20% of the defence budget for purchases and procurement), interoperability of divisions, and research and development of technologies (PESCO and the European Defence Fund).[39] As the result of the all-out war between Russia and Ukraine that began in February 2022, the 'geopolitical EU was born'. The EU countries will create a rapid reaction force of 5,000 troops to be deployed in various crises. Further intensification of cooperation within NATO is supposed to be followed by work on rules for rapid decision-making and the development of the command structures and the system of regular military manoeuvres.

The European Union is a long-term project. According to the neo-functional theory, intensifying integration at the political level will make it possible to create a unified federalist European state and, subsequently, achieve the status of a fully developed power in the eyes of both neoliberals and realists. There are a few researchers (e.g. Andrei Markovits) who already see the EU as a fully developed power (considering the military potential of certain EU states as a part of NATO), but it seems to be very difficult to achieve the status of a 'peaceful and developed' third superpower alongside the Chinese dragon and the American eagle, as a result of the destabilisation of the EU's neighbouring countries in the form of the Russo-Ukrainian war or illegal migration. The economic downturn and demographic problems are also clouding the notion of EU development and progress. It seems impossible for the EU to achieve strategic autonomy if the problems of 'diversified integration' and 'asymmetric confederation' are not solved first. Obviously, military threats can be a successful pressure factor in pushing the EU toward the development of the NATO-aligned defence community and towards deeper integration as such.

Notes

1 Marshall, Tim: *Prisoners of Geography. Ten Maps that tell you everything you need to know about Global Politics.* Elliott and Thompson Limited: Chicago, 2016, pp. 133.

2 Ibid., p. 147.

3 The EU is not a country but a subject of international relations as a voluntary association of free and democratic countries (the realist theory). The neo-functional theory presents it as a self-propelled system in which each stage of development leads to the need for further steps, that is, an increase in its competencies. This leads to constant tensions over the scope and pace of change and the definition of national interests, democracy, and sovereignty. According to game theory, the EU is an internally conflicted power

because national governments are dependent on national actors and, therefore, have different foreign and domestic policy objectives. This leads to crises that paralyse the EU operations and hinder its integration. These are the factors that researchers see as the causes of the EU's significant crises, namely the financial and economic crisis, the axiological crisis, the 'democratic deficit' crisis, the European integration crisis, the leadership crisis, and the Brexit-related crisis. See: Kuźniar, Roman: *Polityka i siła. Studia strategiczne – zarys problematyki.* Scholar: Warszawa, 2006. See also: Józef Fiszera (ed.): *Unia Europejska-Chiny w XXI wieku.* Institute of Political Studies at Polish Academy of Sciences: Warszawa, 2018.

4 Hans Morgentau determined eight factors of power: geographical conditions, territory, type of borders, natural assets, economy, quality of diplomacy, national fighting spirit, population, and military power. See: Morgenthau, Hans: *Politics Among Nations. The Struggle for Power and Peace.* Alfred A. Knopf: New York, 1960, pp. 25–39.

5 Barnett, Michael / Duvall, Raymond: 'Power in International Politics', *International Organization,* Issue 1, vol. 59, 2005, pp. 39.

6 'Letter by President Donald Tusk to the 27 EU leaders on the future of the EU – "United we stand, divided we fall"', *European Council,* 31 January 2017, retrieved November 1, 2021, from: <https://www.consilium.europa.eu/en/press/press-releases/2017/01/31/tusk-letter-future-europe/>.

7 Kagan, Robert: *The Jungle Grows Back*: *America* and *Our Imperilled World.* Alfred A. Knopf: New York, 2018.

8 Haken, Nate et al.: *Fragile States Index 2022 – Annual Report.* 13 July 2022. The Fund for Peace: Washington, retrieved November 1, 2023, from: <https://fragilestatesindex.org/wp-content/uploads / 2022/07/22-FSI-Report-Final.pdf>.

9 Zakaria, Fareed: *The Post-American World.* W.W. Norton and Company: New York, 2008.

10 *Global Strategic Trends. The Future Starts Today.* Ministry of Defence, United Kingdom: London, 2018, pp. 212–218. Retrieved November 1, 2022, from: <https://assets.publishing.service.gov.uk /government/uploads/system/uploads/ attachment_data/file/771309/Global_Strategic_Trends_-_The_Future_Starts_Today.pdf>.

11 'London Declaration issued by the Heads of State and Government participating in the meeting of the North Atlantic Council in London 3-4 December 2019'. . Retrieved November 1, 2022, from: <https://www.nato.int/cps/en/natohq/official _texts_171584.htm? selectedLocale=en/>.

12 *EU-China—A strategic outlook, European Commission,* 2019, retrieved November 1, 2022, from: <https://ec.europa.eu/ commission/ sites/beta-political/files/communication-eu-china-a-strategic-outlook.pdf>.

13 During the Cold War, apart from minor disputes within the transatlantic community, US and Western European societies had no doubt that their main threat came from the Soviet Union. Today, there is no such clear-cut attitude to the threat posed by China. See: Mahneken, Thomas G.: 'Forging the tools of 21st-century great power competition', *The Center for Strategic and Budgetary Assessments,* 2020, retrieved November 1, 2023, from: <https://csbaonline.org/ uploads/documents /GPC_Final_Report_Web.pdf>.

14 Blocher, John W.: 'Unexpected Competition: A US Strategy to Keep its Central and Eastern European Allies as Allies in an Era of Great-Power Competition, *'Atlantic*

Council, 22 November 2020,retrieved November 1, 2023, from: <https://www.atlanticcouncil.org/in-depth-research-reports/report/unexpected-competition/>.

[15] After the presidency of Donald Trump, who preferred unilateral action to multilateralism, American analysts and politicians are convinced Joe Biden's administration should focus on the multilateral approach. With regard to relations with Russia, they suggest reacting like NATO, which discourages the Kremlin from carrying out aggressive operations against US allies. The Americans also announced work on the new version of the Anti-Ballistic Missile Treaty to reassure the US allies in Europe. The age of shock, suggested by the global COVID-19 pandemic and climate change, encourages action and the search for new solutions, so there is also discussion of the creation of the NATO Bank, which could finance the modernisation of weapons or strategic infrastructure investments, such as the development of the 5G technology. It would also serve as an emergency reserve. See: 'Summary of the National Defence Strategy of The United States of America, Sharpening the American Military's Competitive Edge'. Department of Defence: Washington, 2018. Retrieved November 1, 2023, from: <https://dod.defence.gov/Portals/1/Documents/pubs/2018-National-Defence-Strategy-Summary.pdf>. See also: Green, Michael /Alterman, John / Miller, Franklin (eds.): *Ironclad: Forging a New Future for America's Alliances*. Center for Strategic and International Studies: Lanham, Boulder, New York, London, 19 October 2019, retrieved November 1, 2023, from: <https://www.csis.org/ analysis/ ironclad-forging-new-future-americas-alliances>. See also: Skaluba, Christopher / Rodihan, Conor/ Doyle, Gabriela (eds.): *NATO 20/2020. Twenty bold ideas to reimagine the Alliance after the 2020 US election*. Atlantic Council Washington: 2020. Retrieved November 1, 2023, from: >wp-content/uploads /2020/10/NATO-20-2020-Twenty-bold-ideas-to-reimagine-the-alliance-after-the-2020-US-election.pdf>. See: O'Rourke, Ronald: 'U.S. Role in the World: Background and Issues for Congress Updated', *Congressional Research Service*, August 5, 2020. Retrieved November 1, 2023, from: <https://www.hsdl.org/?view&did=842596>.

[16] 'The White Paper on the future of Europe. Reflections and scenarios for the EU27 by 2025', *European Commission*, 1 March 2017, COM (2017)2025. Retrieved November 1, 2023, from: <https://ec.europa.eu/info/sites/default/files/ white _paper _on_the_future_of_europe_en.pdf>.

[17] Keohane, Robert O. / Nye, Jr., Joseph S.: *Power and Interdependence*. Littel Brown: Boston, 1977.

[18] Wendt, Alexander: 'Anarchy is what States Make of It: the Social Construction of Power Politics', *International Organization*,46, no. 2, Spring 1992, pp. 391–425.

[19] Barnett, Michael / Duvall, Raymond: 'Power in International Politics', *International Organization*, Issue 1, vol. 59, 2005, pp. 39.

[20] Dahl, Robert A.: 'The concept of Power', *Behavioral Science*, No. 2, Vol. 3,1957, pp. 203.

[21] Smouts, Marie-Cloude: 'International Organizations and Inequality among States', *International Social Science Journal*, No. 144,1995, pp. 234.

[22] Haugaard, Mark / Lentner, Howard H. (eds.): *Hegemony and Power. Consensus and Coercion in Contemporary Politics*. Lexington Books: Lanham, 2006, pp. 10. Similar understanding of the term of power was characteristic of Hannah Arendt. See: Arendt, Hannah: *On Violence*. Harvest, Harcourt Brace & Company: New York, 1970.

[23] Nye, Joseph S.: 'The Benefits of Soft Power', *Harvard Business School Working Knowledge for Business Leaders*, February 8, 2004.

[24] According to Steven Spiegel, power in international relations is defined by five elements: material assets (territory, population, energy production and consumption, political system, and government position), military power, state driving force, range of driving force, and state achievements. Joseph Frankel determines the following factors: demographic, geographical, economic, organisational, psychological, and sociological, as well as state strategic position. See: Spiegel, Steven: *Dominance and Diversity. The International Hierarchy.* Little, Brown: Boston, 1972, pp. 43. See: Frankel, Joseph: *International Relations.* Oxford University Press London: 1969, pp. 82–51.

[25] 'Will The EU Ever Become a Superpower?', *Carnegie Endowment For International Peace*, July 17, 2008, retrieved November 1, 2023, from: <https:// carnegieendowment.org/files/0717carnegie-stubb.pdf/>.

[26] Moravcsik, Andrew: 'Europe: The quiet superpower', *French Politics*, Vol. 7, 3/4, 2009, pp.403–422.

[27] Reding, Andrew: 'EU in position to be world's next superpower', *Chicago Tribune*, January 6, 2002,retrieved November 1, 2023, from: <https://www.chicagotribune.com/news/ct-xpm-2002-01-06-0201060227-story.html>. See also: Rifikn, Jeremy: *The European dream: how Europe's vision of the future is quietly eclipsing the American dream.* Jeremy P. Tarcher/Penguin: New York, 2004. See: Rauch, Jonathan: 'Europe Is the Next Rival Superpower. But Then, So Was Japan', *The Atlantic.com*, February 1, 2005, retrieved November 1, 2023, from: <https://web.archive.org/web/ 20080828194231>/<http:// www.theatlantic.com/doc/200502u/nj_rauch_2005-02-01>. See also: Leonard, Mark: *Why Europe Will Run the 21st Century.* Public Affairs: New York, 2005. See also: McCormick, John: *The European superpower.* Palgrave Macmillan: New York, 2007. See: Kagan, Robert: *Paradise and Power: America and Europe in the New World Order.* Vintage Books: New York, 2004. Khanna, Parag: 'The Empire Strikes Back', *The Economist*, May 27, 2008. Retrieved November 1, 2023, from: <https://www.economist.com/books-and-arts/2008/03/27/the-empires-strike-back>.

[28] Biscop, Sven: 'Geopolitics with European Characteristics An Essay on Pragmatic Idealism', *Equality and Strategy*, March 15, 2016, Retrieved November 1, 2023, from: <https://eu.boell.org/en /2016/v03/15/geopolitics-european-characteristics>. See also: Gstöhl, Sieglinde/ Lannon, Erwan (eds.):

The Neighbours of the European Union's Neighbours Diplomatic and Geopolitical Dimensions beyond the European Neighbourhood Policy. Routledge: London, 2014. See: Gerrits, André (ed.): *Normative Power Europe in a Changing World: A Discussion*, Netherlands Institute of International relations, Clingendael, December 2009. Retrieved November 1, 2023, from: <https://www.clingendael.org/sites/default/files/pdfs/ 20091200 _cesp_ paper gerrits.pdf>. Haine, Jean-Yves: 'The EU's Soft Power: Not Hard Enough?', *Georgetown Journal of International Affairs*, Vol. 5, No. 1, Winter/Spring 2004, pp. 69–77. Keukeleire, Stephen: 'The European Union as a diplomatic actor: internal, traditional, and structural diplomacy', *Diplomacy & Statecraft*, Volume: 14 Issue: 3, 2003, pp. 31–56. Toje, Asle: *The European Union as a Small Power. After the Post-Cold War.* Palgrave MaCmillan: London, 2010. Diez, Thomas: 'Normative power as hegemony', *Cooperation and Conflict*, Volume: 48 Issue: 2, 2013, pp. 194–210. Henry,

Nicholas: 'Politics beyond the state: Europe as civilization and as empire', *Comparative European Politics,* Volume: 8 Issue: 2, 2010, pp. 262–280.

29 Borrell Fontelles, Josep: 'Europe in the Interregnum: our geopolitical awakening after Ukraine, Grouped'études géopolitiques', 24.03.2022, retrieved November 1, 2023, from: <https://geopolitique. eu/ en/2022/03/24/europe-in-the-interregnum-our-geopolitical-awakening-after-ukraine/>.

30 Piskorska, Beata: *Soft power w polityce UE wobec państw Partnerstwa Wschodniego.* Katolicki Uniwersytet Lubelski: Lublin, 2017.

31 'The White Paper on the future of Europe. Reflections and scenarios for the EU27 by 2025', *European Commission*, 1 March 2017, COM (2017)2025. Retrieved November 1, 2023, from: <https://ec.europa.eu/info/sites/default/files/ white _paper _on_the_future_of_europe_en.pdf>.

32 'Letter by President Donald Tusk to the 27 EU leaders on the future of the EU – "United we stand, divided we fall"', *European Council*, 31 January 2017, retrieved November 1, 2021, from: <https://www.consilium. Europa.eu/en/press/press-releases/2017/01/31/tusk-letter-future-europe/>.

33 The term 'Europe's variable geometry', expressing the EU countries' division based on the integration level, has been used since the introduction of the single EU currency in 2002. Currently, the euro is used in 19 countries of 27 member states. See: Grosse, Tomasz Grzegorz: *Polityki europejskie w dobie kryzysu.* Scholar: Warszawa, 2016. See: Vitte de, Bruno / Ott, Andrea / Vos, Ellen: *Between Flexibility and Disintegration. The Trajectory of Differentiation in EU Law.* Edward Elgar: Cheltenham-Northampton, 2017. See: Zhelyazkova, Asya: 'From selective integration into selective implementation: The link between differentiated integration and conformity with EU laws', *European Journal of Political Research*, Volume 53, Issue 4, November 2014. See: Schimmelfennig, Frank: 'Good governance and differentiated integration: Graded membership in the European Union'. *European Journal of Political Research*, Volume 55, Issue 4, November 2016. See: Khoo, Jerald: 'Towards a Two-Speed Europe: National Sovereignty and the Absence of Political Integration in the Eurozone', *Columbia Journal of European Law*, Volume 22, Issue 1, 2015–2016, pp. 165–192. See also: Kabat-Rudnicka, Danuta: 'Zróżnicowana integracja europejska jako odpowiedź na zmieniający się porządek międzynarodowy'. In: Mania, Andrzej / Bajor, Piotr / Pugacewicz, Tomasz / Wyrwisz, Anna (eds.): *Stany Zjednoczone oraz państwa europejskie między globalizacją a regionalizacją.* Polskie Towarzystwo Studiów Międzynarodowych. Rambler Press: Warszawa, 2018, pp. 123–146. La Baume de, Maia: 'Juncker chides 'ignorant' EU leaders for criticizing his speech. The Dutch and Danish leaders described the Commission president's proposals last week as unnecessary', *Politico*, 21.09.2017, Retrieved November 1, 2023, from: <https://www.politico.eu/article/jean-claude-juncker-chides-ignorant-eu-leaders-for-criticizing-his-state-of-union-speech/>.

34 'The White Paper on the future of Europe. Reflections and scenarios for the EU27 by 2025', *European Commission*, 1 March 2017, COM (2017)2025. Retrieved November 1, 2023, from: <https://ec.europa.eu/info/sites/default/files/ white _paper _on_the_future_of_europe_en.pdf>.

35 Council Decision Establishing Permanent Structured Cooperation (PESCO) and determining the list of participating Member States, 14866/17, Brussels, 8 December

2017.Retrieved June 1, 2022, from: <https://eur-lex.europa.eu/legal-content/EN/TXT/PDF/?uri=CELEX:32017D2315&from=EN>.

Council Regulation (EU) 2017/1939 of 12 October 2017 implementing enhanced cooperation on the establishment of the European Public Prosecutor's Office ('the EPPO') Brussels, 15 October 2017.Retrieved June 1, 2022, from: <https://eur-lex.europa.eu/legal-content/EN/TXT/?uri =CELEX %3A32017R1939&qid=1659704641124>.

36 Grosse, Tomasz Grzegorz: *Polityki europejskie w dobie kryzysu.* Scholar: Warszawa, 2016.

37 Ferguson, Niall: *Colossus: The Price of America's Empire.* Penguin Press: New York, pp. 24.

38 Casarini, Nicola: 'A European strategic "third way?" The European Union between the traditional transatlantic alliance and the pull of the Chinese market', *China International Strategy Review.* The Institute of International and Strategic Studies: Peking University, 2022. See also: Bergsen, Pepijn: *The EU's unsustainable China strategy*, Chatham House: London, July 2021. Ayrault, Jean-Marc / Steinmeier, Frank-Walter: *A strong Europe in a world of uncertainties*, 26 June 2016, retrieved June 1, 2022, from: <https://static.presspublica.pl/red/rp/pdf/DokumentUE.pdf>.

39 A Strategic Compass for the EU, The Diplomatic Service of the European Union, October 28, 2021. Retrieved June 1, 2023, from: <https://www.eeas.europa.eu/eeas/strategic-compass-security-and-defence-1_en>. See also: Shared Vision, Common Action: A Stronger Europe. A Global Strategy for the European Union's Foreign And Security Policy, June 2016, retrieved June 1, 2023, from: <https://www.eeas.europa.eu/sites/default/ files /eugs _ review_web_0.pdf. See: Borrell Fontelles, Josep: 'Europe in the Interregnum: our geopolitical awakening after Ukraine', *Grouped'études géopolitiques*, 24.03.2022, retrieved June 1, 2023, from: July 30, 2022: <https:// geopolitique.eu/en/2022/03/24/europe-in-the-interregnum-our-geopolitical-awakening-after-ukraine/>.

Bibliography

A Strategic Compass for the EU, The Diplomatic Service of the European Union, October 28, 2021. Retrieved June 1, 2023, from: <https://www.eeas.europa.eu/eeas/strategic-compass-security-and-defence-1_en>.

Arendt, Hannah: *On Violence.* Harvest, Harcourt Brace & Company: New York, 1970.

Barnett, Michael / Duvall, Raymond: 'Power in International Politics', *International Organization,* Issue 1, vol. 59, 2005, pp. 39.

Bergsen, Pepijn: *The EU's unsustainable China strategy*, Chatham House: London, July 2021. Ayrault, Jean-Marc /Steinmeier, Frank-Walter: *A strong Europe in a world of uncertainties*, 26 June 2016, retrieved June 1, 2022, from: <https://static.presspublica.pl/red/rp/pdf/DokumentUE.pdf>.

Biscop, Sven: 'Geopolitics with European Characteristics An Essay on Pragmatic Idealism', *Equality and Strategy*, March 15, 2016,Retrieved November 1, 2023, from: <https://eu.boell.org/en> /2016/v03/15/ geopolitics-european-characteristics.

Blocher, John W.: 'Unexpected Competition: A US Strategy to Keep its Central and Eastern European Allies as Allies in an Era of Great-Power Competition, '*Atlantic Council*, 22 November 2020,retrieved November 1, 2023, from: <https://www.atlanticcouncil.org/ in-depth-research-reports/report/unexpected-competition/>.

Borrell Fontelles, Josep: 'Europe in the Interregnum: our geopolitical awakening after Ukraine, Grouped'études géopolitiques', 24.03.2022, retrieved November 1, 2023, from: https://geopolitique. eu/ en/2022/03/24/ europe-in-the-interregnum-our-geopolitical-awakening-after-ukraine/.

Casarini, Nicola: 'A European strategic "third way?" The European Union between the traditional transatlantic alliance and the pull of the Chinese market', *China International Strategy Review.* The Institute of International and Strategic Studies: Peking University, 2022.

Council Decision Establishing Permanent Structured Cooperation (PESCO) and determining the list of participating Member States, 14866/17, Brussels, 8 December 2017.Retrieved June 1, 2022, from: <https://eur-lex.europa.eu/legal-content/EN/TXT/ PDF/?uri=CELEX>:32017D2315&from=EN.

Council Regulation (EU) 2017/1939 of 12 October 2017 implementing enhanced cooperation on the establishment of the European Public Prosecutor's Office ('the EPPO') Brussels, 15 October 2017.Retrieved June 1, 2022, from: <https://eur-lex.europa.eu/legal-content/EN/ TXT/?uri> =CELEX %3A32017R1939&qid=1659704641124.

Dahl, Robert A.: 'The concept of Power', *Behavioral Science*, No. 2, Vol. 3, 1957, pp. 203.

Diez, Thomas: 'Normative power as hegemony', *Cooperation and Conflict*, Volume: 48 Issue: 2, 2013, pp.194–210.

EU-China—A strategic outlook, European Commission, 2019, retrieved November 1, 2022, from: <https://ec.europa.eu/> commission/ sites/ beta-political/files/communication-eu-china-a-strategic-outlook.pdf.

Ferguson, Niall: *Colossus: The Price of America's Empire*. Penguin Press: New York, pp. 24.

Fiszera, Józef (ed.): *Unia Europejska-Chiny w XXI wieku.* Institute of Political Studies at Polish Academy of Sciences: Warszawa, 2018.

Frankel, Joseph: *International Relations.* Oxford University Press London: 1969, pp. 82–51.

Gerrits, André (ed.): *Normative Power Europe in a Changing World: A Discussion*, NETHERLANDS INSTITUTE OF INTERNATIONAL RELATIONS, CLINGENDAEL, December 2009. Retrieved November 1, 2023, from: <https://www.clingendael.org/sites/default/files/pdfs/> 20091200 _cesp_ paper gerrits.pdf.

Gstöhl, Sieglinde / Lannon, Erwan (eds.): *The Neighbours of the European Union's Neighbours Diplomatic and Geopolitical Dimensions beyond the European Neighbourhood Policy*. Routledge: London, 2014.

Global Strategic Trends. The Future Starts Today. Ministry of Defence, United Kingdom: London, 2018, pp. 212–218. Retrieved November 1, 2022, from: <https://assets.publishing.service.gov.uk> /government/uploads/system/uploads/ attachment_data/file/771309/ Global_Strategic_Trends_-_The_Future_Starts_Today.pdf.

Green, Michael / Alterman, John / Miller, Franklin (eds.): *Ironclad: Forging a New Future for America's Alliances*. Center for Strategic and International Studies: Lanham, Boulder, New York, London, 19 October 2019, retrieved November 1, 2023, from: <https://www.csis.org/> analysis/ ironclad-forging-new-future-americas-alliances.

Grosse, Tomasz Grzegorz: *Polityki europejskie w dobie kryzysu.* Scholar: Warszawa, 2016.

Vitte de, Bruno / Ott, Andrea / Vos, Ellen: *Between Flexibility and Disintegration. The Trajectory of Differentiation in EU Law.* Edward Elgar: Cheltenham-Northampton, 2017.

Haine, Jean-Yves: 'The EU's Soft Power: Not Hard Enough?', *Georgetown Journal of International Affairs*, Vol. 5, No. 1, Winter/Spring 2004, pp. 69–77.

Haken, Nate et al.: *FragileStates Index 2022 – Annual Report.* 13 July 2022. The Fund for Peace: Washington, retrieved November 1, 2023, from: <https://fragilestatesindex.org/wp-content/uploads> / 2022/07/22-FSI-Report-Final.pdf.

Haugaard, Mark / Lentner, Howard H. (eds.): *Hegemony and Power. Consensus and Coercion in Contemporary Politics.* Lexington Books: Lanham, 2006, pp. 10.

Henry, Nicholas: 'Politics beyond the state: Europe as civilization and as empire', *Comparative European Politics,* Volume: 8 Issue: 2, 2010, pp.262–280.

Kabat-Rudnicka, Danuta: 'Zróżnicowana integracja europejska jako odpowiedź na zmieniający się porządek międzynarodowy'. In: Mania, Andrzej / Bajor, Piotr / Pugacewicz, Tomasz / Wyrwisz, Anna (eds.): *Stany Zjednoczone oraz państwa europejskie między globalizacją a regionalizacją.* Polskie Towarzystwo Studiów Międzynarodowych. Rambler Press: Warszawa, 2018, pp. 123–146.

Kagan, Robert: *The Jungle Grows Back*: *America* and *Our Imperiled World.* Alfred A. Knopf: New York, 2018.

Kagan, Robert: *Paradise and Power: America and Europe in the New World Order.* Vintage Books: New York, 2004.

Keukeleire, Stephen: 'The European Union as a diplomatic actor: internal, traditional, and structural diplomacy', *Diplomacy & Statecraft,* Volume: 14 Issue: 3, 2003, pp. 31–56.

Keohane, Robert O. / Nye, Jr., Joseph S.: *Power and Interdependence.* Littel Brown: Boston, 1977.

Khanna, Parag: 'The Empire Strikes Back', *The Economist,* May 27,2008. Retrieved November 1, 2023, from: <https://www.economist.com/books-and-arts/2008/03/27/the-empires-strike-back>.

Khoo, Jerald: 'Towards a Two-Speed Europe: National Sovereignty and the Absence of Political Integration in the Eurozone', *Columbia Journal of European Law,* Volume 22, Issue 1, 2015–2016, pp. 165–192.

Kuźniar, Roman: *Polityka i siła. Studia strategiczne – zarys problematyki.* Scholar: Warszawa, 2006.

La Baumede, Maia: 'Juncker chides 'ignorant' EU leaders for criticizing his speech. The Dutch and Danish leaders described the Commission president's proposals last week as unnecessary', *Politico,*21.09.2017, Retrieved November 1, 2023, from: <https://www.politico.eu/article/jean-claude-juncker-chides-ignorant-eu-leaders-for-criticizing-his-state-of-union-speech/>.

Leonard, Mark: *Why Europe Will Run the 21st Century*. Public Affairs: New York,2005.

'Letter by President Donald Tusk to the 27 EU leaders on the future of the EU – "United we stand, divided we fall"', *European Council*, 31 January 2017, retrieved November 1, 2021, from: <https://www.consilium.europa.eu/en/press/press-releases/2017/01/31/tusk-letter-future-europe/>.

'London Declaration issued by the Heads of State and Government participating in the meeting of the North Atlantic Council in London 3-4 December 2019'. *North Atlantic Treaty Organization*. Retrieved November 1, 2022, from: <https://www.nato.int/cps/en/natohq/official> _texts_171584.htm? selectedLocale=en/.

McCormick, John: *The European superpower.* Palgrave Macmillan: New York, 2007.

Toje, Asle: *The European Union as a Small Power. After the Post-Cold War.* Palgrave MacMillan: London, 2010.

Mahneken, Thomas G.: 'Forging the tools of 21st-century great power competition', *The Center for Strategic and Budgetary Assessments*, 2020, retrieved November 1, 2023, from: <https://csbaonline.org/uploads/documents> /GPC_Final_Report_Web.pdf.

Marshall, Tim: *Prisoners of Geography. Ten Maps that tell you everything you need to know about Global Politics.* Elliott and Thompson Limited: Chicago, 2016, pp. 133.

Morgenthau, Hans: *Politics Among Nations. The Struggle for Power and Peace.* Alfred A. Knopf: New York, 1960, pp. 25–39.

Moravcsik, Andrew: 'Europe: The quiet superpower', *French Politics*, Vol. 7, 3/4, 2009, pp.403–422.

Nye, Joseph S.: 'The *Benefits of Soft Power*', Harvard Business School Working Knowledge for Business Leaders, February 8, 2004.

O'Rourke, Ronald: 'U.S. Role in the World: Background and Issues for Congress Updated', *Congressional Research Service*, August 5, 2020. Retrieved November 1, 2023, from: <https://www.hsdl.org/?view&did=842596>.

Piskorska, Beata: *Soft power w polityce UE wobec państw Partnerstwa Wschodniego*. Katolicki Uniwersytet Lubelski: Lublin, 2017.

Rauch, Jonathan: 'Europe Is the Next Rival Superpower. But Then, So Was Japan', *TheAtlantic.com*, February 1, 20025, retrieved November 1, 2023, from: <https://www.theatlantic.com/magazine/archive/2005/02/europe-is-the-next-rival-superpower-but-then-so-was-japan/303774/>.

Reding, Andrew: 'EU in position to be world's next superpower', *Chicago Tribune*, January 6, 2002, retrieved November 1, 2023, from: <https://www.chicagotribune.com/news/ct-xpm-2002-01-06-0201060227-story.html>.

Rifikn, Jeremy: *The European dream: how Europe's vision of the future is quietly eclipsing the American dream.* Jeremy P. Tarcher/Penguin: New York, 2004.

Schimmelfennig, Frank: 'Good governance and differentiated integration: Graded membership in the European Union'. *European Journal of Political Research*, Volume 55, Issue 4, November 2016.

Shared Vision, Common Action: A Stronger Europe. A Global Strategy for the European Union's Foreign And Security Policy, June 2016, retrieved June 1, 2023, from: <https://www.eeas.europa.eu/sites/default/> files /eugs _ review_web_0.pdf.

Skaluba, Christopher / Rodihan, Conor / Doyle, Gabriela (eds.): *NATO 20/2020. Twenty bold ideas to reimagine the Alliance after the 2020 US election.* Atlantic Council Washington: 2020. Retrieved November 1, 2023, from: wp-content/uploads /2020/10/NATO-20-2020-Twenty-bold-ideas-to-reimagine-the-alliance-after-the-2020-US-election.pdf.

Smouts, Marie-Cloude: 'International Organizations and Inequality among States', *International Social Science Journal*, No. 144,1995, pp. 234.

Spiegel, Steven: *Dominance and Diversity. The International Hierarchy.* Little, Brown: Boston, 1972, pp. 43.

'Summary of the National Defence Strategy of The United States of America, Sharpening the American Military's Competitive Edge'. Department of Defence: Washington, 2018. Retrieved November 1, 2023, from: <https://dod.defence.gov/Portals/1/Documents/pubs/2018-National-Defence-Strategy-Summary.pdf>.

'The White Paper on the future of Europe. Reflections and scenarios for the EU27 by 2025', *European Commission*, 1 March 2017, COM (2017)2025. Retrieved November 1, 2023, from: \<https://ec.europa.eu/info/sites/default/files/> white_paper _on_the_future_of_europe_en.pdf.

Wendt, Alexander: 'Anarchy is what States Make of It: the Social Construction of Power Politics', *International Organization*, 46, no. 2, Spring 1992, pp. 391–425.

'Will The EU Ever Become a Superpower?', *Carnegie Endowment For International Peace*, July 17, 2008, retrieved November 1, 2023, from: https:// <carnegieendowment.org/files/0717carnegie-stubb.pdf/>.

Zakaria, Fareed: *The Post-American World.* W.W. Norton and Company: New York, 2008.

Zhelyazkova, Asya: 'From selective integration into selective implementation: The link between differentiated integration and conformity with EU laws', *European Journal of Political Research*, Volume 53, Issue 4, November 2014.

US-European Relations in the Context of the Russian Invasion of Ukraine

Przemysław Furgacz

The new phase of the Russian aggression against Ukraine, which began on 24 February, brought about a fundamental change in the relations between the overwhelming majority of European states and the Russian Federation. At the same time, the issue of the Russian-Ukrainian war became the subject of very intensive diplomatic talks between various European states and the U.S. Both Europe and the U.S. had to work out a coordinated response to Moscow's extremely bold move. The absence of such a response to a new challenge would not only make the Russian Federation even more belligerent and combative in the future but would also likely encourage Beijing to take equally bold and peace-endangering steps, for example towards Taiwan. As a result, US-European relations have undoubtedly become much more important since 2022.

In this chapter of the book, the US-European policy towards the Russian-Ukrainian war, both in the period before the outbreak of the war and after it, will be presented very succinctly.[1] It must be emphasised that what exactly went on behind the scenes before and after the outbreak of the war in US and European political, diplomatic, military and intelligence circles is to a large extent still not fully known. Our knowledge in this area is unavoidably incomplete, fragmentary and partial. Researchers must therefore necessarily rely on leaks and information published in the media, as well as official diplomatic and political communiqués, statements and announcements. However, a more objective and comprehensive review of this policy will only be possible in the future, as successive generations of scholars and historians gain greater access to the currently classified documents.

US-European policy toward Russian preparation to war

The first public information about the increasing concentration of Russian troops near Ukraine appeared in September 2021. Western intelligence services had to take note of some worrying signs that Russia was preparing some military operations earlier. According to Serhiy Hrabsky – a retired colonel in the Ukrainian Armed Forces – the first signals of an imminent invasion reached the state leadership as early as March 2021.[2] Similarly, Polish analyst and columnist Jarosław Wolski claims that the first indications of an imminent Russian invasion reached some Western intelligence services in March 2021. Assessments of Russia's intentions and plans differed between the US and its European partners. According to the information published by the Washington Post,[3] the US intelligence services received credible and rather extensive information about Russia's offensive plans in advance.[4] By late summer of 2021, US intelligence analysts were increasingly certain that Moscow was indeed planning the new invasion of Ukraine, but this time on a much larger scale than in 2014.[5] When Joe Biden met with the leaders of three Western European powers – Germany, France and the United Kingdom – at the Group 20 conference in Rome in October 2022, he shared with them certain information he had received from US intelligence about the coming new major war in Europe. In mid-November, Avril Haines – US Director of National Intelligence – shared more detailed intelligence information with NATO allies at the NATO North Atlantic Council meeting.

Generally speaking, the predictions of the US's European allies in the run-up to the war can be divided into three camps. In the first camp we can place those states that were deeply and completely convinced that the US was right and that Moscow really intended to launch a full-scale invasion of Ukraine. Only the United Kingdom and the Baltic states can be included in this camp. In the second camp, we can group the states that believed that Russia was planning a new offensive against Ukraine, but that it would be limited in scope and objectives. In fact, most Central and Eastern European states, including Poland, shared this view. In the third camp we can place states that were suspicious of US intelligence and either ignored or underestimated signals of an imminent Russian invasion. These states included Germany and France, as well as most Western and Southern European states, according to the Washington Post.[6] The information that German and French leaders were sceptical about the Russian invasion even in February 2022 and did not believe the US and the UK is confirmed by the British newspaper The Economist.[7] Interestingly, the head of the French military intelligence service, General Eric Vidaud, was suddenly and unexpectedly dismissed in March 2022, which can be interpreted as a sign of Emmanuel Macron's dissatisfaction with the forecasts formulated by this service before the war, which later turned out to be overtly too sanguine and quite detached from brutal reality. At least this interpretation was widespread in the French media.[8] In retrospect, we know that it was the United States, the United Kingdom, Estonia, Latvia and Lithuania that most accurately predicted Moscow's belligerent plans towards Ukraine for 2022. Poland in general, irrespective of the government, has been warning for many years about Putin's aggressive and belligerent intentions, but the scale of the Russian invasion of Ukraine in 2022 probably surprised even the most hawkish Polish political leaders.

US politics towards the war

According to Polish investigative journalist Wojciech Sumliński, who managed to obtain a secret report prepared by the Internal Security Agency – Poland's civilian counterintelligence service – Washington actually wanted this war as much as Moscow. From the point of view of Washington's hawks, it would be an excellent opportunity to embroil Russia in a long, protracted conflict that would weaken Russia militarily, economically and politically, ultimately leading to a blunting of Russia's expansionist ambitions and anti-American zeal. It is significant that Washington appears to be fighting this war with Russia with Ukrainian hands. Certainly, US policymakers want to control the escalation and avoid direct military confrontation with Russia. That is why they decided to support Ukraine with considerable supplies of arms, ammunition, intelligence and financial aid, and to encourage European states to follow the American example and do the same.

Since the beginning of 2022, the US has gradually begun to send new troops to NATO's Eastern flank. Russia's aggression has given the NATO alliance a new lease of life. Above all, the public perception in Sweden and Finland of the traditional neutral status of these two Scandinavian states changed rapidly. Stockholm and Helsinki applied for NATO membership very soon after the outbreak of the war. Finland joined NATO in April 2023, while Sweden's accession to NATO was blocked for a long time by Turkey, and Sweden finally joined NATO only in March 2024. Ankara wanted to obtain some political concessions from Stockholm, especially regarding the Kurdish political activists living in Sweden.

Following the outbreak of the Russian-Ukrainian war, the US and its European allies have either initiated or significantly intensified cooperation in three key areas:

- jointly waging economic warfare against Russia in a coordinated manner to undermine its economy and reduce its ability to wage war against Ukraine;
- the provision of humanitarian, economic and military aid to Ukraine to help it repel the Russian invasion;
- joint and coordinated efforts to make Europe much less dependent on imports of Russian hydrocarbons and mineral resources.

US-European economic war against Russia

In an effort to punish Russia for its brazen aggression and at the same time deter other countries – such as China – from taking similar steps in the future, the US and European countries decided to impose a whole series of acute economic sanctions on the Russian Federation. The US and European financial sanctions against Russia were truly intense and severe. Never before had so many and such comprehensive sanctions been imposed on such a large economy and such an important power. As a result, the Russian economy was de facto cut off from the Western economies and, to some extent, even from the global economy. This would not have been possible if the US and Europe had not cooperated in this matter. The US and EU have sanctioned the Russian government and its agents for past actions on several occasions, including after the annexation of the Crimean peninsula or the failed attempt to assassinate Sergei Skripal in the UK. However, the scope and range of sanctions implemented against Russia after February 2022 is absolutely unprecedented. The French Minister for the Economy and Finance, Bruno Le Maire, admitted openly and with admirable, if unusual for a politician, sincerity that the West was waging an 'all-out economic and financial war' against the Russian Federation.[9]

Undoubtedly, it was the US that led the way in imposing sanctions on Russia. Washington urged its European allies to follow suit. Washington's encouragement was to some extent successful, but it must be stressed that at the same time Washington faces challenges in assembling a durable Western coalition to put pressure on Moscow, mainly because of serious economic dependence on Russian energy and political reluctance in selected European states, such as Hungary or Germany.

The EU has implemented sanctions in successive packages. For example, the first severe energy import ban adopted by the EU was against imports of Russian coal. Then the EU banned imports of other hydrocarbons. The EU and the US also banned imports of Russian steel, caviar, diamonds, vodka and other beverages. In general, both Europe and the US worked hard to inhibit or even sever normal trade relations with the Russian Federation. The G7 leaders removed Russia's normal trade status. In addition, the Western states banned the export of many types of goods and technologies to Russia, including vital components for the Russian automotive and military industries. Among the goods banned from export to Russia were semiconductors and high-tech equipment, the kind of goods that Russia does not produce in sufficient quantities and has to import from abroad. The West also banned the export of high-value luxury goods to Russia.

The joint Western sanctions target key members of the Russian political and business elite, as well as key members of Vladimir Putin's inner circle. Many members of the Russian elite are subject to travel bans. The European Union, the United Kingdom, the United States and several other Western countries have frozen the assets of the Russian Central Bank and Russian sovereign wealth funds. According to most estimates, about half of the official foreign exchange reserves of the Russian Central Bank – worth about $350 billion[10] – have been frozen, but the Atlantic Council claims that this percentage is actually much lower and that only about $100 billion of these reserves have actually been frozen. The cloudy and non-transparent nature of these reserves makes the issue difficult to determine. Many Russian banks, businessmen and large companies have been blacklisted among those categorically barred from doing business with Western companies and institutions.

The US quickly banned imports of Russian oil, certain petroleum products, liquefied natural gas and coal. The EU also banned imports of Russian fuels but did so gradually in a series of successive rounds of sanctions and with some exemptions for selected countries. The US and the EU announced a broad ban on investment in Russian companies, including those in the Russian energy sector. Later, the US and EU together banned the purchase of Russian crude oil exported by tanker unless the price fell below a strictly defined price cap set by the US; shippers of such oil could not be insured by Western insurers.

Russia was swiftly kicked out of the extraordinarily important SWIFT cross-border financial messaging system, but Moscow has been preparing for such a move since 2014. At that time, Putin ordered the creation of the Russian International Financial Payments System, known by the acronym SPFS. Thanks to SPFS, Russia managed to partially isolate itself from financial sanctions. Cutting Russia off from SWIFT in 2022 was not as painful as it would have been if such a step had been taken ten years earlier.

It should be emphasised that some steps in the economic war against Russia were controversial even among the major European powers. For example, the German authorities, unlike Chancellor Olaf Scholz, were long opposed to a European cap on the price of natural gas. French President Emmanuel Macron pushed for the introduction of this price cap. The German government finally gave in on this issue at the end of 2022, but on the condition that a special mechanism be built into the draft that would allow the price cap to be lifted if certain circumstances arose.[11] This is just one of many examples showing that even the major European players have often disagreed on various details of the implementation of sanctions against Russia.

However, Russia has developed creative and resourceful workarounds to evade at least the most acute sanctions. Many vital components and parts that the Russian economy needs are currently imported from the West through intermediaries in Turkey, Armenia, Kazakhstan and many other countries.[12] For example, Turkish exports to Russia increased by 45% in 2022, reaching $7.6 billion.[13] This sudden and measurable increase in Turkish exports to the Russian Federation can be explained solely by the fact that Turkey, which did not join the Western economic war against Russia, is re-exporting to Russia parts and components imported from the West that Russia desperately needs to keep its economy running and its army fighting. The long-term effectiveness of Western sanctions against Russia is still unknown. The extent to which they will undermine the Russian economy and hamper its expansionist plans remains to be seen. That's partly because Russia has been hiding its economic statistics since 2022, deliberately trying to obscure the true state of its economy. In addition, there are a variety of cunning ways to circumvent sanctions, which have been developed and honed over decades by the sanctioned states.[14] Today, we are witnessing a rapidly accelerating process of de-dollarisation, which in practice means that the dollar is being pushed out of international payments in favour of ruble, yuan, rupees, rials, reals and many other currencies of developing countries. Last but not least, the overall effectiveness of Western sanctions against Russia is reduced by the fact that many important non-Western economies, such as China, India, Turkey, Saudi Arabia, the United Arab Emirates and Israel, have simply not joined the anti-Russian sanctions regime.

US-European aid for Ukraine repelling Russia's aggression

Since the outbreak of the war, the West has consistently provided Ukraine with substantial economic, financial, humanitarian and military aid. In the first year of the war alone, Western donor countries pledged a total of $170 billion in various forms of aid to Ukraine.[15] While it remains to be seen whether all of these promises will be fulfilled, the economic aid given to Ukraine so far has undoubtedly been substantial. As of mid-March 2023, Kyiv had been promised €18bn in macro-financial assistance from the EU and almost $10bn from the US. In addition, the International Monetary Fund, which is dominated by the US and Europe, also contributes significantly to keeping Ukraine's economy and budget relatively stable in very difficult circumstances. For example, in March the IMF reached a preliminary agreement with Ukraine on an Extended Fund Facility (EFF) programme. According to the preliminary agreement, Ukraine will receive a total of $15.6 billion in concessional loans over the period 2023–26, including $4.5 billion by the end of 2023.[16] Although media commentators focus mainly on the transfer of military equipment to Ukraine, we should not forget that Western financial assistance is equally important for the survival of the Ukrainian economy, which has been painfully hit by Russian aggression.

During the first year of the Russian-Ukrainian war, the US provided Ukraine with a total of $44.2 billion in various forms of aid, including $29.3 billion in military aid – mainly in the form of arms and ammunition transfers – $13 billion in economic aid and $1.9 billion in humanitarian aid. From the beginning of Russia's unprovoked aggression against Ukraine until mid-February 2023, President Joe Biden asked Congress four times to authorise and approve aid packages for Ukraine totalling $113 billion – the amount pledged by Congress. Interestingly, Congress expanded Biden's aid packages three times.[17] The aid quotas for Ukraine are really serious. Some of this money – it is difficult to estimate how much – may have been embezzled, defrauded or earmarked for black budget operations, as some members of the Republican Party and investigative journalists suggest.[18]

Sometimes Washington has pushed its European partners very hard, trying to convince them to send some weapons systems to Ukraine to make it easier for Kyiv to succeed on the battlefields. One such case is the issue of the German-made Leopard 2 main battle tanks. For months, the Americans have wanted the Germans to supply Leopard 2 tanks in cooperation with other European partners, although they have not made this public in order to avoid embarrassing Berlin. Despite consistent and insistent requests from the US to supply these tanks to Ukraine, Chancellor Olaf Scholz relentlessly resisted the pressure. Most of the media claimed that it was only after the White House agreed to send Ukraine a batch of US M1A2 Abrams tanks that Berlin relented and decided to send its Leopard 2 tanks. Most of the media claimed that this was a concession by Washington to Berlin, which allegedly did not want to be the first major Western power to send its tanks to Ukraine and incur Moscow's wrath. However, the former head of the Polish Civilian Intelligence Service – the Foreign Intelligence Agency – Andrzej Derlatka, in one of his interviews with Robert Cheda, clearly stated that Scholz was forced by Washington to deliver Leopard 2 tanks to Ukraine and that the US announcement of sending M1A2 Abrams tanks was nothing more than a gesture given to Scholz to save his face by presenting to domestic and foreign public opinion that he had obtained an alleged material concession from the US.[19]

US-European energy partnership

Washington is keen to reduce European economic contacts with Russia in almost all areas of the economy, but especially in the energy sector. Regardless of who occupies the White House or which party is in control of Congress, Washington is undoubtedly determined to significantly reduce – if not completely stop – Russian energy exports to Europe. It would seem that, from a US leadership perspective, by cutting off Russia's energy exports to Europe, the US would actually be killing two birds with one stone. Firstly, it would reduce Russia's export revenues – especially for natural gas, which cannot be redirected as easily and quickly as oil exports. Second, the US could increase its economic and political influence in Europe, because – to some extent – Europe could import natural gas from the US instead of from Russia. In such a case, US export revenues would soar, and the US would gain additional leverage over many European states. Moreover, by stopping Russia's hydrocarbon exports to Europe, it would also end Russia's traditional weaponisation of Europe's dependence on fossil fuels. This, in turn, would be very favourable from the US point of view.

Following the outbreak of the Russian-Ukrainian war, European states had to gradually reduce their imports of hydrocarbons from Russia, whether they wanted to or not. Some European states – such as Poland or the Baltic states – did it willingly and at a fast pace, while others – such as Germany or Hungary – did it unenthusiastically and reluctantly. The process is still underway, and it will take several years before energy imports from Russia are completely phased out. Nevertheless, the year 2022 was undoubtedly a real breakthrough in this matter. By 2022, the most prominent European states – led by Germany and Italy – had taken steps to increase their natural gas dependence on the Russian Federation.[20] At present, even the most reluctant European states are reducing their purchases of Russian hydrocarbons, albeit at different rates. Overall, Europe's dependence on Russian fuels has been significantly reduced in a short period of time. Before the outbreak of the Russian-Ukrainian war, Russian energy accounted for 45% of Europe's energy supply, whereas it now accounts for less than 10%.[21] This is partly due to the strengthened transatlantic partnership.

After the Russian invasion of Ukraine, US-European energy cooperation and consultation accelerated. For example, the EU-US Energy Council – a special body established in 2009 for consultative functions – met eight times in the period 2009–2021, while it met twice in 2022–23.[22] A certain intensification of talks within this body is noticeable. On 25 March 2022, the President of the United States, Joe Biden, and the President of the European Commission, Ursula von der Leyen, established a new forum, the EU-US Task Force on Energy Security, whose main objective is to develop viable strategies and plans aimed at reducing the EU's imports of Russian energy, especially natural gas. Washington has committed itself to helping Europe alleviate the energy crisis provoked by Moscow, which has gradually begun to reduce its natural gas exports to Europe as a form of blackmail and a show of geoeconomic strength. In particular, in March 2022, US President Joe Biden promised to do everything in his power to send an additional 15 billion cubic metres (bcm) of liquefied natural gas (LNG) to the EU.[23] In retrospect, we know that the US has indeed increased its LNG exports to Europe quite significantly. Whereas in 2021, the year before the war, the US sold 22 bcm of LNG to the EU, in 2022 it sent 56 bcm of LNG to the EU, an increase of 155% in LNG exports to the EU. In fact, the EU became a major destination for US LNG exports in 2022, with 52% of US LNG exports going to the EU in that year.[24] In other words, it appears that the US is to some extent replacing Russia as the main source of natural gas imports to Europe. The disruption of Russian natural gas supplies has made Europe increasingly dependent on LNG, which is mainly imported from the United States.[25] It should be emphasised that US-EU cooperation is not only aimed at increasing the EU's energy security, but also at helping non-EU European states to increase their energy security and reduce their dependence on the Russian Federation. The EU and the US worked together to provide Ukraine with specialised electrical equipment urgently needed to repair Ukraine's power plants and electricity distribution network, which had been badly damaged by successive rocket attacks. The Atlantic allies also helped Moldova, which was undermined by a Moscow-inspired energy crisis. Both the EU and the US are helping the Western Balkans to gradually switch to non-Russian energy sources. Washington and Brussels are also cooperating in the nuclear energy sector, trying to help Southeastern and Central European states replace Russian nuclear fuel and civilian nuclear technology with American or Western European equivalents.[26] One thing that needs to be discussed in this context is the sabotage of the Nord Stream 1 & 2 pipelines on 26 September. Most Western media and politicians blame Russia. However, sabotage by the USA is much more likely. The following authoritative figures claim that the US is indeed the main culprit in these sabotage acts: former Polish Minister of Defence and Foreign Minister Radoslaw Sikorski, famous American economist Jeffrey Sachs and well-known American financier James Rickards. Perhaps the most comprehensive description of the sabotage was provided by the world-famous and experienced US investigative journalist Seymour Hersh, who wrote unequivocally that the US and Norway jointly organised the sabotage.[27] Maria Zakharova – the Director of the Information and Press Department of the Russian Foreign Ministry – claimed that the UK was involved in the underwater explosions, while Russian President Vladimir

Putin openly said that the US had destroyed the Nord Stream 1 & 2 pipelines. The official version of this sabotage promoted in the media, or the claim that it was carried out by a small group of Ukrainian patriots hired by one of the Ukrainian oligarchs,[28] is a kind of fairy tale for naive and gullible people.[29] Even Joe Biden said this unequivocally a few months before the war: 'If Russia invades ... there will be no Nord Stream 2. We will put an end to it'. To a journalist's justified question: 'But how exactly are you going to do that?' Biden replied: 'I promise you, we will be able to do it'. Without mincing words, Joe Biden kept his promise. The reasons for such a bold and reckless move have been convincingly argued by James Rickards.[30] In this context, it must be emphasised that this act of sabotage was also an aggressive step towards Berlin. Western European, including German, companies were co-owners of the damaged pipelines. By blowing up the Nord Stream 1 & 2 pipelines, Washington put an end to a potential and possible German détente with Russia or withdrawal from the US-led anti-Russian coalition. Now, whether it likes it or not, Germany has no other viable option but to buy natural gas not from Russia but from Norway, the US and other suppliers.

In 2006, when the Polish oil company PKN Orlen acquired a controlling stake in the Mažeikių oil refinery in northern Lithuania, much to Moscow's displeasure, a mysterious fire broke out in the refinery shortly afterwards. Interestingly, on 12 October 2006, at the end of his visit to Vilnius, Konstantin Kosachev, the then chairman of the Duma's foreign affairs committee, said that the Lithuanian government had made a 'serious economic mistake' by selling the Mažeikių refinery to the Polish group PKN Orlen, 'which will lead to unstable operation of the plant in the future'. A few hours later, a fire broke out in the refinery. Only the most naive person could consider this a coincidence.[31] The Lithuanian government commission investigating the causes of the fire concluded that it was not an accident.[32] Even Polish President Lech Kaczyński, in one of his last interviews to Andrzej Nowak before his unexplained death in Smolensk, Russia, on 10 April 2010, openly said that the Russians had set fire to the refinery. This example shows that Russia was sabotaging Europe's vital energy infrastructure even before the war broke out. In addition, on 8 June 2022, there was an explosion at a major US LNG export facility in Freeport, Texas, which was probably also an act of sabotage carried out by Russian saboteurs, despite official dismissals, refutations and denials.[33] Nevertheless, Germany's long-term loyalty to the US has been called into question after the equally mysterious and consequential explosions at the bottom of the Baltic Sea.

Conclusion

Although the US-European coalition in waging economic warfare against Russia to undermine its economy and restrain its belligerence appears to be relatively stable so far, its long-term maintenance should by no means be taken for granted. The US-European diplomatic alignment is not guaranteed forever. Some US political and economic moves, such as the Biden administration's implementation of the Inflation Reduction Act in 2022, which provides substantial subsidies for American-made electric vehicles with batteries that use mineral resources from North America, hit European companies and the EU economy quite hard, reducing Europe's long-term competitiveness. As a result, the European eagerness to wage economic warfare against Russia may diminish over time. This is particularly the case in France and Germany, where anti-American sentiment has always been more or less present and could become more popular in the future. In the face of bilateral political tensions, changing electoral sentiments and, above all, the onset of a major economic crisis, the US-EU diplomatic alignment against Russia may not always be sufficiently enticing. Maintaining public support for Ukraine should not be taken at face value, especially if the financial crisis of enormous proportions hits the US and Europe in 2023–2026, as predicted by James Rickards, Gen. Michael Flynn, Peter Schiff and many other authoritative experts. The Central and Eastern European states are much more concerned about Russian revanchism and expansionism. Thus, the alignment of Poland, Romania and the Baltic states – all of which are smaller and less ambitious than the stronger and richer Western European powers – with the United States is much firmer and more reliable. For these states, which see the US as their main security guarantor, the American military presence in Europe is a very relevant national security interest. Relations between Washington and Paris or Berlin are less firm and less ironclad.

Despite these misgivings, some degree of transatlantic coordination of foreign policy towards Russia can still be expected. Russia's aggression against Ukraine has – to some extent – also affected the interests of those European states that do not share a border with Russia and have never been occupied by it. The swift and coordinated response of the US and Europe after Russia's invasion of Ukraine proved that the unified Western camp still has quite a robust capacity to inflict substantial economic pain on any power that acts too aggressively on the world stage. In theory, it could also be a subtle warning to Beijing to discourage the PRC's leaders from taking too bold and audacious actions in its foreign and security policy. Washington's efforts to alleviate Europe's energy crisis also prove that the transatlantic alliance still has certain advantages for relatively resource-poor Europe. The year 2022 confirms that if European states are faced with a choice between good relations with Russia and bad relations with the US, or good relations with the US and bad relations with Russia, almost all will choose the latter alternative as less harmful and more beneficial to them. Less obvious and more uncertain is the choice that some European states would make in the event of a serious economic and political conflict between China and the U.S. For example, Germany would find it particularly difficult to prioritise partners because its economy is equally dependent on Chinese and American markets.

Notes

1 For the sake of clarity, although the war between Russia and Ukraine actually began in 2014 as a result of the forcible annexation of Crimea and Russia's instigation of the violent secessionist movement in Donbass, the author will assume, for the sake of simplicity, that the war broke out on 24 February 2022. Such a position can be justified by the fact that between 2015 and 2022 the military operations in Donbass in general have calmed down considerably in comparison with what happened there in 2014 and the beginning of 2015.

2 Hrabski, Serhij: 'Wojny wygrywa gospodarka'. *Dziennik Gazeta Prawna*, 5953(39), February 24–26, 2023, p. A2.

3 According to James Rickards, this newspaper is often chosen by the CIA as the object of targeted intelligence leaks.

4 Harris, Shaneet al.: 'Road to war: U.S. struggled to convince allies, and Zelensky, of risk of invasion'. *The Washington Post*, August 16, 2022, retrieved 01.09.2022, from <https://www.washingtonpost.com/national-security/interactive/2022/ukraine-road-to-war/>.

5 Ibidem.

6 Ibidem.

7 'How to make sense of intelligence leaks'. *The Economist*, March 9, 2023, retrieved 13.04.2023, from <https://www.economist.com/the-economist-explains/2023/03/09/how-to-make-sense-of-intelligence-leaks>.

[8] Kucharczyk, Mateusz: 'Francja: Dymisja szefa wywiadu wojskowego. Zlekceważył działania Rosji wobec Ukrainy'. *Euractiv.pl*, March 31, 2022, retrieved 19.04.2023, from <https://www.euractiv.pl/section/bezpieczenstwo-i-obrona/news/francja-rosja-ukraina-armia-wywiad-wojna-vidaud-macron/>.

[9] Lough, Richard: 'French minister declares economic "war" on Russia, then beats a retreat'. *Reuters*, March 03, 2022, retrieved 19.04.2023, from <https://www.reuters.com/world/france-declares-economic-war-against-russia-2022-03-01/>.

[10] Wong, Audrye: 'China's Economic Statecraft: Lessons Learned from Ukraine'. *The Washington Quarterly* 46(1), 2023, p. 125.

[11] Gebauer, Matthias et al.: 'Friends and Strangers: The Franco-German Relationship is Cooling at a Critical Time'. *Der Spiegel*, January 13, 2023, retrieved 16.03.2023, from <https://www.spiegel.de/international/europe/friends-and-strangers-the-franco-german-relationship-is-cooling-at-a-critical-time-a-13a0adfa-dc17-416e-acbd-121cefe9fbce>.

[12] Swanson, Ana / Stevis-Gridneff, Matina: 'Russia Is Importing Western Weapons Technology, Bypassing Sanctions'. *New York Times*, April 18, 2023, retrieved 29.04.2023, from <https://www.nytimes.com/2023/04/18/business/economy/us-russia-chips-sanctions.html>.

[13] 'How to survive a superpower split'. *The Economist*, April 11, 2023, retrieved 17.04.2023, from <https://www.economist.com/international/2023/04/11/how-to-survive-a-superpower-split>.

[14] For example, Russia, with the help of Saudi Arabia and the United Arab Emirates, is skilfully and cleverly circumventing Western crude oil sanctions. It is assisted by Saudi Arabia and the United Arab Emirates, which have not joined the West's economic war against Russia and are trying to profit as much as possible from the West's struggle with Russia, according to the wise proverb: two dogs fight for a bone, a third runs away with it. See: Faucon, Benoit / Said, Summer: 'Saudi Arabia, U.A.E. Scoop Up Russian Oil Products at Steep Discounts'. *Wall Street Journal*, April 17, 2023, retrieved 21.04.2023, from <https://www.wsj.com/articles/saudi-arabia-u-a-e-scoop-up-russian-oil-products-at-steep-discounts-d327a2ee>.

[15] 'How to survive a superpower split'. *The Economist*, April 11, 2023.

[16] Matuszczak, Sławomir: 'Ukraine: the IMF support package and increased defence spending'. *Centre for Eastern Studies*, March 24, 2023, retrieved 17.04.2023, from<https://www.osw.waw.pl/en/publikacje/analyses/2023-03-24/ukraine-imf-support-package-and-increased-defence-spending>.

[17] Piotrowski, Mateusz: 'Congress Key to U.S. Support for Ukraine One Year After the Russian Invasion'. *PISM Bulletin*, 2133(14), 2023, February 17, 2023, retrieved 19.05.2023, from <https://pism.pl/publications/congress-key-to-us-support-for-ukraine-one-year-after-the-russian-invasion>.

[18] Hersh, Seymour: 'Trading with the Enemy'. *Seymourhersh.substack.com*, April 12, 2023, retrieved 19.04.2023, from <https://seymourhersh.substack.com/p/trading-with-the-enemy>.

[19] For a discussion of how arms supplies affect what happens on the battlefield, see: Gady Franz-Stefan / Kofman, Michael: 'Ukraine's Strategy of Attrition'. *Survival* 65(2), 2023, pp. 7–22, retrieved 17.04.2023, from <https://www.iiss.org/online-analysis/survival-online/2023/04/ukraine-strategy-of-attrition/>.

[20] Skalamera, Moren: 'The Geopolitics of Energy after the Invasion of Ukraine'. *The Washington Quarterly* 46(1), 2023, p. 14.

21 Wong, Audrye: 'China's Economic Statecraft: Lessons from Ukraine'. *The Washington Quarterly* 46(1), 2023, pp. 121–136.

22 'United States of America: EU-US Energy Cooperation'. European Commission, retrieved 19.04.2023, from <https://energy.ec.europa.eu/topics/international-cooperation/key-partner-countries-and-regions/united-states-america_en>.

23 Łoskot-Strachota, Agata: 'A strategic gas alliance between the EU & the US'. *Centre for Eastern Studies*, March 28, 2022, retrieved 28.04.2023, from <https://www.osw.waw.pl/en/publikacje/analyses/2022-03-28/a-strategic-gas-alliance-between-eu-us>.

24 'United States of America: EU-US Energy Cooperation'. *European Commission*

25 Skalamera, Moren: 'The Geopolitics of Energy after the Invasion of Ukraine'. *The Washington Quarterly* 46(1), 2023, p. 15.

26 Łoskot-Strachota, Agata: 'The EU's strategic energy partnership with the US after a year of war'. *Centre for Eastern Studies*, April 04, 2023, retrieved 19.04.2023, from <https://www.osw.waw.pl/en/publikacje/analyses/2023-04-06/eus-strategic-energy-partnership-us-after-a-year-war>.

27 Hersh, Seymour: 'How America Took Out The Nord Stream Pipeline'. *Seymourhersh.substack.com*, February 8, 2023, retrieved 09.03.2023, from <https://seymourhersh.substack.com/p/how-america-took-out-the-nord-stream>.

28 Pancevski, Bojan et al.: 'Who Blew Up Nord Stream? Investigators Focus on Six Mysterious Passengers on a Yacht'. *Der Spiegel*, March 16, 2023, Retrieved 21.03.2023, from <https://www.wsj.com/articles/who-blew-up-nord-stream-investigators-focus-on-six-mysterious-passengers-on-a-yacht-25b47e9b?mod=hp_lead_pos7>.

29 Hersh, Seymour: 'The Nord Stream Ghost Ship'. *Seymourhersh.substack.com*, April 05, 2023, retrieved 26.04.2023, from <https://seymourhersh.substack.com/p/the-nord-stream-ghost-ship>.

30 See: transcript 7:00–14:00: 'Former CIA adviser warns of Biden's big blackout'. Retrieved 21.04.2023, from <https://pro.paradigmnewsletters.org/p/awn_energyarmageddon_0123/LAWNZ252/?cake_s1=04_113966024_b1740c05-933a-47ec-a781-4b16cac78691&h=true>.

31 Jabłońska, Agata: 'Pożar ostatniej szansy'. *Wprost,* December 15, 2006, 1245(43), retrieved 02.05.2023, from <https://www.wprost.pl/tygodnik/96627/Pozar-ostatniej-szansy.html>.

32 'Pożar w Możejkach nie był przypadkowy'. *WNP.pl*, November 15, 2006, retrieved 23.04.2023, from <https://www.wnp.pl/wiadomosci/pozar-w-mozejkach-nie-byl-przypadkowy,16940.html>.

33 'U.S.regulatorreleasesreportblamingFreeportLNGblastoninadequateprocesses'.*Reuters*, November 16, 2022, retrieved 18.04.2023, from <https://www.reuters.com/business/energy/freeport-lng-provides-no-timeline-texas-export-plant-restart-2022-11-15/>.

Bibliography

Faucon, Benoit / Said, Summer: 'Saudi Arabia, U.A.E. Scoop Up Russian Oil Products at Steep Discounts'. *Wall Street Journal,* April 17, 2023, retrieved 21.04.2023, from <https://www.wsj.com/articles/saudi-arabia-u-a-e-scoop-up-russian-oil-products-at-steep-discounts-d327a2ee>.

'Former CIA adviser warns of Biden's big blackout'. Retrieved 21.04.2023, from <https://pro.paradigmnewsletters.org/p/awn_energyarmageddon_0123/LAWNZ252/?cake_s1=04_113966024_b1740c05-933a-47ec-a781-4b16cac78691&h=true>.

Gady Franz-Stefan / Kofman, Michael: 'Ukraine's Strategy of Attrition'. *Survival* 65(2), 2023, pp. 7–22, retrieved 17.04.2023, from <https://www.iiss.org/online-analysis/survival-online/2023/04/ukraine-strategy-of-attrition/>.

Gebauer, Matthias et al.: 'Friends and Strangers: The Franco-German Relationship is Cooling at a Critical Time'. *Der Spiegel*, January 13, 2023, retrieved 16.03.2023, from <https://www.spiegel.de/international/europe/friends-and-strangers-the-franco-german-relationship-is-cooling-at-a-critical-time-a-13a0adfa-dc17-416e-acbd-121cefe9fbce>.

Harris, Shaneet al.: 'Road to war: U.S. struggled to convince allies, and Zelensky, of risk of invasion'. *The Washington Post*, August 16, 2022, retrieved 01.09.2022, from <https://www.washingtonpost.com/national-security/interactive/2022/ukraine-road-to-war/>.

Hersh, Seymour: 'How America Took Out The Nord Stream Pipeline'. *Seymourhersh.substack.com*, February 8, 2023, retrieved 09.03.2023, from <seymourhersh.substack.com/p/how-america-took-out-the-nord-stream>.

Hersh, Seymour: 'The Nord Stream Ghost Ship'. *Seymourhersh.substack.com*, April 5, 2023, retrieved 26.04.2023, from <><seymourhersh.substack.com/p/the-nord-stream-ghost-ship>.

Hersh, Seymour: 'Trading with the Enemy'. < *Seymourhersh.substack.com*, April 12, 2023, retrieved 19.04.2023, from ><seymourhersh.substack.com/p/trading-with-the-enemy>.

'How to make sense of intelligence leaks'. *The Economist*, March 9, 2023, retrieved 13.04.2023, from <https://www.economist.com/the-economist-explains/2023/03/09/how-to-make-sense-of-intelligence-leaks>.

'How to survive a superpower split'. *The Economist*, April 11, 2023, retrieved 17.04.2023, from <https://www.economist.com/international/2023/04/11/how-to-survive-a-superpower-split>.

Hrabski, Serhij: 'Wojny wygrywa gospodarka'. *Dziennik Gazeta Prawna*, 5953(39), February 24–26, 2023, p. A2.

Jabłońska, Agata: 'Pożar ostatniej szansy'. *Wprost*, December 15, 2006, 1245(43), retrieved 02.05.2023, from <https://www.wprost.pl/tygodnik/96627/Pozar-ostatniej-szansy.html>.

Kucharczyk, Mateusz: 'Francja: Dymisja szefa wywiadu wojskowego. Zlekceważył działania Rosji wobec Ukrainy'. *Euractiv.pl*, March 31, 2022, retrieved 19.04.2023, from <https://www.euractiv.pl/section/bezpieczenstwo-i-obrona/news/francja-rosja-ukraina-armia-wywiad-wojna-vidaud-macron/>.

Łoskot-Strachota, Agata: 'A strategic gas alliance between the EU & the US'. *Centre for Eastern Studies*, March 28, 2022, retrieved 28.04.2023, from <https://www.osw.waw.pl/en/publikacje/analyses/2022-03-28/a-strategic-gas-alliance-between-eu-us>.

Łoskot-Strachota, Agata: 'The EU's strategic energy partnership with the US after a year of war'. *Centre for Eastern Studies*, April 04, 2023, retrieved 19.04.2023, from <https://www.osw.waw.pl/en/publikacje/analyses/2023-04-06/eus-strategic-energy-partnership-us-after-a-year-war>.

Lough, Richard: 'French minister declares economic "war" on Russia, then beats a retreat'. *Reuters*, March 03, 2022, retrieved 19.04.2023, from <https://www.reuters.com/world/france-declares-economic-war-against-russia-2022-03-01/>.

Matuszczak, Sławomir: 'Ukraine: the IMF support package and increased defence spending'. *Centre for Eastern Studies*, March 24, 2023, retrieved 17.04.2023, from<https://www.osw.waw.pl/en/publikacje/analyses/2023-03-24/ukraine-imf-support-package-and-increased-defence-spending>.

Pancevski, Bojan et al.: 'Who Blew Up Nord Stream? Investigators Focus on Six Mysterious Passengers on a Yacht'. *Der Spiegel*, March 16, 2023, Retrieved 21.03.2023, from <https://www.wsj.com/articles/who-blew-up-nord-stream-investigators-focus-on-six-mysterious-passengers-on-a-yacht-25b47e9b?mod=hp_lead_pos7>.

Piotrowski, Mateusz: 'Congress Key to U.S. Support for Ukraine One Year After the Russian Invasion'. *PISM Bulletin*, 2133(14), 2023, February 17, 2023, retrieved 19.05.2023, from <https://pism.pl/publications/

congress-key-to-us-support-for-ukraine-one-year-after-the-russian-invasion>.

'Pożar w Możejkach nie był przypadkowy'. *WNP.pl*, November 15, 2006, retrieved 23.04.2023, from <https://www.wnp.pl/wiadomosci/pozar-w-mozejkach-nie-byl-przypadkowy,16940.html>.

Skalamera, Moren: 'The Geopolitics of Energy after the Invasion of Ukraine'. *The Washington Quarterly* 46(1), 2023, p.p. 7–24.

Skalamera, Moren: 'The Geopolitics of Energy after the Invasion of Ukraine'. *The Washington Quarterly* 46(1), 2023, pp. 7–24.

Swanson, Ana / Stevis-Gridneff, Matina: 'Russia Is Importing Western Weapons Technology, Bypassing Sanctions'. *New York Times*, April 18, 2023, retrieved 29.04.2023, from <https://www.nytimes.com/2023/04/18/business/economy/us-russia-chips-sanctions.html>.

'U.S. regulator releases report blaming Freeport LNG blast on inadequate processes'. *Reuters*, November 16, 2022, retrieved 18.04.2023, from <https://www.reuters.com/business/energy/freeport-lng-provides-no-timeline-texas-export-plant-restart-2022-11-15/>.

'United States of America: EU-US Energy Cooperation'. *European Commission*, retrieved 11.04.2023, from <https://energy.ec.europa.eu/topics/international-cooperation/key-partner-countries-and-regions/united-states-america_en>.

'United States of America: EU-US Energy Cooperation'. European Commission, retrieved 19.04.2023, from <https://energy.ec.europa.eu/topics/international-cooperation/key-partner-countries-and-regions/united-states-america_en>.

Wong, Audrye: 'China's Economic Statecraft: Lessons from Ukraine'. *The Washington Quarterly* 46(1), 2023, pp. 121–136.

Conclusions

Łukasz Stach

'May you live in interesting times' – this well-known proverb means that it is better to live in time of peace, tranquillity and prosperity, due to the fact that than in 'interesting' times usually unexpected troubles appear. Definitely, we live in interesting times, the rise of China has changed the balance of power in the world. China has awakened and it has global consequences, also for Europe. Suddenly, Europe is confronted with a rapidly changing international environment – the rivalry between the US and China, Russian full-scale invasion on Ukraine, and the growing instability on the EU's southern flank. The Arab Spring, which began in 2011, led to civil wars in Syria and Libya and in turn resulted in the European migrant crisis in 2015. In addition, the rise of the Islamic State has increased the terrorist threat in Europe, especially as the ideas promoted by ISIS have found some followers among EU citizens. Growing illegal migration fuels the popularity of groups described in the European mainstream as far-right, anti-immigrant or populist, some of them are also Eurosceptic. They question the current direction of European integration, sometimes constructively, sometimes just simply challenging the status quo without offering an alternative. It is impossible to disagree with the assertion that Europe is weakening in almost every area and its role in the world is diminishing. There is a lot of data showing that Europe is losing ground to China and the US in almost every area, including innovations, artificial intelligence, new technologies, etc. Europe's share of the world economy is also declining, but given the size of its economy, European Union as a whole can claim to be a global power. However, Europe is mainly a civilian and trading power with limited military and power projection capabilities. As a result, Europe is still dependent on the US military umbrella in security matters, which provides Washington with a convenient tool for exerting political pressure on Europe, especially as the EU is divided in its approach to the United States (and PRC too). Washington put a pressure on Europe to toughen its policy towards PRC, on the other hand, Beijing suggest EU that it should not follow US in its China's policy. Both powers also imply that if Europe will not follow their line, it could suffer the consequences, mainly in the economic field. These are not just hypothetical scenarios. When in 2021 Lithuania withdrew from 17+1 initiative and tightened relations with Taiwan. Beijing's reaction was strong; for example, it restricted Lithuanian companies' access to its market. In general, PRC and the US can exploit the *divide and rule* principle by exploiting existing divisions in the EU, in particular that Europe is divided in many areas, including policy towards People's Republic of China, United States, Russia, mass migration and many other issues. As for relations with the United States, the US invasion of Iraq in 2003, the Barack Obama's pivot to Asia and the presidency of Donald Trump have challenged transatlantic relations and exposed divisions between EU member states towards US. Meanwhile, the United States is the guarantor of the liberal order of which the European Union is a part. The weakening of the US also poses a problem for Europe, for which the U.S. remains the guarantor of security. Central and Eastern European countries, in particular, see perceive Washington as the security provider and they expect closer cooperation with U.S. and NATO, as well as a strong American military presence in Europe. On the other hand, the idea of European 'strategic autonomy' proposed by some politicians (e.g. President of France Emmanuel Macron, High Representative of the UE for Foreign Affairs and Security Policy Joseph Borrell), assumes that Europe is more distant from U.S. and will not become Washington follower in its policy towards Beijing. An open question is whether Europe can ensure its military security without Washington's support. In theory, given the military budgets of EU countries and the potential of the European defence industry, it is possible, but in practice it may be very challenging. Even if Europe were able to reach a consensus on strengthening its defence capabilities, building a de facto alternative security system to NATO would take time and require significant financial resources. So far, European military and powers projection capabilities remain limited.

Europe is also becoming less attractive ideologically and culturally, and its soft power became the less efficient, also in the regions where Europe is remembered from the perspective of its colonial past. European values – democracy, human rights, tolerance, equality, rule of law, human dignity, European values are weaker than Chinese money and investments, especially as Beijing offers much more than Europe and do not ask about values and democracy. For many authoritarian regimes (especially in Africa), the PRC offers a more attractive development model than Europe (and the US). Europe is willing to support democracy worldwide, but it has limited tools to pursue this goal, apart from its own rhetoric. Incidentally, expecting the whole world to adapt to Western ideas and play by the rules set by the West is politically naive. Currently, the People's Republic of China not only challenges the liberal world order but is also building their own system, an alternative to the Western one, and Beijing is committing significant financial resources to achieve this goal. It poses a significant challenge both for United States and Europe, but the perception of China is different in Europe than it is in the US. As Nicola Cassarini noted, for Washington, China is the most ominous challenge to U.S. global dominance and the international democratic order maintained by America. Meanwhile, Europe fully supports the US-led democratic order but is more reluctant to Washington strategy to contain China. Europe would like to not choose between the U.S. and China; it prefers to cooperate with Washington in fields where Beijing is a competitor and at the same time maintain the economic ties with China to support Europe's export-driven economy. In an age of U.S.-China rivalry, however, such an approach will be difficult to sustain. A contest between PRC and the US for global hegemony has an impact on Europe, even if it would like to stand aside. The EU should cooperate both with China and United States to promote pragmatic policies which help to maintain stability. Willingly or not, Europe is caught between the US eagle and PRC dragon. United States struggle to maintain its hegemonic position, while China seeks to replace the U.S. as a world's leading superpower or transform international order towards multipolar ones. Europe has to navigate between the two superpowers, and it finds this difficult.

Europe would like to preserve the *status quo* or return to the age of US-China strategic engagement, but that age has ended, and the era of strategic competition has begun. For now, Europe has to accept that the US and China are the main players, and it only can react to fait accompli created by the two powers. Meanwhile, the growing US-China rivalry is dangerous for Europe due to a number of factors. Export-oriented EU's member states economies may be strongly hampered by political tensions between the great powers. The return of protectionism, deglobalisation, trade wars, disruption in import (like during the COVID-19 pandemic) are the challenges which Europe needs to overcome. Any military hostilities between the PRC and the US (such as China's invasion of Taiwan, naval blockade) would be the worst-case scenario for Europe, both economically and militarily. Not only is Europe dependent on free trade, but so far the US is also the guarantor of its military security.

For the European Union, it will be very difficult to maintain the status of peaceful power, the organization which rely mostly on economic and soft power. The economic slowdown, demographic problems and destabilisation of the EU's neighbourhood combined with the growing US-China rivalry weakens the foundation of European policy based on peaceful means and 'European values'. On the other hand, existing threats may push Europe towards deeper integration and development of its own military capabilities, however, in such scenario EU must overcome the reluctance of its member states to build an alternative military force to NATO. In general, it is extremely difficult to eradicate or even reduce all existing divisions within the European Union itself; the current model requires compromise, which de facto prevents smooth action in crisis situations due to the fact that achieving the consensus amongst 27 member states sometimes being difficult. Rebuilding this model is also difficult task because of existing divisions within the EU itself, as well as concerns about the dominance of the largest countries in the European Community. Following Brexit, the role of Franco-German duo has increased, and it may lead to a situation where a small group of powers takes the main decisions. In fact, Germany and France trying to achieve their own goals within the EU can lead to tensions within an entity as economically, socially and politically diverse as the European Union. Attempts to centralise and strengthen the position of the largest EU countries can only lead to a contestation of this direction of integration, which may hamper the efforts to solving the Europe's problems. The lack of swift solution to crises, such as the migrant crisis, Eurozone crisis, the shift of power, war on Ukraine and the growing instability in international environment raise questions about the EU future. The attempt to respond to the challenges is to deepen integration, which means ever greater centralisation, which, given Europe's economic, social and cultural diversity, can only lead to increasing dysfunctionality of the whole system. A case in point is the introduction of the euro, which has proved beneficial for some European economies (led by Germany), while for the countries like Greece, it has been more of a problem than a factor for growth.

It is worth noting that an important factor limiting growth is also the model chosen for the functioning of the European Union. The EU became a bureaucratic organisation, where centralising and level of regulation is increasing. Over-regulated Europe loses its competitive edge and even in areas that the EU considered to be its strong points (e.g. green technologies), China suddenly and successfully challenged Europe. Overall, EU is losing ground economically and geopolitically. Europe remains attractive to the masses from undeveloped countries all over the world and has become a destination for mass migration. It is an open question whether the newcomers will be able to integrate into European societies, find work and contribute to Europe's development, rather than just enjoying its social benefits. Moreover, access to the European market of more than 448 million mostly rich consumers is also a tempting prospect for any economy, although Brussels is increasingly trying to protect its common market. But for a Europe dependent on free trade, is a return to protectionism the right response? The list of challenges which EU has to face nowadays is long, and it is difficult to predict how Europe find itself in the emerging new world order – so far, Europe has no good answer.

About the Authors

PRZEMYSŁAW FURGACZ is a political scientist, a lecturer in economics, interested in international relations, history, military, international economics, geopolitics and geoeconomics.

PRZEMYSŁAW ŁUKASIK is a historian and political scientist. He is an assistant professor at the Institute of Journalism and International Relations of the National Education Commission University in Kraków, Poland.

ŁUKASZ STACH is a political scientist working at the Centre for International Studies and Development at the Jagiellonian University in Krakow.

INTERNATIONAL RELATIONS IN ASIA, AFRICA AND THE AMERICAS

Edited by Andrzej Mania & Marcin Grabowski

Vol. 1 Olga Barbasiewicz (ed.): Postwar Reconciliation in Central Europe and East Asia. 2018.

Vol. 2 Adam Nobis: A Short Guide to the New Silk Road. 2018.

Vol. 3 Radka Havlová (ed.): Untangling the Mayhem: Crises and Prospects of the Middle East. 2018.

Vol. 4 Marcin Grabowski / Paweł Laidler (eds.): Global Development Policy in the 21st Century. New Challenges. 2018.

Vol. 5 Andrzej Mania / Marcin Grabowski / Tomasz Pugacewicz (eds.): Global Politics in the 21st Century. Between Regional Cooperation and Conflict. 2019.

Vol. 6 Marcin Grabowski / Tomasz Pugacewicz (eds.): Application of International Relations Theo-ries in Asia and Africa. 2019.

Vol. 7 Адам Нобис. Краткий путеводитель по Новому Шелковому Пути. 2019.

Vol. 8 Olga Barbasiewicz / Marcin Grabowski / Ewa Trojnar (eds.): Security Dilemmas and Chal-lenges in 21st Century Asia. 2020.

Vol. 9 Marcin Gabryś / Magdalena Marczuk- Karbownik / Magdalena Paluszkiewicz- Misiaczek (eds.): Canadian Political, Social and Historical (Re)visions in the 20th and 21st Centuries. 2020.

Vol. 10 Agata Wiktoria Ziętek / Grzegorz Gil (eds.): ASEAN in a Changing World. 2021.

Vol. 11 Maciej Kurcz: Urban Now. A Human in the Face of Borderliness and Urbanisation in Juba, South Sudan. 2021.

Vol. 12 Olga Barbasiewicz / Maciej Pletnia (eds.): Internal and External Aspects of Japanese Security. 2021.

Vol. 13 Olga Barbasiewicz / Michał Lipa / Karolina Rak (eds.): Historical and Collective Memory in the Middle and Far East. 2021.

Vol. 14 Tomasz Pugacewicz / Marcin Grabowski (eds.): Great and Small Games in Central Asia and the South Caucasus. 2022.

Vol. 15 Anna Pruska: Swiss Banking Secrecy and the US- Swiss Conflict Over Holocaust Claims. 2022.

Vol. 16 Łukasz Gacek / Rafał Kwieciński / Ewa Trojnar: Taiwan under Tsai Ing- wen. Democracy Diplomacy. 2023.

Vol. 17 Magdalena Musiał- Karg / Natasza Lubik- Reczek (eds.): The War in Ukraine. (Dis)information – Perception – Attitudes. 2023.

Vol. 18 Bogdan Góralczyk: China in the Xi Jiping's Era. 2024.

Vol. 19 Paulina Napierała (ed.): Religion and American Politics. Domestic and International Contexts. 2024.

Vol. 20 Kłosowicz Robert / Mormul Joanna: The Problem of *De Facto States* in International Relations in Africa. 2024.

Vol. 21 Paweł Laidler: The U.S. Supreme Court and the Legitimization of Surveillance. 2024.

Vol. 22 Łukasz Stach, Przemysław Łukasik and Przemysław Furgacz: Europe's Relations with the United States and China in the 21st Century. 2025.

www.ingramcontent.com/pod-product-compliance
Ingram Content Group UK Ltd.
Pitfield, Milton Keynes, MK11 3LW, UK
UKHW022222051026
15624UKWH00002B/303

9 783631 928899